THE REAL PAUL

THE REAL PAUL

RECOVERING HIS RADICAL CHALLENGE

BERNARD BRANDON SCOTT

POLEBRIDGE PRESS
Salem, Oregon

For David Buttrick, Ken Graham,
and Joe Bessler

Amicus magis necessarius,
quam ignis et aqua

(Cicero, *De Amicitiae*, 6.22)

Cover and interior design by Robaire Ream

Library of Congress Cataloging-in-Publication Data
Scott, Bernard Brandon, 1941-
 The real Paul : recovering his radical challenge / by Bernard Brandon Scott.
  pages cm
 Includes bibliographical references.
 ISBN 978-1-59815-154-1 (alk. paper)
 1. Paul, the Apostle, Saint. I. Title.
 BS2506.3.S37 2015
 225.9'2--dc23

                                                        2014038669

CONTENTS

Cameo Essays

Preface

I am writing this as I am retiring from teaching. Well, at least retiring from full-time teaching. I've often been asked recently what I will do when I retire and I always reply, "About the same thing I've always done, I just won't have to go to meetings!" I do indeed owe thanks to a great many people. First of all, the students who have endured my teaching all these years and from whom I have learned so much. The paradox of teaching is that the teacher learns more than the students. In most of what I have written over the years, I see student after student on the pages of what I write. Their questions have provoked my research.

I have been blessed with many fine colleagues over the years. At St. Meinrad, David Buttrick, Fr. Damian Deitlein, OSB, and Fr. Colman Grabert, OSB, were always willing to engage in exploring new avenues. At Phillips Theological Seminary I have enjoyed an extraordinary collegiality, but Joe Bessler has been a constant conversation partner.

The librarians at Phillips Theological Seminary have provided me with excellent and always cheerful service, while running down books in compact storage (why do so many books I need appear to be in storage?), or fulfilling an interlibrary loan request. Sandy Shapoval, Director of the Library, has always gone the extra mile in dealing with my requests. An excellent library is indeed refreshment for the soul.

A number of people have read this book in manuscript and their critique has often kept me out of trouble. David Buttrick has always been both a generous critic and sharp observer of holes in the argument. MaryAnn Morris, a former student, helped provoke my thinking on the conflict between Paul and James in Antioch and caught many small details. Margaret Lee as usual is my best reader and critic, offering substantial and important observations on the work in progress. My indebtedness to her cannot be overstated.

The staff at Polebridge has been supportive in many ways. The publisher Larry Alexander has been understanding when health issues delayed the book and encouraging by keeping it on schedule. Cassandra Farrin made many excellent suggestions in the copy-editing. All of the Polebridge staff have made it a better book.

Special thanks must go to the translators of *The Authentic Letters of Paul: A New Reading of Paul's Rhetoric and Meaning*: Arthur J. Dewey, Roy W. Hoover, Lane C. McGaughy, and Daryl D. Schmidt. Without their translation of the letters of Paul, this book would have been immensely more difficult, if not impossible. Perhaps more than any other author in the New Testament, the understanding of Paul is beset with translation issues.

This book is dedicated to three longtime friends. Life cannot be lived without such friends.

Abbreviations

1,2 Cor	1,2 Corinthians
1,2 Kgs	1,2 Kings
1,2,3,4 Macc	1,2,3,4 Maccabees
1,2 Thess	1,2 Thessalonians
1,2 Tim	1,2 Timothy
BAGD	Bauer, Walter, William F. Arndt, F. Wilbur Gingrich, and Frederick W. Danker. *A Greek-English Lexicon of the New Testament and Other Early Christian Literature.* Chicago: University of Chicago Press, 2000.
BBS	My Translation
Deut	Deuteronomy
Eph	Ephesians
Exod	Exodus
Gal	Galatians
Gen	Genesis
Ign. *Mag.*	Ignatius, *To the Magnesians*
Ign. *Phld.*	Ignatius, *To the Philadelphians*
Ign. *Smyrn.*	Ignatius, *To the Smyrnaeans*
Isa	Isaiah
Jer	Jeremiah
Jub	Jubilees
KJ	The King James Version
Lev	Leviticus
lit:	Literally
LSJ	Liddell, Henry George, Robert Scott, Henry Stuart Jones, and Roderick McKenzie. *A Greek-English Lexicon.* Oxford: Clarendon Press, 1968.
LXX	Septuagint: Pietersma, Albert, and Benjamin G. Wright, eds. *A New English Translation of the Septuagint.* New York; Oxford: Oxford University Press, USA, 2007.

Mal	Malachi
Matt	Matthew
Neh	Nehemiah
NRSV	The New Revised Standard Version
Num	Numbers
Phil	Philippians
Phlm	Philemon
Prov	Proverbs
Ps(s)	Psalm(s)
Q	*Quelle* ("Source")
Rom	Romans
Sir	Sirach
SV	*The Authentic Letters of Paul* or *The Complete Gospels* (Scholars Version)
Wis	Wisdom of Solomon

Chapter 1

Getting Started

My Journey with Paul

I find it odd that I am writing a book on Paul. My publications have mostly been in the area of parables and the historical Jesus. I grew up Roman Catholic, so Paul was not on my agenda. I do not remember reading Paul until I got to graduate school. That had two important consequences on my development. I did not grow up absorbing the Augustinian/Lutheran interpretation of Paul. For me, the apostle Paul was somebody Protestants read. When I did begin to read Paul for the first time with Roy Bowen Ward at Miami University, he introduced me to Krister Stendahl, one of the pioneers of a new way of framing Paul. So when I began to deal seriously with Paul, I began by doubting a tradition I did not take for granted.

In the seminars of Robert Funk and Leander Keck while I was in graduate school at Vanderbilt University, my study of Paul took off. I have probably been living out of their influence ever since. Their approaches were different, but to me they seemed compatible, or in me they found compatibility. Both of them in their own ways were discontent with the traditional interpretations of Paul and were looking for a way out. Yet both of them gave me a thorough grounding in Rudolf Bultmann and therefore in the understanding of Paul represented by Augustine and Martin Luther. I give them thanks for the disquiet they raised in my soul. Over the years I continued to read, study, and teach Paul and began to see that a new way of approaching Paul was aborning. While spending most of my research time on the historical Jesus, I became convinced that a new way of reading Paul made Paul even more radical and threatening to traditional theology than the historical Jesus—whom the churches were already having a difficult time absorbing or ignoring.

This book embodies a brand of scholarship that radically challenges the traditional paradigm for interpreting Paul. I stand on the shoulders and in the debt of a great many scholars who have gone before me. I do not consider this book as particularly creative or original, but as a report on an ongoing struggle with this new scholarship on Paul. This book does not take the form of a survey of recent scholarship but is an effort to understand Paul. Magnus Zetterholm, *Approaches to Paul: A Student's Guide to Recent Scholarship*, provides such a survey in a very competent fashion. As we proceed, I will mention those scholars who made significant contributions in reorienting Pauline scholarship, at least as I see that scholarship.

The traditional paradigm sometimes goes under the name of the Augustinian/Lutheran interpretation because Augustine (354–430 CE) and Luther (1484–1546) are such pivotal and seminal figures in the interpretation of Paul. This model of interpretation is so deeply engrained into our consciousness that it appears as intuitive, making it hard to read or understand Paul in any other way. A new and different way of reading Paul will at times therefore seem counter-intuitive, almost contradictory. I sometimes think of understanding Paul in this fashion as mind blowing, because the effort to get out of the traditional paradigm is so challenging. So deeply embedded is the traditional understanding of Paul, that even with a strenuous effort to get out of it, I find myself constantly slipping back into it. At times I thought this book should be titled, "*Augustine Got It Wrong!*"

The question remains, is this new interpretation a plausible reading of Paul? Gerd Lüdemann and Heikki Räisänen, both writing from within the traditional paradigm, have argued that Paul does not make sense. I think they make an important case. The traditional Paul does not make sense! So is the new understanding of Paul an effort to make Paul acceptable or has this scholarship found the real Paul? Let the reader beware!

A short list of items to keep in mind as you read this book might be helpful at the beginning.

Paul was called.
Paul's concern is with the nations.
Paul addresses a particular situation.

These three points, while simple, have significant and revolutionary implications for understanding Paul's letters. While baldly stated here, they are not assumptions, but conclusions that will be argued step by step in the following chapters. But I list them now to both warn and help the reader to begin to break free from the traditional paradigm.

If Paul was called, then he was not converted. That has important implications. If he did not convert to Christianity, that requires rethinking Paul's relationship to Judaism. Paul is not addressing the universal human situation but as apostle to the nations is addressing the nations. Traditionally Paul has been understood as a theologian and many books have dealt with Pauline theology. His letters were dealt with as theological treatises. Yet as we will see, his letters deal with particular communities experiencing particular issues.

We need a new pair of glasses. The way we have arranged items in understanding Paul will no longer work, and we must see Paul in a new way. Frank McCourt in his '*Tis* tells a story about Humpy Dumpty that illustrates our situation both in understanding Paul and other topics in the early Jesus movement.

> And for a whole class period there's a heated discussion of "Humpty Dumpty".
>
> > Humpty Dumpty sat on the wall,
> > Humpty Dumpty had a great fall;
> > All the king's horses
> > And all the king's men
> > Couldn't put Humpty together again.
>
> So, I ask, what's going on in this nursery rhyme? The hands are up. Well, like, this egg falls off the wall and if you study biology or physics you know you can never put an egg back together again. I mean, like, it's common sense.
>
> > Who says it's an egg? I ask.
> > Of course it's an egg. Everyone knows that.
> > Where does it say it's an egg?

They're thinking. They're searching the text for egg, any mention, any hint of egg. They won't give in.

There are more hands and indignant assertions of egg. All their lives they knew this rhyme and there was never a doubt that Humpty Dumpty was an egg. They're comfortable with the idea of egg and why do teachers have to come along and destroy everything with all this analysis.

I'm not destroying. I just want to know where you got the idea that Humpty Dumpty is an egg.

Because, Mr. McCourt, it's in all the pictures and whoever drew the first picture musta known the guy who wrote the poem or he'd never have made it an egg.

All right. If you're content with the idea of egg we'll let it be but I know the future lawyers in this class will never accept egg where there is no evidence of egg. (353–54)

Humpty Dumpty and the missing egg describe our situation. Once traditions become fixed, they provide a lens through which everything is viewed. It becomes common sense. The Augustinian/Lutheran tradition of understanding Paul is the common-sense way to interpret him. We will often struggle against this common-sense view, trying to put together a new interpretation of Paul.

Translations

Much traditional vocabulary will be challenged in this book; in fact, a great deal of traditional vocabulary will be challenged. For example, along with *The Authentic Letters of Paul*, I suggest that the Greek word *apostolos* should be translated "envoy," not transliterated "apostle." Do I think my suggested changes will be successful? Will gain traction? Hardly. Traditions are stubbornly and at times dangerously conservative and persistent. I am a pessimist about changing religious traditions but an optimist about the importance and liberating effects of trying to understand Paul's letters.

Throughout this book we will be plagued by the problem of translation and actual translations. It might be more accurate to say that I will plague you with the issue. Another title I often have played with for this book is *Problems in Translating Paul*. The way one translates Paul's language produces a different Paul.

Most authors settle this issue by just using one translation and pretending that it is Paul's letters. But all scholars know that is not the case. Paul wrote in Greek and the Greek of a particular time and place. Furthermore a theological tradition has grown up around Paul, especially a tradition of interpretation that extends from Augustine to Luther and into the modern times with Karl Barth and Rudolf Bultmann. Translations of Paul in the West are frequently within and justifications of that theological tradition. A central contention of this book is that that tradition of understanding Paul has misread Paul. That makes translations even more problematic than normal.

The Authentic Letters of Paul (2010) is the first effort to translate Paul's letters from a perspective other than the traditional Augustinian/Lutheran tradition. It is a brave attempt, but not without problems. For this book I have adopted that translation, so unless otherwise noted, you can assume a translation of Paul is from *The Authentic Letters of Paul.* I will at times for clarity abbreviate this translation as SV (Scholars Version).

Translations from the Hebrew Bible will be from the New Revised Standard Version (NRSV). At times it will be important to note that Paul is using the Septuagint, the Greek translation of the Hebrew Bible. This will be noted with the standard abbreviation LXX. All translations of the LXX are from *A New English Translation of the Septuagint.*

Translations for the gospels will be from *The Complete Gospels*, also signified by SV. All translations from the New Testament other than *The Authentic Letters of Paul* will be noted.

At times I will employ the King James (KJ) translation either because it more closely reflects Paul's Greek or because it has caught Paul's rhetoric. While an early seventeenth-century translation in Elizabethan English and employing an inadequate Greek text, it was translated by a committee of scholars who had an excellent grasp of the ancient languages and were still part of the ancient living tradition of rhetoric, a tradition that has died out in modern times and now is only being revived as a scholarly research project.

For comparative purposes I will frequently employ the KJ and the NRSV and less frequently the New International Version

(NIV), a translation favored by many evangelical communities; the Revised English Bible (REB), the translation of the Church of England; and the New American Bible (NAB), the translation of the American Roman Catholic Church. On a few occasions I have employed the translations of other scholars, especially that of Stanley Stowers in the case of Romans.

Occasionally I have judged that for one reason or another no translation is adequate for the point I think Paul is making and so I have presented my own translation. This will always be noted with the abbreviation BBS.

In trying to understand someone like Paul, we cannot avoid what at times might seem pedantic issues concerning what his Greek actually means. Sometimes while using a translation, I will want to note more literally what the Greek says. On those occasions I will use the identifier *lit:* to indicate in parentheses a literal translation.

Much of the traditional theological vocabulary associated with Paul will be retranslated. Apostle becomes envoy, gospel becomes good news, church becomes community, Christ becomes Anointed. At times I will join two words with a forward slash (/) to help the reader focus on a new meaning, such as envoy/apostle. It is not a very felicitous solution, but it is done in an effort to help the reader get out of the traditional theological language and into an English that tries to represent Paul's Greek. While this vocabulary has become part of theological tradition for us, it was standard Greek for Paul. As these issues come up in the text they will be explained.

We often assume there must be a correct translation, but more often there are a range of possible translations. At times I will use a variety of translations, including my own, to represent that range of possible meanings.

A New Reading

This book makes no effort to be an exhaustive study of Paul. It attempts a new reading of Paul based on a consistent approach. The accent is on Paul's actual writing and so we will examine the classic cases (*locus classicus*), not all cases. The point of this book is to provide the reader with a different way to read Paul starting from a different foundation of what Paul is about. I will be asking the reader to start at a particular place—Paul's experience of the risen Jesus as described in his own words in his letter to the Galatians—and from that beginning to spin out our new reading of Paul.

Many issues from a standard introduction to the New Testament will be skipped. There will be no serious treatment of when the letters were written or whether or not Paul wrote them. For those interested in such issues, I recommend *The Authentic Letters of Paul* or *From Jesus to Christianity* by Michael White. On these issues of authenticity and dating of the Pauline letters, I assume the scholarly consensus. This is somewhat ironical since in much of this book I will be disagreeing with the scholarly consensus on the interpretation of Paul. Actually I think that scholarly consensus on the interpretation of Paul, especially as represented by the Augustinian/Lutheran tradition, is breaking down.

This book does not employ footnotes in the normal sense. That would create an apparatus inappropriate to the book's style. At the end of each chapter is a Readings section that has two purposes.

1. To guide the reader to the important literature on the chapter's topic(s). No attempt has been made to be exhaustive.
2. To give bibliographic reference to authors and books quoted in the chapter.

Not employing footnotes has the advantage for the reader of speeding the reading and keeping the focus on the topic. But it has the disadvantage of not providing a way to acknowledge all those other scholars on whom I am dependent. That is a shame and it tempted me on several occasions to consider adding footnoting. But that would have changed the character of the book.

To make amends to those in whose debt I stand and to aid the reader, I have provided as an appendix an annotated bibliography on Pauline scholarship.

In bibliographic references I will simply cite the author's last name and pages, e.g., Scott, 210. The list of readings at each chapter's end will contain the complete bibliographic reference. In the case where an author has more than one reference, the date of the appropriate work will appear before the page number, e.g., Scott, 2010: 310. This simple system of reference should make it easy for a reader to follow up on my bibliographic references.

On occasion an issue or topic that is important or germane but interrupts the flow of the argument will be dealt with in a cameo essay. These will be graphically set apart from the text.

Readings

Lüdemann, Gerd. "Paul—an Obituary." Pp. 11–22 in *Rediscovering the Apostle Paul*. Ed. Bernard Brandon Scott. Jesus Seminar Guides. Salem, OR: Polebridge Press, 2011.

McCourt, Frank. *'Tis*. New York: Scribner, 1999.

Pietersma, Albert, and Benjamin G. Wright, eds. *A New English Translation of the Septuagint*. New York/Oxford: Oxford University Press, USA, 2007.

Räisänen, Heikki. "A Controversial Jew, Paul and His Conflicting Convictions." Pp. 23–36 in *Rediscovering the Apostle Paul*. Ed. Bernard Brandon Scott. Jesus Seminar Guides. Salem, OR: Polebridge Press, 2011.

Stowers, Stanley K. *A Rereading of Romans: Justice, Jews, and Gentiles*. New Haven/London: Yale University Press, 1994.

White, L. Michael. *From Jesus to Christianity*. San Francisco: Harper San Francisco, 2005.

Zetterholm, Magnus. *Approaches to Paul: A Student's Guide to Recent Scholarship*. Minneapolis: Fortress Press, 2009.

Chapter 2

Finding Paul

How to Get at the Apostle Paul? How to tell His story?

This is the point of this book. It is not a comprehensive look at Paul's theology because he did not develop an explicit systematic theology. I also will not attempt to solve all the sticky points in the scholarship on Paul. This book is trying to tell Paul's story in Paul's own words so as to try and figure out what he was about.

Most of what is needed for a biography of Paul is missing. For example, nothing is known of his parents, birth or early childhood traumas. Those certainly happened and were important influences, but we know nothing about them, even though Acts tries to supply some details. But more on that in a minute. The list of unknowns goes on and on. This is not as extraordinary as it sounds. For most important people in the ancient world we are missing much of the data we would consider essential for a modern biography.

Best Evidence

Preferably we should build Paul's story on primary evidence—in this case, his letters, which are ambiguous evidence. The problems are manifold. Which letters are Paul's? And in collecting them were they edited and if so, how much? About the first question we can be reasonably certain; about the second we are only beginning to get a handle on how to ask the question. William Walker has labored almost alone ferreting out later scribal additions or interpolations in the Pauline letters. *The Authentic Letters of Paul* has taken note of Walker's important work. Many scholars simply assume that the letters as found in the canon are from Paul's hand directly, even though they know that is not the case.

As in any biography we are always left sorting, evaluating, interpreting, and reconstructing the evidence. The situation with Paul is no different than writing a biography of any famous modern person—only the evidence is sparser.

Much of the evidence from the ancient world appears tainted. There are letters written in Paul's name that are not his and there are later stories whose provenance is hard to verify. What do we make of the stories in the Acts of the Apostles or the Acts of Paul and Thecla? We should not allow the fact that one is in the canon and the other is not to prejudice our judgment. These stories clearly tell us how Paul was viewed at the end of the first century or, more likely, in the early second. But do they really tell us much about Paul? Because these stories come from a later period and are difficult to verify, it is safer to begin with Paul. This is a minimalist rather than maximalist beginning.

I will work with the best evidence and build up the story from the most certain material. We will never get one hundred percent certainty. Much will remain unclear.

The writings ascribed to Paul in the New Testament can be divided into three groups:

surely from Paul
probably not from Paul
certainly not from Paul

Surely from Paul

In modern scholarship the following letters are usually accepted as surely from Paul.

1 Thessalonians
Galatians
1 and 2 Corinthians
Philemon
Philippians
Romans

At some point late in the first century the letters of Paul were collected and almost certainly edited. In some cases fragments of correspondence were edited together to make a single letter. Sometimes this editing is easy to spot, sometimes it is more controversial. Canonical Phil 3:1 is a good example.

Finally, my brethren, rejoice in the Lord. To write the same things to you, to me indeed is not grievous, but for you it is safe. (KJ)

This sounds like a conclusion with "Finally, my brethren." However canonical Philippians goes on for two more chapters with yet another conclusion at 6:10. Could Paul have written two conclusions to the same letter? Of course, but a careful consideration of the letter shows that what follows in Phil 3:2 is of a very different nature that what precedes. "Beware of dogs, beware of evil workers, beware of the concision" (Phil 3:2 KJ). This tone is so different that it raises the suspicion that it comes from a different letter. Is this absolute proof? No, but we must weigh the probabilities. It seems more probable that this is part of two letters than one.

The Corinthian correspondence is especially difficult. The first letter Paul wrote to this community is missing (1 Cor 5:9), so canonical 1 Corinthians is really their second letter from Paul. There are a number of interpolations—later additions by scribes—in both 1 and 2 Corinthians, one of which will become important in chapter 11. The status of the famous hymn on love in 1 Corinthians 13 is another example of a dubious piece of evidence. Is it from Paul? Is it a later interpolation? Is it even Christian? Finally, 2 Corinthians appears to be a composite of several different letters.

We are at a difficult place in modern scholarship on this issue of the editing of Paul's letters. Surely Paul's letters were edited, and there is probably consensus on the broad outline, however there is no real consensus on the details of the extent of the editing. Furthermore the weight of the canon means that the printed New Testament exhibits Paul's letters in canonical order with no indication of editing. This presents a reader with a solidity that is unreal and ahistorical. The new translation *The Authentic Letters of Paul* presents

- only the letters that are surely from Paul
- in chronological order, not canonical order
- with a plausible reconstruction of the various parts of the letters
- with the interpolations—later additions—removed and moved to an appendix at the letter's end

This is an important first step in beginning to restore the letters to a state more or less as Paul wrote them.

Fortunately, for our purposes, although we need to keep the issue of the composition of Paul's letters before us, it does not need to be conclusively solved. The issue of interpolations plays an important role in determining Paul's position on some controversial issues, such as Paul's view on women.

This editing process was not a one-time occurrence but an ongoing affair. We should not allow our printing press mentality to determine our understanding of the process. Printing fixes a composition, making it permanent and repeatable, so that each printed text is identical to all other versions printed from the same exemplar. But the same is not the case with a hand written and copied manuscript. Each manuscript is different. Each manuscript is individual and unique. This allows numerous variations to be introduced in each reiteration of the manual copying process. An historical understanding of Paul's letters needs to anticipate both the editing of the letters and the introduction of interpolations.

Probably Not from Paul

The status of Colossians, Ephesians and 2 Thessalonians has been debated, although a consensus is clearly trending towards their inauthenticity. I am of the opinion that all three of these letters are not Paul's letters. Ephesians has a literary relation to Colossians, that is, it copies and edits parts of Colossians. Both Colossians as well as Ephesians present a worldview that is very different from that of Paul, a worldview I find both incompatible with Paul's and at a chronological distance from Paul. These issues will become important later in chapter 11, "The Body in Ephesians."

A major difference between Colossians and Ephesians and those letters that are surely from Paul is that the authentic letters are addressed to real communities facing real problems. Their concreteness is palpable, which often makes them difficult to interpret or understand because precisely identifying the concrete situation is difficult. Ephesians on the contrary is not a real letter at all but a literary fabrication based on Colossians, while Colossians itself does not have the specificity of the surely authentic letters, but a more generalized, almost theoretical, outlook. For these reasons we should set these letters aside as not part of the best evidence.

Certainly Not from Paul

Finally there are those letters that surely are not from Paul, 1 and 2 Timothy and Titus, the so-called Pastorals, a modern designation. There are numerous reasons why scholars have long maintained that these letters are not from the hand of Paul. The Pastorals do not appear in the manuscript tradition until after 200 CE, and then sporadically, suggesting a very late composition for them. Irenaeus (about 180 CE) is the first one to quote from them. They are not letters addressed to a real community facing real issues, but are addressed to individuals. These letters look back to the followers and disciples of Paul. Thus they appear to come from the third or fourth generation, sometime around 120–50 CE.

Acts of the Apostles

The standard dating of the Acts of the Apostles has been around 85–95 CE. Recently Richard Pervo in *Dating Acts*, in his Hermeneia commentary on Acts, and in the Acts Seminar Report *Acts and Christian Beginnings* (edited by Dennis Smith and Joseph Tyson) have dated Acts to 115–20 CE. Pervo in his *Dating Acts* has amassed a convincing amount of data for this conclusion. He argues that the author of Acts, who is anonymous and surely not a companion of Paul, knew both the Pauline letter collection and Josephus. Both of these conclusions overturn long held scholarly beliefs, but Pervo has assembled compelling evidence for both conclusions.

If we are seeking the best evidence, there are many reasons for setting the Acts of the Apostles aside. As Leander Keck and Victor Furnish wisely noted some time ago, "The scholar's Paul, therefore, is not derived primarily from the book of Acts" (18).

Mention should be made of the noncanonical Acts of Paul, of which one important part is the Acts of Paul and Thecla. The dating of these Acts is debated. Late in the second century Tertullian quotes disparagingly from the Acts of Paul, particularly attacking the story of Thecla. Dennis MacDonald argues that the story of Thecla circulated as an oral story, popular among women, and perhaps goes back to the late first century. For MacDonald these oral stories portray Paul as a social radical, and the Pastorals were written to reject that image of Paul (59–66).

In order to build our study of Paul on a firm foundation, we will employ only that evidence that is surely from Paul, his authentic letters. We will not supplement it with material from the inauthentic letters or the Acts of the Apostles or the Acts of Paul and Thecla. We are using only the very best evidence and setting aside everything else.

Central Event

The central event in Paul's life was his experience of the risen Jesus that changed his life forever. He himself demarks this event as central, so that will be our starting point. Starting with his description of that event, we will explore it as carefully as we can. Remember, we are trying to tell Paul's story as he told it by using the best evidence.

The second element around which I will build Paul's story is his confrontation with Cephas in Antioch (Gal 2:11–21; see chapter 7, "Conflict with Cephas"). Although he does not describe it as the second most important event in his life, I suspect it was. Notice that I am already making an assumption. This confrontation also included James (Gal 2:12), the clear leader in Jerusalem. This standoff also apparently produced a breech within the early Jesus movement that was not healed, and plagued Paul wherever he went.

Part of the problem in telling Paul's story is the anomaly that for a person who did not know Jesus and was not one of his origi-

---

Jesus Movement

Gerd Theissen popularized the term Jesus movement as a way to designate the group before it became self-identified as Christian. It comes from the German title of his book, *Die Sociologie des Jesusbewegung* (German edition, 1977). It has the advantage of not over-formalizing a movement that was in the beginning stages of social organization.

---

nal followers, he has come to dominate the New Testament and as a consequence our view of early Christianity. This retrospection from the point of view of the canon of the New Testament, a late third- or fourth-century construction, is surely not the way it was. The Acts of the Apostles starts off with the eleven who become the twelve and soon the whole story is about Paul. Is that really the way the early Jesus movement plausibly developed? Most likely the author of Acts has constructed the viewpoint.

Although the statement "the victors write history" is a truism, equally true is that what survives from the past is often accidental. From the accidents of surviving evidence, historians by trying to fill in the gaps reconstruct our understanding of the past.

In telling Paul's story we are not telling the story of all the early communities of believers in the Anointed, but only one portion that, while it looms large in the canon of the New Testament and the mythology of subsequent Christianity, yet may have been minor and controversial.

Readings

Keck, Leander, and Victor Paul Furnish. *The Pauline Letters*. Nashville: Abingdon Press, 1984.

MacDonald, Dennis Ronald. *The Legend and the Apostle: The Battle for Paul in Story in Canon*. Philadelphia: Westminster Press, 1983.

Pervo, Richard I. *Dating Acts: Between the Evangelists and the Apologists*. Santa Rosa, CA: Polebridge Press, 2006.

_____. *The Mystery of Acts: Unraveling Its Story*. Santa Rosa, CA: Polebridge Press, 2008.

_____. *Acts*. Hermeneia. Ed. Harold W. Attridge. Minneapolis: Fortress Press, 2009.

Smith, Dennis Edwin, Joseph B Tyson, and the Acts Seminar, eds. *Acts and Christian Beginnings: The Acts Seminar Report*. Salem, OR: Polebridge Press, 2013.

Theissen, Gerd. *Sociology of Early Palestinian Christianity*. Philadelphia: Fortress Press, 1978.

Walker, William O. *Interpolations in the Pauline Letters*. London: Sheffield Academic Press, 2001.

_____. *Paul and His Legacy: Collected Essays*. Salem, OR: Polebridge, 2014.

CHAPTER 3

STARTING IN
THE Middle

Where we start often determines where we end up. Yet a starting point is not always obvious, other than the tautology that we should start at the beginning. But the beginning of what?

I propose starting with the central event in Paul's life, the event that changed his life forever. As primary evidence we will use his own description of that event in the letter to the Galatians. We are beginning in the middle, with the central and crucial event of his life, not at some other beginning. We are not starting this biography with birthplace, education, and so on. Nor are we starting with a review of scholarship.

We are starting in the middle because that is where Paul began when he told his story. That is the event through which he sees all of his life. For Paul, his life before the event, what happened after the event, and where his life and all of world history were going afterward were all shaped by this pivotal event.

We begin with Paul's account of his experience as related in his letter to the Galatians, not the more picturesque thrice-told tale in the Acts of the Apostles. We begin with Galatians even though what the tradition has remembered, what the art has pictured, is based on the dramatic accounts in the Acts of the Apostles (9:1–25; 22:6–21; 26:12–18), traditionally referred to as Paul's Damascus experience or his conversion. The event may have happened on the way to Damascus, but we only would know that from Acts. Just think of all the art you have seen depicting this event. They all have Paul being struck off a horse by a blinding light. There is no light in Paul's account in Galatians and no horse. There is a blinding light in Acts, but strangely no horse.

Galatians

Paul's Letter to the Galatians was written to his converts in the province Galatia around 55 CE. This letter's authenticity has not been seriously challenged nor has it been viewed as having been heavily edited. Kümmel in his *Introduction to the New Testament* deals with what Galatia means in this context and concludes, "The most readily justified assumption is that in this letter Paul is addressing the Galatians living in the interior of Asia, Minor" (298), that is, the province of Galatia.

As Crossan and Reed note, the horse comes from the assumptions of artists (8–9). This reveals how layered and distant our imagination of the event is from Paul's description in Galatians.

Let's begin with the primary evidence and see where it takes us. At this point we make no assumptions about the secondary accounts, other than that we have agreed to set them aside as secondary.

By pursuing Paul's own description of this central event, my hope is that it will open out onto the mystery of his life. Can this one text provide the clues to construct an image of the real Paul?

Galatians 1:11–17

Let me make it clear, friends, the message I announced does not conform to human expectations. I say this because it was not transmitted to me by anyone nor did anyone teach it to me. Rather, it came to me as an insight from God about Jesus as God's Anointed.

Surely you've heard of my own behavior as a practicing Jew, how aggressively I harassed God's new community, trying to wipe it out. I went way beyond most of my contemporaries in my observance of Judaism, and became notably zealous about my ancestral traditions.

However, when the One, who designated me before I was born and commissioned me to be an envoy, surprising all human expectations, chose to make his son known through me with the intent that I would proclaim God's world-transforming news to the nations, I did not rush off to consult with anyone. Neither did

I set out for Jerusalem to get the approval of those who became envoys for God's Anointed before I did. Instead, I left for Arabia and afterward returned to Damascus.

In order to understand this passage we must first understand its context, that is, ask why Paul was writing this letter, what was his purpose? Why is Paul giving his readers this little bit of autobiography?

CONTEXT

The letter's greeting poses and highlights Paul's central contention.

> Paul, an envoy,
>   not appointed by humans
>   nor by an individual
>   but by Jesus, God's Anointed,
>   and by God the father,
>   who raised Jesus from among the dead,
>   and all those brothers with me,
>   to the communities <of the Anointed> in Galatia.
>   (Gal 1:1–2 BBS)

Right off the bat Paul makes the point that he is an envoy/apostle not by human determination but by divine determination. From his point of view, this is the central point of contention in the letter. This is the issue. It may not be the issue from the Galatians' point of view. We must remember that we do not know their side.

Paul does not hide or suppress his anger in this letter. He is so angry that this is the only one of his letters that does not have a thanksgiving. Apparently he thinks he has nothing for which to be thankful. Later in the letter, while describing those who were in his judgment disturbing the Galatians, he says that he hopes they may "cut it off" (Gal 5:12 BBS). In this argument about circumcision, the "it" refers to their penises. This indeed is an angry letter.

From the Galatians' point of view the issue is circumcision as demanded by the sacred scriptures, while from Paul's point of view that problem exposes a greater issue, the very gospel itself and his claim that he has been sent by God and God's Anointed.

Paul's Story

This is Paul's story—one can call it autobiography as Lyons notes in his study of this passage: "Paul's autobiographical 'I' appears for the first time in 1:10 and continues to dominate the narrative through 2:21" (130). But we must be careful. This narrative occurs in a rhetorical context in which Paul is trying to score points. He thinks his divine commission is under attack. Paul claims that his message was not taught to him; that he did not receive it from any human being. He is claiming, even insisting upon, his independence. The vehemence of this letter has to imply that someone is saying the opposite. They are saying that Paul was taught the gospel by others and that he depends upon other envoys/apostles.

So a debate about the legitimacy of Paul's divine commission is what is at stake. To validate his position and as proof of his claim, he tells his story. His is not a neutral telling of his story but he tells his story to prove a point to win a debate. That does not mean that we should distrust his account, but we should be aware of its perspective and purpose.

The narrative has three parts: before the event, the event itself, and after the event. We use these three stages as shorthand to refer to Paul's narrative—before Paul, Paul in the event itself, and after Paul. We will be tracing the continuity and discontinuity in these three stages.

Before

In describing his former life in Judaism, Paul characterizes himself as "notably zealous about my ancestral traditions," as found in the Torah. He ends the account by noting that he is zealous. We moderns tend to see zeal not so much as a virtue but as a vice. We connect it with zealotry, a scourge of the modern religious and religions. But Paul sees zeal as a virtue and it demonstrates that he was a serious person who took his religion seriously. Some examples will help us understand what he means by "zealous."

In the contest between Jezebel and Elijah, Elijah proclaims he is zealous for God.

> "I have been very zealous for the LORD, the God of hosts; for the Israelites have forsaken your covenant, thrown down your altars,

and killed your prophets with the sword. I alone am left, and they are seeking my life, to take it away." (1 Kgs 19:10)

4 Maccabees presents the speech of the mother of seven sons who are being martyred. The speech is a later reworking of a scene in 2 Maccabees 7. In both the mother encourages her sons to die for their religion. In both, she remains nameless. In this speech she upholds Abraham as an example by pointing to his zeal.

> Remember that it is through God that you have had a share
> in the world and have enjoyed life, and therefore you ought to
> endure any suffering for the sake of God. For his sake also our
> father Abraham was zealous to sacrifice his son Isaac, the ances-
> tor of our nation; and when Isaac saw his father's hand wielding a
> knife and descending upon him, he did not cower.
> (4 Macc 16:18–20)

These two examples illustrate that zeal means to go beyond the everyday. Only Elijah is left, all the people have abandoned the Lord, and the king and queen are pursuing his life, yet he persists. In the case of Abraham, his willingness to sacrifice his own son is seen as an example of his zeal. Thus for Paul to claim that he is zealous for the traditions of his ancestors is to claim he went way beyond most of his contemporaries in his observance of Judaism. It means in his judgment he is a standout example of what it means to be a Jew. He has neither guilt nor shame for persecuting the community of the Anointed. He is proud of his stance. It demonstrates how serious and observant he was.

His behavior is like Abraham's or Elijah's in his harassing or persecuting the *ekklesia*/community of God.

This raises the question of just what Paul did, and how we should translate this passage. Action and translation are intercon-nected and both will plague our study until the very end. Paul wrote in Greek, we speak English and translation is hardly ever a one-to-one proposition. Even more, the theological tradition frequently employs Paul's words with a difference. There is a tendency to fill out the translation with what we think happened. The fact that there are two thousand years between his writing and our translation is sufficient to introduce many ambiguities. Rendering Paul's Greek into English is always a problem, at times a treacherous one.

We should not forget that Paul's audience in Galatia already knew his story. They knew what he did in his "before" life. We don't. Reading a letter is like hearing one side of a telephone conversation. We have to reconstruct the other side and often are left in the dark, at times guessing, sometimes correctly, but at other times wrongly, as to what the other side is saying.

Persecuting the Church

We begin by trying to understand just what Paul is writing, and that raises the problem of translation. Here are five representative translations of Gal 1:13:

KJ   how that beyond measure I persecuted the church of God, and wasted it.

NIV   how intensely I persecuted the church of God and tried to destroy it.

NRSV   I was violently persecuting the church of God and was trying to destroy it.

NAB   how I persecuted the church of God beyond measure and tried to destroy it.

SV   how aggressively I harassed God's new community, trying to wipe it out.

Marytrdom

The notion of martyrdom is part of the way Christians tell their story even today. Google "Christian persecution in America" and you will be surprised at the number of hits you will get. Standard Roman policy was not mass martyrdom, but elimination of a group's leaders. The catacombs were not a good place to hide, since everyone knew where they were. As Candida Moss argues in her *The Myth of Persecution*,

> Eusebius (262–339 CE) has uniquely shaped the way that people tell the story of Christianity. Eusebius helped to make the history of Christianity the history of persecution. The historical evidence suggests that the majority of texts about martyrs were either written down or heavily edited during this period [after Constantine] of relative peace and quiet. (245)

The King James sticks close to the Greek. "Beyond measure" is an accurate if wooden translation of the Greek *kath'hyperbolēn*. The English word "hyperbolic," a transliteration of the Greek word, conveys an accurate sense of the Greek's meaning. So it denotes "in excess." The NRSV's translation of "violently" is, how should we say, hyperbolic. It goes over the edge and, I suspect, is reading into Paul's account the stories from Acts, especially the report of Paul participating in the stoning of Stephen (Acts 7:58; 8:1). The Acts of the Apostles is a much later book with its own agenda, so we should not rely on it to flesh out Paul's Greek when translating it into English.

Perhaps "to the full measure" might be a good translation.

This leads us directly to "persecuting." The primary meaning in the Greek is "to pursue," in the sense of pursuing a thief or a lover. By extension it means to prosecute in the legal sense and, by extension in a different direction, to persecute. But now problems arise. Persecution in the Christian tradition conjures up the persecutions and martyrdoms of Christians by the Roman Empire, especially in the Acts of the Martyrs. These stories have seeped deep into Christianity's DNA. But whatever we think Rome was doing, this is not what Paul was doing. He was not executing or killing the early Anointed followers. Rome tended to have exclusive control of that kind of violence. Paul may best be thought of as harassing these early followers of Jesus. "Persecute" is fine as long as we do not imagine the later martyrdoms.

Why was Paul harassing or persecuting the community of God? He himself does not explicitly say why, so we have to make an educated guess, one of many we will have to make. Just because these folks were proclaiming Jesus the Anointed or Messiah is not sufficient reason. Famously in the Bar Kokhba revolt against Rome (132–36 CE), Rabbi Akiba proclaimed the revolt's leader, Simon ben Kosiba, to be the Messiah, yet the later rabbinic tradition did not condemn him for this. He remained one of the most celebrated and revered rabbis. They just thought Rabbi Akiba was mistaken.

This example is illuminating. Rabbi Akiba in proclaiming Simon ben Kosiba the Messiah gave him the surname Bar Kokhba, which in Aramaic means "son of the star" in reference to Num 24:17—"a star shall come out of Jacob, and a scepter shall rise out of Israel; it shall crush the borderlands of Moab, and the territory of all the Shethites." In later rabbinic tradition he is called Simon bar Kozeba, "son of lies." Simon ben Kosiba is blamed, not Rabbi Akiba. As Pamela Eisenbaum notes, for declaring Simon the Messiah, "R. Akiba has never been judged a heretic, and his teachings continue to be authoritative because they are preserved in the Mishnah and Talmud" (8). Simon ben Kosiba becomes a son of lies because Rome defeated him, and so he could not possibly be the promised Messiah. He lied.

To be clear: The issue was not the claim that Simon was the Messiah, but the evidence, the proof that he wasn't. In his case, the decisive evidence against him was his defeat by Rome. That proved his claim false.

Paul before his life-changing event appears to have taken a similar position in regard to Jesus. Jesus could not have been the Anointed because Rome crucified him. This means that Rome won and Jesus lost, which is the whole point of crucifixion. Paul appeals to this notion in his understanding of Jesus crucified as having been cursed. "Christ redeemed us from the curse of the law by becoming a curse for us—for it is written, 'Cursed is everyone who hangs on a tree'" (Gal 3:13 NRSV). In Paul's "before" logic, Jesus' crucifixion means that the claims made on his behalf are false. It is a very strong argument, as the case with Simon ben Kosiba demonstrates.

Thus Paul's persecuting or harassing of the early communities so as to wipe them out is based on the evidence of their false claim that Jesus was the Messiah.

Within the rhetorical context of Paul's argument with the Galatians, the significance of his persecuting the community is that it proves how unlikely a candidate for membership in this community he was. In the strongest terms he opposed that community and its claims.

But this opposition to the claims that Jesus was God's Anointed indicates why the cross became so important for Paul after his experience. Crucifixion is the piece of evidence that he must overcome. Paradoxically he must see the cross not as evidence that Jesus was defeated and that Rome won, but that Rome lost and Jesus won. That is his central issue, and it comes from his life before.

"My Mother's Womb"

From the point of view of the event itself Paul looks back on his life before as under divine control. This is what Gal 1:15 indicates: "when the One, who designated me before I was born," or as the KJ has it more poetically, "who separated me from my mother's womb." This note in Galatians is important for two reasons. It provides us with an important clue to Paul's self-understanding and gives us a way to understand how Paul often constructs his arguments rhetorically.

In Gal 1:15 Paul alludes to two quotations, one from Isa 49:1 and the other from Jeremiah:

> Now the word of the LORD came to me saying,
> "Before I formed you in the womb I knew you,
> and before you were born I consecrated you;
> I appointed you a prophet to the nations."
> (Jer 1:4–5)

Instead of directly quoting a verse of scripture, Paul alludes to it, almost like a midrash, like a jazz riff, expecting his audience to pick up the allusion. I must admit that I wonder how often that happened. The allusion provides important hermeneutical clues to the interpretation of Paul's self-understanding and rhetorical compositions.

In this case it shows that Paul viewed his whole life as part of a divine plan. Even before God formed him in his mother's womb, God had destined him for this mission.

Even more, the allusion specifies how Paul sees that designation. The quote is set in the context of Jeremiah's call to be a prophet. This notion is reinforced in parallel language found in Isaiah 49:

> Listen to me, O coastlands, pay attention, you peoples from far away! The Lord called me before I was born, while I was in my mother's womb he named me. (Isa 49:1)

> And now the Lord says, who formed me in the womb to be his servant, to bring Jacob back to him, and that Israel might be gathered to him, for I am honored in the sight of the Lord, and my God has become my strength. (Isa 49:5)

This allusion provides us with an important piece of evidence by which to understand Paul's take on the event that changed his life. "Formed in the womb" is a trope in the story of a prophet's call. Paul clearly understands himself as a prophet, as one standing in the line of Israel's great prophets. A prophet has both a call from God and a mission from God.

A Pharisee

In Phil 3:5–6 Paul adds some more details about who he was before his life-changing event.

> I was circumcised eight days after my birth, I belong to the people of Israel by birth and am descended from the tribe of Benjamin, a Hebrew descended from Hebrews. With respect to the law I was a Pharisee. My zeal about this led me to persecute the Anointed's people. In regard to the requirements of the law, I was flawless. (Phil 3:5–6)

Notice the similarity of the pattern to that in Galatians. Paul's zeal led him to persecute the Anointed's people. This is the formulaic version of his story that he wants to accent and call to his audience's attention. When he tells his story, this is the pattern that for him stands out because it means, in his mind, that his turn to the Anointed was totally unexpected and could not be accounted for.

His former life in Judaism constitutes his credentials, which are still in place. In the Greek the following describe his lineage, his source of honor.

> by circumcision on the eighth day
> out of the people of Israel
> of the tribe of Benjamin
> a Hebrew of Hebrews
> according to the Torah a Pharisee. (BBS)

This list defines who Paul thinks he is "according to the flesh," that is, by human standards. These all point to him as an outstanding Jew. In the context in Philippians, Paul is debating with Jewish opponents, and he claims that his Jewish credentials top theirs (Phil 3:4). They boast about these things, but he will not. Now, after the event, he counts them as worthless (Phil 3:8) or rubbish (NRSV). But that does not mean that they are no longer true of

Letter to the Philippians

Philippi was a colony in Macedonia settled by Roman soldiers. Its wealth was derived from mining. Considerable debate exists about whether the canonical letter is a composite of several letters or a single unity. The SV divides it into three letters. Regardless, it does show a unity of theme concerning fellowship. The letter(s) were written sometime around 55–56 from Ephesus where Paul was in prison. The community at Philippi was a strong financial supporter of Paul.

him. They are just no longer the occasion of his boasting. They are not what determine his honor, as they do for his opponents.

These items describe him as having been a pious, male Jew, who interpreted the Torah according to the principles of a Pharisee and who was not guilt-ridden in the observance of the Torah. In fact he thinks his behavior was exemplary, flawless (Phil 3:6). This latter point is extremely important, since the major interpretative tradition of Paul stemming from Augustine and Luther demands that Paul be guilt-ridden.

In Paul's telling of the story his devotion and zeal as a Jew did not lead to any expectation that he would become a follower of this newly proclaimed Messiah. In fact from his point of view it is unaccountable, so it must have been not of his own doing, but God's.

In the next chapter we will turn our attention to the transforming, shattering event that changed Paul's life.

Readings

Crossan, John Dominic, and Jonathan L. Reed. *In Search of Paul, How Jesus' Apostle Opposed Rome's Empire with God's Kingdom.* San Francisco: HarperSanFrancisco, 2004.

Eisenbaum, Pamela. *Paul Was Not a Christian: The Original Message of a Misunderstood Apostle.* New York: HarperOne, 2009.

Kümmel, Werner Georg. *Introduction to the New Testament.* Trans. Howard Clark Kee. Nashville: Abingdon Press, 1973.

Lyons, George. *Pauline Autobiography, Toward a New Understanding.* Atlanta: Scholars Press, 1985.

Moss, Candida R. *The Myth of Persecution: How Early Christians Invented a Story of Martyrdom.* New York: HarperOne, 2013.

Zetterholm, Magnus. *Approaches to Paul: A Student's Guide to Recent Scholarship.* Minneapolis: Fortress Press, 2009.

CHAPTER 4

LIFE-CHANGING EVENT

Traditionally we have referred to this event as Paul's conversion on the road to Damascus and sometimes in shorthand as either Paul's conversion or the Damascus road experience. These titles are problematic, but for different reasons.

As we have seen, the problem with Damascus Road as shorthand is that it imports the Acts of the Apostles stories (Acts 9:1–25; 22:6–21; 26:12–18) into Paul's discourse. For our purposes we have bracketed Acts. We seek the best evidence, the primary evidence, not secondary evidence as found in Acts.

Conversion as a model for what happened to Paul is both problematic and potentially misleading.

The interpretation of Paul that has dominated the West and underpinned the Protestant reformation derives from Augustine and Luther, and was championed in modern times by Karl Barth and Rudolf Bultmann. This is indeed a powerful and entrenched understanding of Paul. For most folks it *is* Paul, so deeply ingrained that it has become intuitive. We automatically read Paul in this fashion.

Krister Stendahl's essay, "The Apostle Paul and the Introspective Conscience of the West" (1963) started a revolution that is undoing and overturning the traditional Augustinian/Lutheran interpretation. Stendahl argued "the West for centuries has wrongly surmised that the biblical writers were grappling with problems which no doubt are ours, but which never entered their consciousness" (95).

Rather than rehearse Stendhal's argument, let's turn our attention to Paul's actual language, with Stendhal looking over our shoulder and leading the way.

Twice, in quick succession, in Galatians Paul characterizes his experience in formulaic language.

> Rather, it came to me as an insight from God about Jesus as God's Anointed. (Gal 1:12b)

> However, when the One, who designated me before I was born and commissioned me to be an envoy, surprising all human expectations, chose to make his son known through me with the intent that I would proclaim God's world-transforming news to the nations. (Gal 1:15–16)

Both these quotes are set as clauses within a larger grammatical structure, yet they contain a clear fragment of Paul's autobiography. Verses 15–16 are an elaboration of the formula in 12b. These two and one-half verses are packed with important and special vocabulary, and paying close attention to this language will get us closer to understanding Paul in his own context.

Insight/Revelation

The phrase "before I was born" or "from my mother's womb" as the King James has it, sticking closer to the Greek's metaphor, comes from the prophetic call tradition and underlines that God has planned the prophet's mission. This demonstrates that Paul sees this event within the horizon of the call of a prophet by God. God calls and commissions Paul as a prophet/apostle/envoy, standing in the line of Israel's great prophets.

Twice, in quick succession, Paul characterizes the event using the words "revelation" and "to reveal," employing the same Greek word root *apocalyps-*.

> by the revelation of Jesus Christ (Gal 1:12 KJ)
> to reveal his Son in me (Gal 1:16 KJ)

The verb "to reveal" or the noun "revelation" are over-determined words in English. In English it can imply a vision or content from another world. The graphic images in the Acts of the Apostles and the artwork that Acts has inspired reinforce the vision aspect. Acts uses the image of a blinding light and a voice, and has Paul refer to his experience as a vision (Acts 26:19). But Paul himself gives no evidence that he experienced a vision, although that is not impossible and according to some may be probable. He does not associate this experience with a vision. For Paul the accent is not on his subjective experience, what he experienced; but on the objective happening, what this event means or makes evident.

He is describing his experience of the risen Jesus. In 1 Corinthians 15 and 9:1 he does use the language of seeing, but again without elaborating the subjective experience, even though the later tradition has been only too happy to supply it. This problem is somewhat beyond the scope of the present study and if you are interested, see my book *The Trouble with Resurrection* (107–22). Paul claims to have experienced "visions and revelations" (2 Cor 12:1 NRSV), but in describing them he engages in a fool's speech. He mocks these visions and revelations: "whether in the body, I don't know, or out of the body, I don't know, God knows—carried off to heaven's third level" (2 Cor 12:2). He only makes it to the third heaven, not seventh as in the third-century *Apocalypse of Paul* (for translation see Hennecke, 755–803). And what is the point of hearing "indescribable words which no one may speak?" (2 Cor 12:4). This fool's speech graphically demonstrates the difference between visions and revelations and the central event of Paul's life—an *apocalypsis*/revelation of God's son.

What is important in the context of Galatians is the recognition that the Greek word root *apocalyps-* has the sense of knowing something that cannot be known in a human way; making the hidden or non-evident manifest or evident. So revelation is a good translation. Psalm 97:2 (LXX; Ps 98:2 in the Hebrew and NRSV) is an excellent example of this sense:

> The Lord has made known his deliverance (*sōtērion, lit:* salvation); before the nations he revealed (*apekalypsen*) his righteousness.

For Paul *apocalypsis* explains what has happened; in his estimation he cannot account for the experience except by the action of God. In the rhetorical context he is trying to defend his call as not from or dependent upon humans or a human.

Instead of translating the *apocalyps-* root as "revelation," the SV uses "insight" and "to make known" in an effort to avoid the problems associated with the possible misleading implications of the English "revelation/reveal." The SV translation is making an important point. "Revelation" as a translation has the disadvantage of reading into Paul's account the vivid image of the in-breaking of the supernatural world in the form of the blinding light and dramatic voice addressing Saul that occurs in the Acts account. "Insight" and "to make known" sidestep Acts's dramatic image and imply that it might not be a single, dramatic moment, but may have occurred over a period of time. But it risks downplaying that, for Paul, the event is from God. That is what "revelation" as a translation makes evident. Because there is no perfect English gloss for *apocalypsis*, I will frequently use *apocalypsis*/revelation or *apocalypsis*/insight to remind the English reader that we are dealing with a word more sophisticated in meaning than either the English "revelation" or "insight." It may be awkward, but it reminds us that Paul did not write his letters in English and that translation is always an issue we must take seriously.

Paul does specify the content of the *apocalypsis*/revelation: "to make his son known through me with the intent that I would proclaim God's world-transforming news to the nations." This content is encoded in concise language. The *apocalypsis*/revelation has two parts: God's son and Paul's commission.

His Son

A question seldom asked but important to notice is why does Paul use "son" in Gal 1:16? Why did he not write "Jesus," or "Jesus Messiah," or "Anointed," or "lord"? Why son? What is the implication of this title? After all, both "Anointed" and "lord" occur much more frequently in the Pauline letters than "son." At the very beginning of the letter to the Galatians, in which Paul invokes the letter's themes, he thrice refers to "father" and "brothers" in the middle of the rhetorical construction, thus implying a familial pattern, yet he refers to Jesus as "lord" and "Anointed."

> From Paul envoy
>> not from humans nor through a human
>> but through Jesus the anointed and God *father*
>>> who raised him from the dead

and all those with me *brothers*
to those called out of Galatia
grace and peace from God our *father* and lord Jesus Anointed
who gave himself on behalf of our sins to take us out of
the present evil age according to the will of God and our
father.
(Gal 1:1–4 BBS, emphasis added)

Right at the beginning Paul notes that he is an envoy not through human means but "through Jesus the anointed and God father." That his commission is not from humans but from God denotes a primary building block in his defense of his revelation. Then three times in this greeting Paul mentions "father" in reference to God. This makes it all the more puzzling why "son" is not employed in the greeting but is the content of the *apocalypsis*/revelation. Why does he not say he revealed "his Anointed/Messiah" since that is precisely what he says in 1:12? It may prove impossible to definitively answer this question, but it will enrich our understanding if we are aware of the possibilities.

The point of the *apocalypsis*/revelation is simple to state— the crucified one is actually God's son. This defines why it is an *apocalypsis*—a revelation that demands an insight. From Paul's perspective before the *apocalypsis*/revelation, the crucified one as God's son is an oxymoron, a contradiction in terms. It cannot be true because God's son, God's messiah, must triumph over his enemies, not be defeated by them. Psalm 2:7–8 is the classic proof text:

I will tell of the decree of the LORD: He said to me, "You are my son; today I have begotten you. Ask of me, and I will make the nations your heritage, and the ends of the earth your possession."

For Paul before his revelation, the crucifixion of Jesus was his proof that those who believed Jesus was God's Anointed were wrong. Jesus could not be the son of God because Rome had triumphed over him. Precisely for this reason Paul says that what convinced him that this oxymoron is actually true was an *apocalypsis*/revelation.

Consider the counter position. The proof that an emperor is god's son is his defeat of the nations. Rome's military victories demonstrate that the gods favor Rome. This is precisely the argument made in stone by the Arch of Titus. Domitian constructed the arch in 81 CE to commemorate the death of his brother the emperor Titus. It was Titus who had led the siege of Jerusalem in 70 CE for his father, the recently made emperor Vespasian. The arch sits on the *Via Sacra* at the entrance to the Roman Forum. The two panels in the Arch's interior memorialize the triumph celebrated by Titus and Vespasian in 71 CE commemorating the destruction of Jerusalem and its Temple. The south panel depicts the spoils from the Temple in Jerusalem being carried in the triumphal procession by the legionaries. A giant, deeply carved menorah dominates the scene, probably originally colored in gold. The south panel portrays Titus in his quadra with winged victory in his chariot. The arch's soffit depicts Titus' apotheosis. The logic of the arch is manifest—it is a revelation in stone. Titus must be a god because he defeated their god. The reverse logic applies to the crucifixion of Jesus.

While Jesus' defeat by Rome, his crucifixion, demonstrates that he is not God's son, the event of *apocalypsis*/insight demonstrates to Paul that he is God's son, and from it flow important consequences. This paradox drives Paul. The power of the title "his son" derives from its juxtaposition with "crucified by Rome." Paul's *apocalypsis*/revelation implies a counter-world to that of the Roman Empire. It is an anti-imperial insight. We have to always keep this in mind because of our tendency to see Jesus as son of God as "just" or "only" religious and therefore devoid of political implication. To call the crucified one son of God challenges the way Roman imperial ideology says the world is constructed.

Likewise "his son" implies that God is his father, which picks up on the greeting at the letter's beginning where God as father is thrice invoked. The titles of son and father are explicitly imperial titles. The emperor is a son of god, often so proclaimed on coins, and father of the fatherland (*pater patriae*). The way these titles are employed in dealing with Paul's *apocalypsis*/revelation walks along the line of sedition. It directly and explicitly contests Rome's ideology.

The traditional interpretation of Paul sees his main opposition as Judaism, but our line of argument suggests that his main opponent is Roman ideology. The Augustinian/Lutheran understanding of Paul has clearly understood Judaism as the opposite of

Paul's new religion, Christianity. But our exploration is suggesting that Rome fills that place. As we move forward, we will have to pay special attention to this opposition and its implications.

Adopted Sons

Out of this central *apocalypsis*/revelation/insight event, implications will emerge throughout this book. My working hypothesis is that the *apocalypsis* event is the key to understanding Paul. Paul does not begin with an established or fully formed theology. He was always improvising, working it out, making it up as he went along. But he is working it out from his *apocalypsis*/insight that the crucified Jesus is God's son. The *apocalypsis* is an oxymoron, namely the crucified one is God's son; that it is true is a revelation, to understand it demands insight.

Out of this *apocalypsis*/insight Paul draws conclusions about himself—which we will pursue in the next chapter—and about those who accepted Jesus as the Anointed. He concludes that they are adopted sons of God. He makes this argument clear in Gal 4:6–7:

> And because ye are sons, God hath sent forth the Spirit of his Son into your hearts, crying, Abba, Father. Wherefore thou art no more a servant, but a son; and if a son, then an heir of God through Christ. (KJ)

Most modern translations in avoiding sexist language obscure the underlying metaphorical structure. The SV translation is a good example.

> Now because you are adopted, God sent into your hearts the same filial attitude toward God that was in Jesus, that can call God, "Abba! Father!" So as a result, you are no longer menial servants, but through what God has done you have become adopted as "children" and that means heirs. (SV)

There is nothing wrong with this translation and it catches the sense and feeling of the Greek better than the more literal translation of the KJ. All translations have to make decisions when they represent an ancient text in a modern language. With that ancient language come the values and conventions of that ancient culture. Likewise with the modern language come the values and conventions of that modern culture. Language and culture are not separable. The KJ refers to the Anointed believers as "sons," a literal translation of the Greek, while the SV refers to the "filial attitude" and "children," neither of which is gender specific.

Is there something specific in Paul's argument that requires "sons," or is he just using "sons" in the sense of all human beings, thus reflecting the inherent patriarchal structure of the ancient world? I think there is a specific argument which is important to follow out.

The fundamental contrast in this passage is between slave and son, or enslaved and free. The KJ and modern translations render the Greek as "servant" instead of the more correct "slave" to avoid the implications of slavery (see Glancy) and so hide the metaphorical structure. Slave personifies enslavement or bondage, while son personifies freedom. Paul is describing the before and after status of the Anointed believer. Before, one is a slave; after, one is free. Baptism marks the movement, alluded to in the cry, "Abba! Father!" which an initiate cries out as she emerges from the water. Thus those who believe in the Anointed are adopted sons of God.

Once again, the Roman Empire lurks around the edges. Augustus was an adopted son of Julius Caesar and that adoption was the basis for his claim to be emperor, to take up Caesar's inheritance and his title as a son of god, for his father Caesar was a god. Likewise Tiberius was an adopted son of Augustus. Adoption was often important in determining who succeeded the emperor.

Is Paul being sexist in his language? Not completely. Because he thinks that all Anointed believers are sons of God, he draws the conclusion that there is no longer male and female.

> So, everyone of you who has been baptized into solidarity with God's Anointed has become invested with the status of God's Anointed. You are no longer Jew or Greek, no longer slave or freeborn, no longer "male and female." Instead, you all have the same status in the service of God's Anointed, Jesus. Moreover, if you now belong to God's Anointed, that also makes you Abraham's offspring and—as promised—his heirs.
> (Gal 3:26–29)

We will have to unpack this statement later, but for now notice that the SV translators have placed male and female in quotation marks, because they think Paul is quoting the creation story in Gen 1:27 (LXX). So Paul is making a powerful claim here: that by baptism the order of creation is being set aright.

Readings

Glancy, Jennifer A. *Slavery in Early Christianity*. Oxford: Oxford University Press, 2002.

Hennecke, Edgar, and Wilhelm Schneemelcher. *New Testament Apocrypha, Vol. 2: Writings Relating to the Apostles; Apocalypses and Related Subjects*. Philadelphia: Westminster Press, 1965.

Scott, Bernard Brandon. *The Trouble with Resurrection*. Salem, OR: Polebridge Press, 2011.

Stendahl, Krister. "The Apostle Paul and the Introspective Conscience of the West." *Harvard Theological Review* 56 (1963) 123–44. Reprinted as pp. 78–96 in *Paul among Jews and Gentiles*. Philadelphia: Fortress Press, 1976. In this same volume see his essay "Call Rather than Conversion," 7–23.

Chapter 5

After the Event

We have already begun dealing with the aftermath of the *apocalypsis* event in Paul's description of the Anointed believers as adopted sons of God. In this chapter we turn to the aftereffects of the event on Paul. What was the outcome for him? We return to that pivotal passage in Gal 1:15–16:

> [God, who] commissioned me to be an envoy, surprising all human expectations, chose to make his son known through me with the intent that I would proclaim God's world-transforming news to the nations.

Commissioned to Be an Envoy

Apostle

Once again, a translation issue. Traditionally the Greek word *apostolos* is translated "apostle," because the early Latin usage transliterated the Greek *apostolos* into Latin as *apostolus*, that is, it brought the Greek letters over letter for letter into Latin. Thus the Greek *apostolos* became in Latin *apostolus* and in English apostle. Apostle is not a translation but a transliteration. By the time that the Latin usage was established, I suspect that *apostolus* had become an established Christian ecclesiastical title and so there was no need to translate it.

This transliteration has the unfortunate consequence of turning apostle into a distinctive theological and ecclesiastical title, an overtone it lacks in the Greek of Paul's day. The Greek word has the meaning of "one who is sent from": *apo* (from) *stellein* (to send). Therefore envoy, messenger or ambassador are all possible translations (BAGD).

The New Testament usage is unique. Ann Brock in a careful study of the Greek word *apostolos* summarizes the situation:

> The word *apostolos* in Greek literature is primarily connected with seafaring, where it arose as a description of a type of transport ship and came eventually to refer to the dispatch of a fleet. Only Herodotus, employing the word twice in the sense of "messenger," provides a pre-Christian Greek connection to the meaning of the word in New Testament texts. (3)

The word is used once in Josephus and once in the LXX. So the New Testament usage apparently is *sui generis*. (See Brock for a careful summary of the evidence and recent scholarship, 3–6.)

Paul's writings contain the earliest extant use of the word in the Jesus movement, although he is clearly not the first to use the word. The later tradition conflated what in the Jesus movement of Paul's time were two separate groups, the twelve and the envoys/apostles, into one group, the twelve apostles. This conflation is mostly a byproduct of the author of Luke/Acts. 1 Corinthians 15:5 and 7 plainly indicate that at the time Paul was writing the twelve and the apostles were two separate groups.

The Acts of the Apostles, written well after Paul, most likely in the early second century, relates the story of the succession of Judas. Before making a selection Peter announces: "So one of the men who have accompanied us during all the time that the Lord Jesus went in and out among us, beginning from the baptism of John until the day when he was taken up from us—one of these must become a witness with us to his resurrection" (Acts 1:21–22 NRSV). While this eventually became the *de facto* definition of an apostle, it appears to be a construction of the author of Acts. It does not even literally fit with the Gospel of Luke. In that gospel, after John is arrested (Luke 3:20), Jesus is baptized (Luke 3:21), so Jesus' baptism is not by John and the disciples have not yet been called. Why this construction by the author of Acts? Suspicions are raised for several reasons. This is a onetime event in Acts. No other member of the twelve is replaced. In fact, the twelve apostles soon disappear from the Acts narrative. Besides, the requirement that they be eyewitnesses to the ministry of Jesus deliberately excludes Paul, who in Acts is only twice referred to as an apostle (along with Barnabas, Acts 14:4, 14; see Pervo, 350). Given Paul's fierce insistence in his letters that he is an envoy/apostle, this reluctance on the part of Acts raises suspicions.

For Paul not only are the twelve and the *apostoloi*/envoys two separate groups, but he also knows female apostles. "Greet Andronicus and Junia, my compatriots and fellow-prisoners. They are persons of distinction among [the Anointed's] emissaries and they identified themselves with the Anointed before I did" (Rom 16:7). The name Junia is clearly a female name.

The Apostle Junia

Junia has had to struggle to take her rightful place among the apostles. The history of her transformation into a male and rediscovery as a female almost reads like a detective novel with a denial of her existence, the invention of a phony Latin male name and other convoluted grammatical contortions. (See Eldon Epp's *Junia, the First Woman Apostle* for an engaging treatment of issue.)

In early Christianity there was no real challenge to her status as an apostle. The oft-quoted words of John Chrysostom (ca. 347–407) clearly make the point.

> "Greet Andronicus and Junia . . . who are outstanding among the apostles": To be an apostle is something great. But to be outstanding among the apostles—just think what a wonderful song of praise that is! They were outstanding on the basis of their works and virtuous actions. Indeed, how great the wisdom of this woman must have been that she was even deemed worthy of the title of apostle.
> *(In ep. ad Romanos* 31.2)

The quote makes it clear that Chrysostom considered Junia a full-fledged apostle. As far as we can tell, Chrysostom represents the standard position in Christianity until the late medieval period. While the first identification of the name as male occurs in the late thirteenth century, the decisive influence is Luther's translation. He identifies the name as masculine.

Despite Luther's influence, *textus receptus* as well as all Greek printed editions of the New Testament, save one,

---

take the name as feminine until the 1927 edition of Nestle. Likewise early English translations, including the King James, take the name as Junia, female. In the nineteenth century translations suddenly began to move to a masculine interpretation of the name.

Bernadette Brouton's 1977 article changed the situation by producing a mass of evidence that a female Junia was the correct reading and that there was no evidence of the supposed male name that scholars had proposed to avoid the outcome of a female apostle. The 1998 Nestle-Aland (27th edition) and UBS (4th edition) restored Junia as a female. English translations also have begun shifting. Beginning in 1970 with the NAB (a Catholic translation) more and more English translations have interpreted the name as female. The REB and NRSV made the shift in 1989, while the NIV has remained with the name as male.

PAUL AS ENVOY

What is an envoy for Paul? He notes two characteristics:

> called by God to be an envoy
> have seen the Lord

Paul never explicitly conjoins these two conditions and they may be the same thing, that is, being called to be an envoy takes place in a revelation or seeing of the Lord. In the list in 1 Corinthians 15 of those who have seen the Lord, the apostles come last with James, whom Paul also apparently thinks of as an apostle (at least that is the most natural reading of Gal 1:19). "Then he was seen by James, then by all the apostles" (1 Cor 15:7). The Greek word translated "he was seen" (*ōphthē*) is used in the LXX to refer to a revelation, with the classic example being the appearance of God to Moses in the burning bush. "And an angel of the Lord has been seen for him in a flaming fire out of a bush; and he sees that the bush is burning and the bush is not burning up" (Exod 3:2 LXX BBS). As Philo comments, this is seeing while not seeing!

> He in His love for mankind, when the soul came into His presence, did not turn away His face, but came forward to meet him and revealed His nature, so far as the beholder's power of sight

allowed. That is why we are told not that the Sage saw (*eide*) God, but that God was seen (*ōphthē*) by him. For it were impossible that anyone should by himself apprehend the truly Existent, did not he reveal and manifest Himself.

("On the Migration of Abraham," 17.77–80, pp. 42–45)

A careful reading of the Exodus passage, which Philo clearly did, indicates that what Moses saw was the bush burning but not being consumed. What he did not actually see is Yahweh, because, as Philo notes, Yahweh cannot be seen. Paul is careful never to give a description of the subjective experience of seeing/revealing. In contrast, in 2 Cor 12:1–7 he engages in a fool's speech to characterize his visions and revelations (see chapter 4, "Insight/ Revelation").

Several important conclusions spring from this.

- Not everyone who has seen the Lord is an envoy/apostle. Only those in the last part of the list in 1 Corinthians 15 are envoys.
- Part of the *apocalypsis*/event is a commission, to be sent out with a specific task.

So the call comes with the event. This self-understanding is evident as Paul introduces himself as the addresser of his letters. The letters show an interesting development in this regard. 1 Thessalonians, the earliest letter, has a quite simple form.

Paul, Silvanus, and Timothy,
To the community of the Thessalonians.
(1 Thess 1:1 BBS)

Philippians elaborates with a title:

Paul and Timothy,
    slaves of the Anointed Jesus
To all the holy ones in the Anointed Jesus who are in Philippi.
(Phil 1:1 BBS)

The construction of the addresser in Romans exhibits yet more elaboration:

Paul
    slave of Anointed Jesus
    called to be an envoy
    set apart for the good news of God.
(Rom 1:1 BBS)

This construction is more balanced and elaborate, abetting the elegance of the letter to the Romans. "Slave" contrasts sharply with the status of "envoy" and "good news," and the honor of the addressee, "to all God's beloved in Rome" (Rom 1:7 BBS). So sharp is the contrast that the juxtaposition is almost shocking. "Called" and "set apart" denote divine activity on behalf of the addresser.

There is a tendency to view the title slave of the Anointed as a throwaway for two reasons. The title in which the ecclesiastical tradition has been most interested is apostle/envoy, and most often in English translations the Greek *doulos* is translated as servant, thus masking the offensive character of slave. But as we shall see, Paul takes the title of slave of the Anointed seriously. The slave is at the very bottom of the social hierarchy, almost a nonhuman. The slave is one who is cursed and being a slave is shameful. For Paul, "slave of the Anointed" matches "the Anointed crucified." They are parallel titles demonstrating that Paul as slave and the Anointed as crucified have the same status. We ought not to be too quick to think that Paul calling himself a slave is a sign of false humility. No, we should take this seriously as part of his self-understanding, of what it means to be "in the Anointed."

Although we have already examined the address of Galatians, this context calls for another look.

> Paul,
>> an envoy
>>> not from humans nor through a human
>>> but through Jesus Anointed and God the father who raised
>>> him from the dead.
>>> (Gal 1:1 BBS)

As noted previously, Paul, the letter's addresser, lays out his credentials, which are under dispute. The construction accents that he is an envoy/apostle through the activity of Jesus and God and that the demonstration of God's power is the resurrection. Implication: the resurrection of Jesus demonstrates that Rome's power as exhibited in Jesus' crucifixion is now void.

The way Paul as addresser of the letter describes himself discloses his self-understanding as an envoy/apostle. What stands out is the called dimension—that an envoy, one who is sent-from (*apo-stel-*), is called by Jesus and God and sent from Jesus and

God. Called by and sent from are two aspects of the same *apocalypsis* event.

Also noted above, in describing his call, Paul alludes to the language of Jeremiah: "who set me apart from my mother's womb" (Gal 1:15 BBS; see Jer 1:4 and Isa 49:1). This reinforces the notion that Paul sees himself as God's envoy as called by God. While Paul never refers to himself as a prophet, clearly he sees himself and all the envoys of Jesus Anointed and God as carrying out the last stage of the task of the Hebrew prophets.

Gospel

For what purpose was Paul called to be an envoy? Again the *locus classicus* from which to begin our discussion is Paul's own description in Galatians.

> when the One, who . . . commissioned me to be an envoy, surprising all human expectations, chose to make his son known through me with the intent that I would proclaim God's world-transforming news to the nations. (Gal 1:15–16)

Part of the problem in translation is that Greek employs the same root *euaggel-* for both the verb and noun, whereas in English translators must employ two different words—for the verb "to preach" and the noun "gospel." Unfortunately "to gospelize" is not English.

The Greek word *euaggelion*, traditionally translated as "gospel" or "good news," is a freighted word in the Greek of Paul's time. The translators of *Authentic Letters of Paul* often chose to translate the Greek with the phrase "world-transforming news," thus signaling to a reader the provocative and challenging nature of the Greek word. What gets missed in the English usage "gospel" is the usage of this word in the imperial cult. We cannot understand the gospel of God without understanding the gospel of Rome. The former was understood in the context of the latter.

Priene Inscription

In 1889 some fragments from an inscription from Priene in Turkey (ancient Asia Minor) were published in Germany. The inscription commemorated a calendar change and used some language strikingly similar to that used by the early Jesus movement.

In 1908 Adolf Deissmann in his famous book *Light from the Ancient East* (English translation, 1910) argued for the importance of the fragments in a discussion that still holds up well. Deissmann also published pictures of the inscriptions (366–72). The fragments from Priene are in the Pergamon Museum in Berlin.

Since Deissmann's time archaeologists have discovered thirteen more fragments of the inscription from five different cities in Asia Minor, and research on the inscription and the imperial cult have made much progress. Thirteen different fragments from five different cities in Asia Minor indicate that this inscription originally discovered at Priene is not about just a local affair but a major policy development in this province of the empire.

The situation in the Province of Asia is this: The Proconsul or Governor of Asia, Paulus Fabius Maximus, wrote in 9 BCE to the provincial council that they should switch from their local calendar to the Julian calendar. Calendars were important in the ancient world, but a request from a proconsul is always more of a command. Here is his request to the council:

> It is subject to question whether the birthday of our most divine Caesar spells more of joy or blessing, this being a date that we could probably without fear of contradiction equate with the beginning of all things, if not in terms of nature, certainly in terms of utility, seeing that he restored stability, when everything was collapsing and falling into disarray, and gave a new look to the entire world that would have been most happy to accept its own ruin had not the good and common fortune of all been born: CAESAR. Therefore people might justly assume that his birthday spells the beginning of life and real living and marks the end and boundary of any regret that they had themselves been born. And since no other day affords more promise of blessing for engagement in public or private enterprise than this one which is so fraught with good fortune for everyone; and since this day practically coincides with the inaugural day for local magistrates in all the cities of Asia, and quite apparently through divine intervention, and in such a way that the (provincial) observance seems to have provided a model for others so that there might be a starting point for rendering appropriate honors to Augustus; and whereas on the one hand it is difficult to render thanks in

proportion to the many benefits he has conferred—unless, of course, we ponder carefully how we might in some way requite them one by one; and whereas on the other hand it may be presumed that people will more readily celebrate as a birthday a day that is already observed in common by all, especially if it offers them a measure of leisure because it coincides with the (local) inaugural observance, it is my judgment that the one and the same day observed by all the citizens as the New Year's day be celebrated as the birthday of the Most Divine Caesar, and on that day, September 23, all elected officials shall assume office, with the prospect that their association with observances connected with the existing celebration, the birthday observance might attract all the more esteem and prove to be more widely known and thereby confer no small benefit on the province. Therefore it would behoove the Asian League to pass a resolution that puts into writing all his arête, so that our recognition of what redounds to the honor of Augustus might abide for all time. And I shall order the decree to be inscribed in (Greek and Latin) stele and set up in the temple.

(Danker, 216–17; Greek text with bibliography and commentary, Sherk, 328–37)

"The falling into chaos . . . a new look to the whole world" refers to the conclusion, in 36 BCE at the battle of Actium, of the civil war that had raged through the Roman Empire between Octavian and Mark Anthony. The forces of Anthony and Cleopatra had been arrayed against those of Octavian. For his great victory the Roman Senate had bestowed on Octavian the title of Augustus, the august or venerable one. In Greek the title was translated as *sebastos* (venerable one). In this letter of request from Paulus Fabius Maximus we can see how the title has escalated towards increasing divine honors. The East was always more willing to venerate its rulers as gods than Italy. Caesar is the most divine one and the birth of Caesar is a blessing for all mankind, and so his birthday is the beginning of all things.

Whereas Providence that orders all our lives has in her display of concern and generosity in our behalf adorned our lives with the highest good: Augustus, whom she has filled with arête for the benefit of humanity, and has in her beneficence granted us and those who will come after us [a Savior] who has made war to cease and who shall put everything [in peaceful] order; and whereas Caesar, [when he was manifest], transcended the expectations of all [who had anticipated the good news], not only by surpassing the benefits conferred by his predecessors but by leaving no expectation of surpassing him to those who would come after him, with the result that the birthday of our God signaled the beginning of good news for the world because of him; whereas, after the assembly of Asia decreed in Smyrna—[during the administration of the pro-counsel] Lucius Volcasius Tullus, when Papion, [son of Diosierites], was clerk—but a crown be awarded to the person who came up with the best proposal for honoring our God; (and whereas) the proconsul Paul Fabius Maximus, benefactor of the province, who had been dispatched for its security by (Caesar's) authority and decision, besides all the other benefits that he had already conferred on the province, so many in fact that no one would be able to calculate them, as contributed yet one more, and so has discovered a way to honor Augustus that was hitherto unknown among the Greeks, namely to reckon time from the date of his nativity; therefore, with the blessings of Good Fortune and for their own welfare, the Greeks in Asia decreed that the new year began for all the cities on September 23, which is the birthday of Augustus; and, to ensure that the dates coincide in every city, all documents are to carry both the Roman and the Greek date, and the first month shall in accordance with the decree be observed as the Month of Caesar, beginning with 23 September, the birthday of Caesar, and that the crown be awarded to Maximus the proconsul for his proposal of the best way to honor Caesar.

(Danker, 216–18; Greek, Sherk, 328–37)

The council of Asia not only immediately accedes to the request of the proconsul, but decrees that his letter and their reply be set up in marble inscriptions in the temples of Rome and Augustus, the site of the imperial cult.

There is a considerable amount of religious language in this reply (see the excellent discussions in Stanton, 25–33, and Crossan, 236–42). Augustus is a benefactor for all humans and savior of the world. He put an end to war, an astonishing claim given the war-like reputation of the Romans. But this type of language is not unusual in the imperial propaganda. In Virgil's famous image of Augustus inaugurating the golden age, Anchises, Aeneas' father, foresees the great glory of the Roman people:

> Turn your two eyes
> This way and see this people, your own Romans.
> Here is Caesar, and all the line of Iulus,
> All who shall one day pass under the dome
> Of the great sky: this is the man, this one,
> Of whom so often you have heard the promise,
> Caesar Augustus, son of the deified,
> Who shall bring once again an Age of Gold
> To Latium, to the land where Saturn reigned
> In early times. He will extend his power
> Beyond the Garamants and Indians,
> Over far territories north and south
> Of the zodiacal stars, the solar way,
> Where Atlas, heaven-bearing, on his shoulder
> Turns the night-sphere, studded with burning stars.
> At that man's coming even now the realms
> Of Caspia and Maeotia tremble, warned
> By oracles, and the seven mouths of Nile
> Go dark with fear.
>   (*Aeneid*, 6.789–800; Fitzgerald, 187–88)

The Priene inscription proclaims that Augustus' birthday is good tidings (*euaggelia*) and that his very epiphany, divine manifestation, exceeds all expectations of good tidings (*euaggelia*). This is the gospel of the empire and it announces its good news, peace for all humans—which is indeed a great benefit from a great benefactor. The *Ara Pacis*, Augustus' altar to peace in Rome, proclaims exactly this same message. The benefits of the empire were real, which is why it lasted for so long.

Euaggelion for Paul

What is the good news for Paul? For him the noun gospel is always used in the singular, whereas the Priene inscription uses the plural. He modifies the gospel with three different possessives:

the gospel of God
the gospel of his son
the gospel of the Anointed

"His son" of course implies God as father. In Gal 1:7 he indicates a counter-gospel (*heteron euaggelion*, a different gospel, Gal 1:7 NRSV).

> Even if one of us, or for that matter a messenger from heaven, were to advocate a message different from the one we delivered they must be rejected and shunned! We told you before and now I repeat it: anyone who champions a message other than the one you heard from us—they must be rejected and shunned!
> (Gal 1:8–9)

He also thinks the gospel is something to be heard. The passage in Rom 10:14–18 makes a number of wordplays on this theme. I have italicized the words in the underlying Greek to make the wordplay on hearing/sound more evident.

> How, then, could people appeal to one in whom they have no confidence? And how could they put their confidence in someone they have never *heard* of? And how could they *hear* without a *preacher*? And how could they *preach* if they have not been sent by a higher authority? Just as it is written, "How well-timed are the footsteps of those who *announce good news*?" But not all of them have *paid attention* to this *news*. It is as Isaiah says, "Who has put any confidence in what he has *heard* from us?" In other words, confidence comes from *hearing* the message, and the message comes through *what is said* about God's Anointed. But I ask, "Is it not true that they have *heard*?" They certainly have. [As scripture says],
>
> > "The *sound of their voice* has reached to the ends of the earth, and *what they have said* to the outer limits of the inhabited world."
> > (Rom 10:14–18)

In the ancient world communication took place almost exclusively out loud. Even reading for the most part was out loud. Since most of the ancient world was illiterate—literacy never being more than ten percent in the large urban areas and much less in rural areas— oral communication was the only way in which most folks could ever get the news, good or bad.

The topic of this passage in Romans concerns whether Israel has heard the gospel, and the passage makes a number of wordplays on hearing. Let me elaborate by looking more closely at the Greek of verse 15.

How can they announce (*kērysōsin*) unless they are sent
(*apostalōsin*)
As it is written: how beautiful are the feet of those who preach
(*euaggelizomenōn*) good things. (BBS)

In the first line the verb "to announce" translates the root *kēryx-*:
the one who makes announcements, the town crier. The Greek
verb *apostalōsin* (in the English translation "they are sent") makes
a word play on the noun *apostolos*, apostle or envoy. And in the
second line "feet" is a metonym for apostle/envoy, as the one who
is sent travels on his feet. "Those who preach" employs the verb
euaggelizomenōn, from the noun *euaggelion*, gospel/good news.
Finally, "good things" (*agatha*) is a synonym for the prefix *eu-*
of the verb form *euaggelizomenōn* ("to preach or announce the
good news"). This whole passage invokes an elaborate series of
wordplays based on the metaphor of sound, a wordplay largely
and inevitably missed in an English translation, inevitably missed
because translations always surrender something in meaning, often the sound of the original. The SV does a good job at trying to
represent these wordplays, but it falls well short.

For Paul the gospel is out loud, oral. At one level this is simply
a cultural assumption, since as we have noted in the ancient world
almost all communication is out loud. But the out-loud character
of the gospel indicates the intimate connection between the one
who speaks out loud and the one who hears. The gospel and faith
in this context are always public, taking place in the medium of
sound. They are not a private affair, as is so often the case in the
modern world. This public, proclaimed, out-loud character of the
gospel also reminds us that for Paul the gospel is not written, and
the notion of a written gospel, so important in light of the four
written gospels in the much later New Testament canon, plays no
part in Paul's usage. Finally for Paul, gospel does not imply a narrative of Jesus' life. There is no evidence that he is telling, or even
knows or cares about, the story of Jesus (2 Cor 5:16).

The Good News Proclaimed
In 1 Corinthians 15, Paul does indicate the content of the gospel.
Because the gospel/good news is an oral phenomenon, we should
not think of its content as fixed but as proclaimed. In a series of
formulaic statements he lays out the gospel. "Now I would remind

you, brothers and sisters, of the good news that I proclaimed to you, which you in turn received, in which also you stand" (15:1 NRSV). In Greek "the good news that I proclaimed" involves a repetitive word play: *to euaggelion ho euēgellizamēn*, literally, the gospel which I gospelized, while not very good English, makes the point of the wordplay in Greek, which in turn is lost in translation. As in the Priene inscription, a connection between gospel and salvation exists: "through which also you are being saved" (15:2).

In these introductory formulaic phrases that lead up to the content of the gospel, Paul accents that he and the Corinthians stand in a tradition: "I passed on to you as of paramount importance what I also had received" (15:3 SV). Part of the problem is how to reconcile this formula, a standard formula for the passing on of tradition, with Paul's statement in Galatians that he did not receive his apostleship from humans or a human (Gal 1:1). Is Paul contradicting himself, or must we look more carefully at the matter? In Galatians Paul is defending his apostleship, his call to be an envoy. As we have seen, he vigorously contests any attribution of his call to human means. Is he arguing that his apostleship, his call, is of divine origin, while the gospel is something he receives from the tradition, as the formula of 1 Corinthians indicates? This line of argument seems problematic. He also accuses the Galatians of turning to another gospel:

> I'm amazed by how quickly you have abandoned the one who called you by the favor of God's Anointed and have embraced an entirely different message (*lit:* another gospel). There is no other world-transforming message, but there are people who are confusing you and want to pervert the truth about God's Anointed (*lit:* gospel of the Anointed). (Gal 1:6–7)

Paul understands the gospel as something handed on, as part of tradition, and as tied to his apostleship. My solution around this conundrum, and I confess that it is not the most satisfying, is that Paul sees his call and conviction about the gospel as part of a divine *apocalypsis*/revelation, while the gospel's expression, of which he is reminding the Corinthians in 1 Corinthians 15, he derived from the tradition in which he and they stand.

Now the content of the gospel:

that the Anointed died to free us from the seductive power of
  corruption
    according to the scriptures,
and that he was buried,
and that he was raised "on the third day"
    according to the scriptures;
and that he was seen by Cephas,
then by the twelve;
then he was seen by more than five hundred brothers and sisters
    at the same time. Most of them are still alive today, but some
    have passed away.
Then he was seen by James,
    then by all the apostles.
Last of all, as to one in whose birth God's purpose seemed to
    have miscarried, he was seen by me as well.
    (1 Cor 15:3b–8)

The gospel's content employs vocabulary and language that is not
Pauline, which is what we would expect since he is passing on
tradition. Therefore this is not Paul's construction. There has been
a great deal of speculation about whether this formulaic piece of
tradition was originally in Aramaic, but that is unclear. At any
rate, it was not created by Paul but represents the tradition he has
handed on.

The content of the gospel has two parts: a tripartite death,
burial and resurrection, and then a tripartite list of those who
have seen (ōphthē) Jesus. Both are clearly formulaic, as one would
expect of oral tradition, but they are probably two different pieces
of tradition, perhaps joined together by Paul. While Paul uses the
formula for passing on tradition, this cannot be a very old tradition, since Paul's writing to Corinth takes place within twenty
years of the events reported. Furthermore, both tripartite formu-
lae imply narratives but are constructed in a confessional form.
For example, "the Anointed died for our sins according to the
writings" (1 Cor 15:3 BBS), has three parts:

The anointed died
for our sins
according to the writings

This implies a story but the language is confessional. Anointed, as a title, is a confession, not a name, and the way he died is avoided; he was crucified. "Jesus was crucified" is not confessional but a statement of what happened. Likewise, "for our sins" is again a theological confession. Crucified by Pontus Pilate is a statement of what happened. And finally "according to the writings" states the warrant for the confession without ever stating which scriptures are attested. Certainly Pilate never referred to the Jewish scriptures in passing sentence, if there was such a thing as a formal trial.

The confessional character of the content of the gospel, according to Paul, is important to notice because it indicates how far his understanding of gospel is from the Gospel of Mark's beginning: "The good news of Jesus the Anointed begins with something Isaiah the prophet wrote" (Mark 1:1). Mark's gospel is also confessional, but now the confession is elaborated into a story of Jesus the Anointed. Paul shows no evidence of such a story or even knowledge of such a story.

Not Ashamed of the Gospel

The following four translations indicate several different ways of representing the Greek of Rom 1:16. Coming to terms with the differences represented by these translations will take us a long way in our discovery of who Paul actually was and what he was about.

KJ   For I am not ashamed of the gospel of Christ: for it is the power of God unto salvation to every one that believeth; to the Jew first, and also to the Greek.

NRSV   For I am not ashamed of the gospel; it is the power of God for salvation to everyone who has faith, to the Jew first and also to the Greek.

SV   I'm not embarrassed by this news, because it has the power to transform those who are persuaded by it, first Jews and then Greeks.

Stanley Stowers in *A Rereading of Romans* proposed this translation of the verse:

> For I am not ashamed of the good news, because it is a power which God has to save all who are faithful, the Jew first, afterwards also the Greek. (Stowers, 199)

We will have to return to this verse when we consider the issue of what Paul means by "faith," but for now our attention is on good news/gospel. We have two questions to answer.

1. Why might Paul be embarrassed or ashamed of the gospel?
2. How does this further our understanding of his definition of the gospel?

We will begin with the second question.

The good news has two aspects. First it is a power of God. Paul understands the good news as a power or capability that belongs to God to save. Again we see the association of gospel and salvation as in the Priene inscription. The imperial overtones cannot be escaped. Both the emperor and God claim this same power to save or rescue their people. For the emperor it is the Roman people, the *res publica*, who are saved by his power. This is again and again demonstrated by the emperor's triumph in battle, paradigmatically for Augustus at the battle of Actium in which all the nations of the empire were saved. But Paul places two qualifiers for those who are saved. First,

> everyone who has faith (NRSV)
> those who are persuaded by it (SV)
> all who are faithful (Stowers)

All three translations are struggling with how to translate *pisteuonti*. All three translations are defensible and we will have to eventually sort out what differences the translations make and which one makes Paul more intelligible. As you can begin to intuit, a great deal hangs on this issue. For our consideration now, we need only note that this phrase describes a positive response to the gospel.

Secondly, Paul notes this group of positive responders has two distinct elements: first Jews and then Greeks. This is Paul's way of denoting the makeup of the whole world. From Paul's point of view the whole world is divided into two groups, Jews and Greeks, or as he also notes otherwise, Jews and the nations (e.g., Rom 9:24). "Nations" is often translated gentiles (see below). There does not appear for Paul to be any difference in dividing humankind between Jews and Greeks and Jews and the nations. But Paul does note the priority of the Jews in that they come first.

Greek and Barbarian

In Rom 1:14–15, which marks the conclusion of the thanksgiving to the letter, Paul makes the following contrast between Greeks and barbarians.

I am under obligation   both to Greeks   and barbarians,
                         both to the wise   and the foolish;
that's why I'm eager to proclaim God's world-changing news also to you in Rome.

Paul wants to make a good impression upon the community in Rome, and one purpose of this letter is to make that good impression. His audience in Rome is Greek-speaking. This usage, Greek and barbarian, reflects the audience's point of view and Paul is appealing to their prejudice. The phrase "Greek and barbarian" is a stereotyped phrase that contrasts civilized with uncivilized. The saying has it: *pas mē hellēn barbaros* (whoever is not Greek is a barbarian). Barbarian is an onomatopoeia word—its sounding makes it meaning. A barbarian is one who does not speak smoothly like a Greek, but babbles and is thus uncivilized. Paul rhetorically connects Greek with wise and barbarian with foolish, while announcing his eagerness to preach the gospel to those wise Greeks in Rome. Jewett (131) thinks barbarian is mentioned here because of Paul's intention to take the gospel to the barbarians in Spain.

What is not implied and should not be read into the text is that the Jews are rejected.

This observation brings us back to our first question, why is Paul ashamed of the gospel? If one must assert that he is not ashamed of the gospel, then rhetorically that means someone has said he should be ashamed of the good news. That is the way this type of rhetorical assertion works. Shame involves a sensitivity to one's honor or reputation and is a highly motivating influence in the ancient world. This represents a serious charge against the good news.

The most logical answer to this question is a charge has been laid against Paul that his gospel is failing. Does that failing consist in the lack of Jews who have accepted that Jesus is the Anointed? Or have some charged that his gospel is a false gospel? Or that he is not a true envoy of the Anointed? Or is it that in comparison with the gospel of Rome, his gospel is weak? This is the deepest cause of shame. The very good news itself is an object of shame because it is about the crucified one.

> At a time when Jews expect a miracle and Greeks seek enlightenment, we speak about God's Anointed *crucified*! This is an offense to Jews, nonsense to the nations; but to those who have heard God's call, both Jews and Greeks, the Anointed represents God's power and God's wisdom; because the folly of God is wiser than humans are and the weakness of God is stronger than humans are. (1 Cor 1:2–5)

The language of this passage from Corinthians is remarkably parallel to Rom 1:16. The good news is a power of God for both Jews and Greeks. But it stands against the expectations of both; it is an offense to both.

Romans 1:16 announces the letter's theme—in order to come to Rome to preach the good news, Paul will need to establish the validity of his preaching of a shameful message.

From this survey we have learned that for Paul the gospel is

about salvation
about God's son
announced publicly, orally
for both Jews and Greeks
about the crucifixion and resurrection of the anointed
shameful

To the Nations

"that I would proclaim God's world-transforming news to the nations." (Gal 1:16b)

We are pursuing Paul's autobiography or self-understanding as expressed in Galatians. Paul understands his call through an *apocalypsis*/revelation to be an (or *the*?) envoy of the Anointed announcing the *euaggelion*/good news to the nations. So who are the nations? Let us observe an interesting shift in translations in a clip of Rom 1:5:

KJ   for obedience to the faith among all nations, for his name
RSV   to bring about the obedience of faith for the sake of his name
        among all the nations
NIV   to call all the Gentiles to the obedience that comes from faith
NRSV to bring about the obedience of faith among all the Gentiles

From the 1952 publication of the Revised Standard Version through the 1970 New International Version and the 1989 New Revised Standard Version, the translation shifted from "nations" to Gentiles with capitalization. This has important implications. "Gentiles" means "not a Jew" and this casts the debate in the Pauline letters between Judaism and all those who are not Jews. This translation has a tendency towards supersessionism, the doctrine in which Christianity replaces or supersedes Judaism. As Christopher Stanley points out, "in social terms, there was simply no such thing as a 'Gentile' in the ancient world" (105). There were Greeks or Romans or Galatians. These were all members of the nations. This way of viewing Judaism as a distinct ethnic and religious group in counter-distinction to gentiles (even with capitalized "Gentiles") is anachronistic. It reads the distinctions of a later time back into the period of Paul. We should always remember that Paul is pre-70 CE and the Temple is still a fully functioning element. Nowhere does he envision its replacement.

The Greek word *ta ethnē* refers to "the nations" in the sense of "people groups foreign to a specific people group" (BAGD). It is both similar and different from *laos*, the people. *Laos* has the sense of "our folks," while *ethnē* has the sense of "those folks." In the LXX *ethnē* frequently translates Hebrew word *gôyîm*. The singular does not refer to a gentile, that is, a non-Jewish individual, but to a nation, "thus, significantly, Paul never uses the term" (Elliott, 46). Paul does not view himself as addressing individuals, much less modern individuals, but the nations. Despite the traditional title of Letter to the Romans, the letter's addressee is "to all of God's beloved in Rome" (Rom 1:7 SV). Paul addresses a group, not individual Romans.

A good example of the meaning of both the singular *ethnos* and plural *ethnē* occurs in Gen 18:18 dealing with the promise to Abraham:

> As for Abraam, he shall become a great and populous nation (*ethnos, gôy*), and all the nations (*ta ethnē, gôyîm*) of the earth shall be blessed in him. (LXX)

As this example makes clear, gentile or gentiles would not work— nation or nations is the correct translation. Furthermore, this indicates how the nations turning towards Israel is part of the eschatological vision. Isaiah 11:10 makes this point about the Anointed.

> And there shall be on that day the root of Iessai, even the one who stands up to rule nations; nations shall hope in him, and his rest shall be honor. (Isa 11:10 LXX)

In the conclusion to Paul's argument in the Letter to the Romans (15:12), he quotes Isa 11:10 in order to indicate that God will remain faithful to the promises made to the Jewish people. Paul's mission to the nations to subject them to the Anointed is part of the ancient Hebrew dream of all the nations of the earth worshipping at Mount Zion. He sees himself as called to fulfill that ancient promise.

> I maintain that the Anointed became the servant of the Jewish people to demonstrate God's veracity in confirmation of God's promise to our ancestors, and so that the nations might praise God's mercy, just as it is written, . . .
> And again Isaiah says,
>
> > The root of Jesse will spring up,
> > the one who will rise to rule the nations,
> > the nations will place their hope on him.
> > (Rom 15:8–7, 12)

Paul's apocalyptic scenario of the nations being ruled by Israel's Anointed and those nations coming to place their hope in that Anointed is not only not a form of supersessionism, but it implicitly challenges Rome's imperial claim to be the ruler of all the nations. Virgil vividly presents Rome's version of this claim.

But Caesar then in triple triumph rode
Within the walls of Rome, making immortal
Offerings to the gods of Italy—
. . . .
The man himself, enthroned before the snow-white
Threshold of sunny Phoebus, viewed the gifts
The nations of the earth made, and he fitted them
To the tall portals. Conquered races passed
In long procession, varied in languages
As in their dress and arms.
    (*Aeneid* 8.714–15, 720–23 Fitzgerald, 255)

Paul sees himself as the envoy to the nations in an apocalyptic plan to bring the nations to worship God at Mount Zion. This self-understanding has important consequences for understanding Paul's audience, those to whom his letters are written. Paul is addressing the nations and so unless explicitly counter-indicated, we should assume the audience for his letters is the nations. His mission is not universal; he is not addressing all humanity in some generalized, philosophical sense. For him the world is divided into Jews and the nations, or as he says of the result of the meeting in Jerusalem,

> On the contrary, they recognized that God had entrusted me with the task of announcing God's world-transforming message to the uncircumcised, just as Peter had been entrusted with taking it to the circumcised. For it was evident that the God who worked through Peter as envoy to the circumcised worked through me as envoy to the rest of the world (*lit*: the nations).
> (Gal 2:7–8)

This does not mean that there were no Jews in Paul's communities. There undoubtedly were. But his concern is with the nations. The nations are his addressees. Even more, he is in a contest for those nations because they have been conquered by the Roman imperium.

Readings

Brock, Ann Graham. *Mary Magdalene, The First Apostle: The Struggle for Authority*. Cambridge: Harvard University Press, 2003.
Brooten, Bernadette J. "'Junia . . . Outstanding among the Apostles' (Romans 16,7)." Pp. 148–51 in *Women Priests: A Catholic*

Commentary on the Vatican Declaration. Ed. L. S. and A. Swidler. New York: Paulist Press, 1977.

Crossan, John Dominic, and Jonathan L. Reed. *In Search of Paul, How Jesus' Apostle Opposed Rome's Empire with God's Kingdom.* San Francisco: HarperSanFrancisco, 2004.

Danker, Frederick W. *Benefactor: Epigraphic Study of a Graeco-Roman and New Testament Semantic Field.* St. Louis, MO: Clayton Publishing House, 1982.

Deissmann, Adolf. *Light from the Ancient East.* Trans. Lionel Strachan. London: George H. Doran, 1910.

Elliott, Neil. *The Arrogance of Nations: Reading Romans in the Shadow of Empire.* Paul in Critical Contexts. Minneapolis: Fortress Press, 2008.

Epp, Eldon Jay. *Junia, the First Woman Apostle.* Minneapolis: Fortress Press, 2005.

Jewett, Robert. *Romans: A Commentary.* Hermeneia. Ed. Roy David Kotansky and Eldon Jay Epp. Minneapolis: Fortress Press, 2007.

Pervo, Richard L. *Acts.* Hermeneia. Ed. Harold W. Attridge. Minneapolis: Fortress Press, 2009.

Philo. *Philo.* Vol. 4. 10 vols. Trans. F. H. Colson and G. H. Whitaker. Loeb Classical Library. Cambridge: Harvard University Press, 1935.

Sherk, Robert K. *Roman Documents from the Greek East: Senatus Consulta and Epistulae to the Age of Augustus.* Baltimore: Johns Hopkins Press, 1969.

Stanley, Christopher D. "'Neither Jew nor Greek': Ethnic Conflict in Graeco-Roman Society." *Journal for the Study of the New Testament* 64 (1996) 101–24.

Stanton, Graham. *Jesus and Gospel.* Cambridge: Cambridge University Press, 2004.

Stowers, Stanley K. *A Rereading of Romans: Justice, Jews, and Gentiles.* New Haven/London: Yale University Press, 1994.

Virgil. *The Aeneid.* Trans. Robert Fitzgerald. New York: Vintage Books, 1990.

Chapter 6

Was Paul Converted?

Having sorted through Paul's description of his *apocalypsis/* revelation/insight, we can clearly see that, in his own self-understanding, he was called and commissioned by God. By alluding to the call language of the prophets Isaiah and Jeremiah, he sees what is happening to him as parallel to what happened to them, as standing in the line or tradition of their calls. They were called by God and given a commission. The prophetic call always also involves a mission. His mission was to announce the good news of the Anointed to the nations, that Jesus was the Anointed lord and that the nations were to worship at Mount Zion, fulfilling the ancient Jewish dream.

Was Paul's call also a conversion? If it was a conversion, to what was he converted? Given the tradition's insistence that he was converted, this question is important to ask.

Conversion

Bernard Lonergan in his *Method in Theology* has constructed a useful model for the analysis of conversion. There are points at which we experience change, even intense change, but we also experience ourselves acting in continuity with what has gone before. The fundamental horizon of meaning remains the same. We may be changing and shifting, but we basically experience continuity with the past, with what has been.

> But it is also possible that the movement into a new horizon involves an about-face; it comes out of the old by repudiating characteristic features; it begins a new sequence that can keep

revealing ever greater depth and breadth and wealth. Such an
about-face and new beginning is what is meant by a conversion.
(Lonergan, 237–38)

What distinguishes ordinary change from conversion is not
its depth or intensity or suddenness, but continuity with the past
versus an about-face with a new beginning. Paul no doubt experienced a life-changing event, but did he experience it as a continuity with his past or a repudiation of the past and a new beginning?

Lonergan further distinguished three types of conversion that
help clarify the issue. The three types are:

intellectual
moral
religious

Intellectual conversion "is a radical clarification and, conse-
quently, the elimination of an exceedingly stubborn and misleading myth concerning reality, objectivity, and human knowledge"
(Lonergan, 238). In this type of conversion one is led to see reality
for what it is. Intellectual conversion deals with truth. The classic
example of such a conversion is the deconstruction of a myth,
when what we had held as true is seen as not true. There is no
Santa Claus.

Moral conversion deals with values, when the values by which
life is lived change. This is the realm of ethics. A moral conversion
is when a person changes the values that guide one's life.

Finally "religious conversion is being grasped by ultimate
concern" (Lonergan, 240). Religious conversion deals with the
realm of the transcendent. These three types of conversion are not
totally separate but often interrelated and connected.

Augustine

Both Augustine and Luther offer good examples of these three
forms of conversion. Augustine's account of his conversion while
in the garden in Milan (*Confessions*, 8.12) follows the classic
model for a conversion, as analyzed by Nock in his classic study
of the topic (259–66):

> I was asking myself these questions, weeping all the while the
> most bitter sorrow in my heart, when all at once I heard the sing-

song voice of a child in a nearby house. . . . Again and again it repeated the refrain 'take it and read, take it and read.' . . . I stemmed my flood of tears and stood up, telling myself that this could only be a divine command to open my book of Scripture and read the first passage on which my eyes should fall upon. . . . I had put down the book containing Paul's epistles. I seized it and opened it, and in silence I read the first passage on which my eyes fell: *Not in reveling and drunkenness, not in lust and wantonness, not in quarrels and rivalries. Rather, arm yourselves with the Lord Jesus Christ; spend no more thought on nature and nature's appetites* [Rom 13:13–14]. I had no wish to read more and no need to do so. For in an instant, as I came to the end of the sentence, it was through this the light of confidence flooded into my heart and all the darkness of doubt was dispelled. . . .

Then I went in and told my mother, who was overjoyed. And when [I] went on to describe how it had happened, she was jubilant and triumphant and glorified you, *who are powerful enough, and more than powerful enough, to carry out your purpose beyond our hopes and dreams* [Eph 3:20]. For she saw that you had granted her far more than she used to ask in her tearful prayers and plaintive lamentations. You converted me to yourself, so that I no longer desired a wife or placed any hope in this world but stood firmly upon that rule of faith.

Augustine had a moral conversion. His famous prayer, "Grant me chastity and continence, but not yet" (*Confessions* 8.7) can stand for this type of conversion. He had two concubines. Upon his conversion and baptism he abandoned his then concubine, the mother of his son Adeodatus. As his *Confessions* make clear, he had much of which to repent. Augustine's robbing of a pear tree, not to eat the fruit but to throw it at pigs, strikes us as scrupulosity, but as an adult he looks back on this youthful event terrified at what it says about greed. "I was preserved from whatever sins I did not commit, for there was no knowing what I might have done, since I love evil even if it serves no purpose" (*Confessions*, 2.7). As a result of his conversion he reformed his moral life to the point of practicing celibacy.

He also experienced a religious conversion that became the deep source of his theological program. He had been a pagan, then a Manichaean, and finally a Christian. His mother, herself a Christian, had a deep influence on her son's conversion. So he clearly underwent a religious conversion.

Before his conversion to Christianity, Augustine had been deeply influenced by the Neoplatonism of Plotinus. One might question whether Augustine's conversion also involved an intellectual conversion, because before his Christian conversion he was a Neoplatonist and after his conversion he remained a Neoplatonist. Peter Brown in his biography of Augustine notes this strong continuity in Augustine's life before and after his conversion.

> Augustine enjoyed the immense advantage of being rooted in a mature tradition. But the Neo-Platonists provided him with the one, essential tool for any serious autobiography: they had given him a theory of dynamics of the soul that made sense of his experiences. (168)

One might argue that because of Augustine's influence Christianity itself underwent an intellectual conversion to Neoplatonism.

So strong was Augustine's sense of his conversion that he wrote his *Confessions* to explain and justify it. According to Brown, "the writing of the *Confessions* was an act of therapy" (165).

Luther

Martin Luther's situation was different. Unlike Augustine he remained within Christianity but ended up radically reforming it. His conversion was rather complete. Luther was on the cusp between the late Middle Ages and the Renaissance. Revolutions were happening, not only the Reformation but also the Copernican revolution. As a young man, Luther became a humanist. Like many of his generation he rejected his early education, especially the Modern Devotion and scholasticism. His humanistic scholarship involved him in the study of Greek and Hebrew. As a Doctor of the Bible at Wittenberg University, he studied and taught the Bible in the original languages. His famous German translation of the Bible is an outcome of this intellectual conversion, as it represents the overthrow of the Latin Vulgate.

Luther's moral and religious conversions were entangled. He was a pious Augustinian monk and did not lead a particularly sinful life, but he had a strong sense of sin and the devil. He was undoubtedly scrupulous. His great insight was that God's righteousness was not some distant, threatening judgment, but that it made the believer righteous. Thus it was not the believer's works that saved, but God's righteousness. This fundamentally overturned ethics. The traditional connection between reward, merit, and good works was broken. Human motivation could no longer be understood in this simple carrot and stick model.

Luther famously remarked that the Holy Spirit "gave me this realization in the cloaca" (i.e., the privy, see Oberman, 155). The cloaca or privy is the place where the Devil was and it was a humiliating place—not the modern sanitary bathroom. Heiki Oberman in his *Luther: Man between God and the Devil* well summarizes the contradictory nature of the experience of grace in such a place:

> It is right here that we have Christ; the mighty helper, on our side. No spot is unholy for the Holy Ghost; this is the very place to express contempt for the adversary through trust in Christ crucified. (155)

Luther finds in Paul the vindication of his understanding and experience, and it produces a profound conversion on all three levels.

Paul's Conversion

Traditionally Paul has been portrayed as converting. Much of that depiction comes from the three stories in the Acts of the Apostles—the dramatic light, the voice calling out "Saul, Saul, why do you persecute me?" Augustine's and then Luther's dependence upon Paul only reinforced this image. But was Paul converted? Here Lonergan's distinctions are helpful. While it might not appear to make much sense to go through Lonergan's three types of conversion, it will clarify the situation.

Intellectual Conversion

In Phil 3:5 Paul writes, "With respect to the Law I was a Pharisee." The SV translates this in a past tense, but the Greek does not imply that. In fact the more normal reading of the Greek would be a present tense. What Paul is stating is that in the interpretation of the Torah he follows the Pharisees (see Reumann, 53–52).

Let us grant for sake of argument that the SV translators are right, that Paul would no longer have described his interpretation of the Torah as Pharisaic. What would that mean? He interprets the Torah through the lens of the Anointed. Therefore one could argue that Paul had undergone an intellectual conversion based upon his *apocalypsis*/insight, so that he sees the truth of the Torah in a different light, namely, that of the Anointed. This would parallel Augustine's intellectual conversion to Neoplatonism or Luther's conversion/insight into the meaning of Paul's understanding of the righteousness of God.

On the other hand, if Paul is referring to the present tense, then he would not have seen himself as undergoing an intellectual conversion. He would be a Pharisee before and after the *apocalypsis*/revelation. It is hard to know whether Paul sees continuity or change in this regard. Alan Segal in *Paul the Convert: The Apostolate and Apostasy of Saul the Pharisee*, maintains that Paul "began as a Pharisee and became a convert *from* Pharisaism. He spent the rest of his life trying to express what he converted *to*" (283; emphasis in original). Segal wants to have his cake and eat it too. He maintains that

> [Paul] was both converted and called. By using the term *conversion* I wish to stress the wrenching and decisive change of Paul's entrance into Christianity, thereby linking Paul with many modern accounts of conversion. (6)

I have no argument with Segal as long as he limits the conversion from Pharisaism, in Lonergan's terms, to an intellectual conversion. But Paul did not convert to Christianity. That is anachronistic on Segal's part and intuitively he knows it because he admits that Paul "never felt that he had left Judaism" (284). Segal's argument is helpful, because he demonstrates how important being precise about the categories is. Yes, Paul underwent a radical, even wrenching change, but that change was not a shift from Judaism to Christianity. Moreover, what is the nature of the shift? Is it based on continuity or discontinuity? A prophet's call involves radical shift, but it can be continuous.

Whether or not Paul had an intellectual conversion in this regard is not really central, because intellectual conversion is not the essence of what one means when traditionally referring to Paul's conversion.

Moral Conversion

Moral conversion hits closer to home in the traditional understanding of Paul's conversion. There has been a tendency to project Augustine's experience and to a more limited degree Luther's onto Paul. Paul is presented as tormented by his inability to fulfill the law, to meet the demands of the law. Romans 7 is often read like a part of Paul's autobiography to illustrate this point. Paul despairs at his inability to keep the Torah.

> Yet, if it had not been for the law, I would not have known sin. I would not have known what it is to covet if the law had not said, "You shall not covet." But sin, seizing an opportunity in the commandment, produced in me all kinds of covetousness.
> (Rom 7:7–8 NRSV)

Or yet again:

> So I find it to be a law that when I want to do what is good, evil lies close at hand. For I delight in the law of God in my inmost self, but I see in my members another law at war with the law of my mind, making me captive to the law of sin that dwells in my members. Wretched man that I am! Who will rescue me from this body of death? (Rom 7:21–24 NRSV)

These passages appear to picture a deeply conflicted Paul under the spell of trying to fulfill the Law. And yet his self-description in Philippians presents a different picture. "In regard to the requirements of the Law, I was flawless" (Phil 3:6); "as to righteousness under the law, blameless" (Phil 3:6 NRSV). In this passage where Paul is presenting his credentials as a Jew, he says that his behavior in regards to the Torah was flawless or blameless.

So is Paul contradicting himself or trying to have it both ways? In regard to the Philippians quote, John Reumann in his Anchor Bible Commentary on *Philippians* remarks, "This self-description has stung many commentators, and not only Protestants, as outrageous" (515). But the rabbis viewed the Torah as a duty and a delight (see chapter 12, "Covenantal Nomism"). The problem lies in correctly identifying the context and audience in Romans 7. The audience in Romans 7 is the non-Jewish audience in Rome, those members of the nations who dwell in Rome. Moreover Paul is performing in this passage what is known as "speech-in-character" (see chapter 13, "Self Mastery"). He is not describing his own autobiographical experience, but is in character as the non-Jewish person trying to fulfill the Torah. For Paul, the Jew and the non-Jew approach the Law from two different perspectives. For the Jew the Torah is part of the covenant with God; for the non-Jew striving for self-mastery is a moral code demanding moral perfection.

The passage in Philippians and the use of the proper model for understanding Romans 7 indicate that in regards to Torah Paul was flawless or blameless. That is, he was not in need of moral conversion. This for Paul is not the case for his audience among the nations. They are in need of moral conversion and their turn to the Anointed should produce such a moral conversion. He castigates them when it does not!

> Don't you know that wrongdoers are not going to inherit the Empire of God? Don't let anyone mislead you; neither those who consort with prostitutes nor those who follow phony gods, neither adulterers nor promiscuous people, nor pederasts, neither the thieving nor the greedy, neither drunkards nor those who engage in verbal abuse nor swindlers are going to inherit the Empire of God. And these are what some of you were. But you have been cleansed, you have a new relation with God through the name of the lord, Jesus the Anointed, and through the presence and power of our God. (1 Cor 6:9–11, see also 1 Cor 12:2)

In regard to a moral conversion, sometimes reference is made to Paul's presence at (Acts 7:58) and approval of (Acts 8:1) the stoning of Stephen. Acts 8:1 is a clear Lukan construction; it fulfills Luke 11:48, "You are therefore witnesses to and approve of the deeds of your ancestors: they killed <the prophets> and you build <monuments> to them" (see Pervo, 200). In his letters, Paul never mentions this event and it should not be assumed as the reference when Paul mentions his persecuting the community of the Anointed. Paul always sees his persecuting the community as a sign of his zeal (Gal 1:3; Phil 3:6; 1 Cor 15:9, see above chapter 3, "Persecuting the Church").

Paul, therefore, did not undergo a moral conversion.

Religious Conversion

The issue of Paul's moral conversion is important in considering how we understand him and interpret his letters, but his religious conversion is where the rubber meets the road. When considering Paul's religious conversion, once again the passage in Phil 3:5–6 is of critical importance. Paul is warning those who are receiving his letter to beware of those preaching circumcision, a situation similar to that in the letter to the Galatians. These preachers he calls curs or dogs. In contrast to them, who also perhaps call themselves apostles, Paul argues that he truly understands circumcision. And if they have grounds for boasting, he has even more grounds. The SV refers to "religious credentials" as a way of specifying what is more literally referred to in the Greek as "according to the flesh." SV is correct in its implication for what is meant by "according to the flesh" in this passage. These preachers, much like the super-apostles in 2 Cor 11:5, boast in their Jewish credentials and status. Paul claims his credentials are even higher:

> Watch out for those curs, watch out for those perpetrators of fraud, watch out for those who would carve up your flesh. We are the ones who know what circumcision really means; we are serving <God> with our whole heart and mind and base our confidence on the Anointed Jesus and do not put our trust in religious credentials. I say this even though I also have grounds for putting my trust in religious credentials. If any of these other people think that they have grounds for putting trust in religious credentials, I can top them. (Phil 3:2–4)

Then Paul lists his credentials:

> I was circumcised eight days after my birth, I belong to the people of Israel by birth and am descended from the tribe of Benjamin, a Hebrew descended from Hebrews. With respect to the Law I was a Pharisee. My zeal about this led me to persecute the Anointed's people. In regard to the requirements of the Law, I was flawless. (Phil 3:5–6)

In the Greek Paul actually presents his credentials in a tightly constructed list which the SV translation has unpacked to help with comprehension.

> by circumcision on the eighth day,
> out of the people of Israel,
> of the tribe of Benjamin,
> a Hebrew from a line of Hebrews,
> as to the Torah a Pharisee,
> as to zeal a persecutor of the community,
> as to righteousness which comes from the Torah blameless.
> (Phil 3:5–6 BBS)

This list of credentials, while answering a different question from the autobiography section in Gal 1:11–16, has points of contact with that passage, thus indicating a common implied narrative. As in Galatians his zeal for the traditions of his people, the people of Israel, is attested by his persecution of the community of the Anointed. And what makes him a Jew is listed. These credentials of his Jewishness, except for the persecution of the community, are still in place. In both Galatians and Philippians after the *apocalypsis*/revelation, Paul remains a Jew.

Tentmaker

How should we envision Paul's ministry? What did his day look like? Certainly not like a modern fulltime ministry. Paul supported himself at a trade and that took up most of his time. According to Acts, Paul joined with Aquila and Priscilla in a workshop in Corinth "and they worked together—by trade they were tentmakers" (Acts 18:1–3). Paul himself writes to the Thessalonians, "we worked night and day so as not to impose on anyone while we were sharing God's message with you" (1 Thess 2:9).

Tentmaking meant working with hides, and was arduous work of low status. As Ronald Hock has shown, people who worked at such a trade "could not avoid experiencing the hostility and contempt directed toward them by representatives of the dominant ethos" (35).

Yet in the very next verse in Philippians he disparages these credentials:

> But all of these things that I once thought were valuable assets I have come to regard as worthless because of God's Anointed. Indeed, I now regard everything as worthless in light of the incomparable value of realizing that the Anointed Jesus is my lord. Because of him I wrote off all of those assets and now regard them as worth no more than rubbish so that I can gain the <incomparable asset of> the Anointed. (Phil 3:7–8)

As Reumann succinctly summarizes: "*All things* past are now assessed as *crap*" (516). Is Paul renouncing his Judaism, his Jewish religion in favor of a Christian religion? To return to Lonergan's discussion of conversion, religious conversion concerns root values for apprehending the transcendent. In this regard we should ask some fundamental questions. What has changed religiously for Paul? He remains a Jew according to the flesh, he still believes in the one true God, unlike his converts who have "turned to God from idols, to serve a living and true God" (1 Thess 1:9). What has changed is his conviction (*pistis*) that

---

Paul's low status as a worker and his free preaching (1 Cor 9:18) became part of the debate in Corinth with the super-apostles. This low status is taken up into Paul's self-understanding as a slave and envoy of the Anointed.

> Right up to this very moment we are hungry and thirsty and poorly clothed, cuffed around, have no place to call home, and are worn out by the hard work we do with our own hands. When we are abused, we bless; when we are harassed, we put up with it; when we are slandered, we are conciliatory. We have been treated as if we were the scum of the earth, the filth everyone wants to get rid of, and still are.
> (1 Cor 4:11–13)

Paul, the envoy of the Anointed, is also Paul the tentmaker. The workshop is the context of his ministry and that workshop is integrated into his *apocalypsis*/insight. His low status as laborer correlates with Anointed crucified.

- Jesus is God's Anointed, God's Son.
- Now God is acting decisively to bring about the end, the subjection of all under Jesus the lord.
- The promises made to Abraham and prophesied by Israel's prophets that the nations would be brought back to Zion are now being fulfilled.
- He, Paul, is God's envoy called to announce this good news to the nations.

But all this takes place within the religion of Israel. At no point does he envision the end of Israel or Judaism. Paul is active pre-70 CE while the Temple is still functioning. Nothing in Paul's writings indicate that he thinks this situation is to change, that the Temple will cease functioning.

Paul in describing his *apocalypsis*/revelation uses language from the call stories of the prophets. He does not employ the language of conversion but of call. The call of a prophet is a momentous, life-changing experience, but it is not a religious conversion. We should think the same way about Paul.

Paul did not undergo a religious conversion; he remained a Jew who believed that Jesus was God's anointed. That is what changed. That can all be explained within Judaism. Paul did not cease being a Jew and become a Christian.

Once again the analogy with Rabbi Akiba is informative. When he proclaimed Simon ben Kosiba the Messiah, Akiba did not cease being a Jew and join a new religion. The same is true of Paul.

The Real Conflict

When we understand that Paul was called, not converted, that he remained a Jew and did not become a Christian, then we must fundamentally reorientate and rethink our understanding and interpretation of Paul. Seeing Paul as rejecting Judaism has been the cornerstone of Pauline interpretation. Now we must undo that cornerstone.

In the traditional interpretation of Paul, Christianity is positioned as the opposite of Judaism. Christianity is based on faith and Judaism is based on works, so faith is the opposite of works. Once this model is in place, it becomes the hermeneutical model by which all of Paul is understood. This not only determines the interpretation of Paul, but of Christianity itself. Additionally it has determined Jewish/Christian relations. Judaism is understood as a religion of works, despite the protests of Jews that this is not so, and Christianity as a religion of faith. This model is so strong that Christianity is understood as "not-Judaism" and anti-Judaism becomes a fundamental plank in Christian self-understanding, with tragic results. David Nirenberg in his book *Anti-Judaism: The Western Tradition* states the purpose of anti-Judaism in the Christian understanding: "the logic of Jewish enmity and the killing carnality of the Jews only grew stronger, driven now not so much by conflict with real Jews, but because it proved ever generally useful for thinking about God, the world, and the nature of the texts and powers that mediate between them" (86).

Paul's real program is very different. His problem is not how to convert Jews and Gentiles to Christianity, but how to get the nations into the covenant. For all we know, this may have also been his issue before his call. For him the answer to this problem is revealed in his *apocalypsis*/insight: God has acted in his son the crucified Anointed to save the nations, and Paul has been called to announce this good news to the nations.

If Paul did not convert to Christianity, then what is the opposition? A consistent feature we have observed in Paul's language is an implied opposition to the empire of Rome. Notice how much language we have examined so far is also employed in imperial language:

Son of God
gospel (*euaggelion*)
salvation
nations

We should also add to the list *kyrios* (lord or master), a major imperial title. This language Paul must contest with the imperial usage, but he employs an antipode that is explicitly anti-imperial: crucified Anointed.

I would propose as a new model of oppositions that the opposite of the gospel of God is the gospel of Rome. This is the true opposition that drives Paul. The Anointed as son of God is the opposite of the emperor as son of god. For Paul the gospel of God implies freedom and life; the gospel of Rome implies slavery and death. In the rest of this book we will test this hermeneutical model as a way to interpret Paul.

These oppositions can be laid out in a schema that makes the oppositions visible. The old model represents the traditional interpretation of Paul, while the new model represents the one for which I will be making arguments.

Old Model

Christianity	Judaism
Faith	Works of the Law
Spirit	Flesh
Life	Death

New Model

Gospel of God	Gospel of Rome
Crucified Anointed	Emperor
Son of God	Son of God
Life	Death
Freedom	Slavery

Readings

Augustine. *Saint Augustine Confessions.* Trans. R. S. Pine-Coffin. London: Penguin Books, 1961.

Brown, Peter Robert Lamont. *Augustine of Hippo: A Biography.* London: Faber, 1967.

Eisenbaum, Pamela. *Paul Was Not a Christian: The Original Message of a Misunderstood Apostle.* New York: HarperOne, 2009.

Hock, Ronald F. *The Social Context of Paul's Ministry: Tentmaking and Apostleship.* Philadelphia: Fortress Press, 1980.

Lonergan, Bernard J. F. *Method in Theology.* New York: Herder and Herder, 1972.

Nirenberg, David. *Anti-Judaism: The Western Tradition.* New York: W. W. Norton, 2014.

Nock, Arthur Darby. *Conversion, Catechumenate, and Baptism in the Early Church.* London: Oxford University Press, 1933.

Oberman, Heiko Augustinus. *Luther: Man between God and the Devil.* New Haven: Yale University Press, 1989.

Reumann, John Henre Paul, ed. *Philippians: A New Translation.* The Anchor Yale Bible, vol. 33B. New Haven: Yale University Press, 2008.

Segal, Alan F. *Paul the Convert: The Apostolate and Apostasy of Saul the Pharisee.* New Haven: Yale University Press, 1990.

Stendahl, Krister. *Paul Among Jews and Gentiles.* Philadelphia: Fortress Press, 1976.

CHAPTER 7

Showdown in Antioch

Having dealt with the central event in Paul's life, his *apocalypsis*/revelation, we now turn to what I judge to be the second most important event for Paul, a dramatic, perhaps even traumatic, conflict that took place in Antioch which apparently split apart the young community of followers of Jesus. Whether that rupture was ever reconciled is unknown, but no reconciliation is recorded.

What happened to provoke this conflict?

Meeting in Jerusalem

In the myth of early Christian origins the Council of Jerusalem plays a much larger role than the conflict in Antioch. The Council in Jerusalem coheres with the picture the Acts of the Apostles is portraying of a harmonious early community gathered around the twelve apostles in Jerusalem. Conflict in Antioch does not.

Paul's account in Gal 2:11–21 of this debate in Antioch is part of his exposition and defense of his call to be an envoy as a commission from God and not from humans. Paul is concerned to defend his independence as an envoy and his non-dependence upon the envoys/apostles in Jerusalem. His first line of defense, which we have already examined, was his *apocalypsis*/revelation. After that he details his relations with those Jerusalem envoys:

> I did not rush off to consult with anyone. Neither did I set out for Jerusalem to get the approval of those who became envoys for God's Anointed before I did. Instead, I left for Arabia and afterward returned to Damascus. (Gal 1:16b–17)

In his report, only three years later did he finally go up to Jerusalem to visit Cephas. This get-acquainted meeting lasted for two weeks, and Paul claims to have met with no other envoys of the Anointed, except for James, the brother of the Lord. This reference and perhaps the list in 1 Cor 15:7 are the only places where James is listed among the apostles. This reporting of events which appears so neutral to us, almost like a grocery list, is so important to Paul and apparently controversial that he feels compelled to take an oath to vouch for its truth: "What I am writing to you is not a lie, so help me God!" (Gal 1:20). One can only suppose that rumors or stories are circulating that attest to the opposite. So what appears neutral to us is actually highly contested. This reminds us that

Pauline Chronology

The story in Acts 18:12–16 which reports Paul's trial in Corinth before Gallio, the proconsul of Achaia, has furnished a starting point for constructing Paul's chronology. An inscription from Delphi recording a letter from the emperor Claudius (41–54 CE) mentions Gallio. The inscription can be dated to 52 CE. (For translation of the inscription see Elliott, *Documents and Images for the Study of Paul*, 55; and discussion in White, *From Jesus to Christianity*, 151–53; especially Murphy-O'Connor, *St. Paul's Corinth: Texts and Archaeology*, 141–52.) Since the term of a proconsul was normally two years, this would put Paul in Corinth in 51 CE, give or take a year. Using Paul's counting "after three years," (Gal 1:18) and "fourteen years later" (Gal 2:1), that would put the meeting in Jerusalem around 48–49 CE and Paul's call around 31–32. Robert Jewett in his *A Chronology of Paul's Life* arranges this data into a most precise chronology (see the chart at his book's conclusion).

This whole edifice has recently been questioned. The dating of the Gallio inscription is secure, but the historicity of the Acts narrative is in doubt. Recent archaeological re-evaluation of the tribunal in Corinth has dated it to the late first century, after Paul's visit to the Corinth. The trial itself appears to be a Lukan construction (Smith, 222–23).

our evidence is always from a point of view. Because our evidence from Paul is in the form of a letter, we only have Paul's side of the conversation. We do not know what the Galatians are saying on their side. That must be reconstructed. The analogy of overhearing a telephone conversation is a helpful warning. Moreover we do not know how Cephas or James related these events.

Paul's report provides an accounting in years ("after three years," Gal 1:18; "fourteen years later," Gal 2:1) that has provided fodder for endless speculation. The problem is that we have neither a *terminus a quo* nor a *terminus ad quem*. Without a starting or ending point we end up with only estimates.

Next Paul relates the so-called Council of Jerusalem. This title is problematic in many ways, but most especially because it risks an anachronistic projection of the later great ecumenical councils like Nicaea or Chalcedon on to this meeting in Jerusalem. In Paul's account of this meeting he is intent upon stressing his independence. He went up in "response to a revelation" (2:2 BBS), employing the same word, *apocalypsis*, as in Gal 1:12. There is no hint that he was called or summoned to Jerusalem. He laid out the good news he preached among the nations, and the proof that they accepted the gospel as he laid it out was that "they did not require my companion Titus, though a Greek, to be circumcised" (Gal 2:3). Titus is physical proof that Paul was not compelled to change his circumcision-free gospel for the nations. For Paul the whole point of relating an account of this meeting in Jerusalem was to demonstrate to his audience in Galatia that those in Jerusalem had accepted his version of the gospel.

Conflict with Cephas

Paul now turns to the issue for which all this has been a buildup: his conflict with Cephas in Antioch. He apparently sees the issues involved in this conflict as parallel to what is happening in Galatia. So what was the conflict with Cephas about and what was happening in Galatia?

The situation is easy to explain, the why is more difficult. "Before representatives of James came to Antioch, Cephas would eat with those from the nations" (Gal 2:12). Meals in the ancient world were part of the public web that held society together. Meals involved public rituals that enforced the common bond

Cephas and Peter

Paul normally employs Cephas, whereas the gospels use Peter and only once Cephas. Cephas is an Aramaic name meaning "rock," and Peter represents *petros,* a wordplay on the Greek *petra,* "rock." The tradition has always assumed that Cephas and Peter are the same person. The NIV translates "Cephas" in Paul's letters as "Peter." When Jesus meets Peter for the first time, the Fourth Gospel explains the wordplay. "When Jesus laid eyes on him, he said, 'You're Simon, John's son; you're going to be called Kephas' (which means Peter <or Rock>)" (John 1:42 SV).

The Gospel of Matthew represents another version of the wordplay, but without employing Cephas. "Let me tell you, you are Peter (*petros*), and on this very rock (*petra*) I will build my congregation" (Matt 16:18, SV modified).

Only in Galatians does Paul employ both Cephas and Peter, and they appear in close proximity. While defending his reception of the gospel, he reports his dealing with the pillars of Jerusalem.

> On the contrary, they recognized that God had entrusted me with the task of announcing God's world-transforming message to the uncircumcised, just as Peter had been entrusted with taking it to the circumcised. For it was evident that the God who worked through Peter as envoy to the circumcised worked through me as envoy to the rest of the world. When they realized that God had given me this special role, James, Cephas and John, the reputed pillars <of the Movement> extended the right hand of fellowship to Barnabas and me and agreed that we should go to the nations and they to the circumcised. (Gal 2:7–9)

The shift in names is difficult to explain as the same person without the explanation in John and Matthew. Without that information, a straight reading would assume that Peter and Cephas are two different people. Are they two different people, or is the report from later tradition about the wordplay correct?

and they could be, on occasion, avenues for social comment and challenge. These common meals brought Jews and the nations together eating in the name of Jesus the Anointed. There are two perspectives at stake. From a Jewish perspective, purity code issues are involved when Jews and the nations eat together. Over a long period of time accommodations had been worked out in the diaspora to make common eating together feasible. From a Roman perspective libations offered to the emperor were necessary as part of the proper order. Caesar as lord and god must be acknowledged. For Paul these common meals of Jews and the nations in the name of Jesus the Anointed followed Jewish practice, so there was no ritual libation to Caesar. Romans tolerated the monotheism of Jews. It was an uneasy truce, but it worked. Jews were not required to worship the emperor as long as sacrifices and prayers for the emperor were offered in the Jerusalem Temple. But no such exemption was in place for the nations.

This mixed meal of Anointed believers could be viewed as an affront, even a blasphemy to the empire. We need to set aside our modern sensibilities. The Roman Empire is not some secular, democratic institution. We need also to recognize *Pax Romana* (Roman Peace) as imperial propaganda. This peace masked the ruthless brutality of the empire. What Martin Goodman in his *The Roman World* observes about Octavian is true for all the emperors, for Augustus was the model:

> When Octavian achieved sole control over the Roman world
> after Actium in 31 BC it was patent to all that his success was
> due to the ruthless manipulation of a huge fighting machine in
> the preceding ten years. To disguise such a fact was neither pos-
> sible nor wholly desirable: the memory of the past would deter
> future challengers. . . . But it was possible to choose . . . not to
> emphasize the crudity of the power struggle. . . . He gradually
> established a new image for himself in which no hint of violence,
> or any need for violence, could be glimpsed. (133)

The secret of Roman power, how a city in Italy conquered the whole known world, was that it never gave up, never used diplomacy to compromise. Tacitus records the comments of a group of captives that makes this point vividly:

> You Romans are not beaten and no disasters will overcome you!
> they declared. Fleet destroyed, weapons lost, shores strewn with

the bodies of horses and men, and you still have the same courage, matching spirit, and apparently greater numbers for invading! (*Annals*, 2.25.3)

By bringing together Jews and the nations, eating according to the customs of monotheism, and with no libation on the part of the nations to the emperor, these meals were not only subversive and offensive to the empire, but dangerous for those who participated.

After his discussion of the meeting with the "pillars" in Jerusalem, Paul concluded with his telling of their full acceptance of his circumcision-free gospel for the nations. Paul jumps immediately into his confrontation with Cephas. "When Cephas came to Antioch, I confronted him publicly because he was clearly in the wrong" (2:11). This is an abrupt transition in telling the story. Apparently his audience already knows the story's outline, while we do not. The Greek paints an image: "I stood against him to his face" (2:11 BBS)—it pictures Paul and Cephas standing face to face, toe to toe, and going at it. Not a polite image. In an honor/ shame culture standing up to someone's face is insulting, a challenge to that person's honor.

Paul then describes the situation in Antioch before the confrontation. "Cephas would eat with those from the nations" (2:12). We have already seen what this involves. Just to reinforce the point: We must avoid reading our church situations into what Paul is describing. Meals are part of ritual life in the ancient world with certain expected public obligations. The meals in Antioch where Jews and the nations ate together in the name of Jesus the Anointed violated Roman social and legal expectations. Eating together put the community at risk.

Now the "representatives of James" come to Antioch. The simplicity of the Greek is tantalizing in what it does not say but perhaps implies. "Certain ones from James" (BBS). Who are these certain ones? Are they connected to the spies referred to in the account of the meeting in Jerusalem who are so wonderfully described in the language of the King James, a language that knew all about spies? "And that because of false brethren unawares brought in, who came in privily to spy out our liberty which we have in Christ Jesus, that they might bring us into bondage" (2:4 KJ). We do not know who these certain ones were and whether there was a connection to the spies. But the result seems to be somewhat the same. The language of freedom and slavery is parallel in both.

After the certain ones from James arrived, Cephas would no longer eat with the nations. The issue is circumcision. "He avoided and kept his distance from those people because he feared those who were advocating circumcision" (2:12). Once again the Greek is simpler, more elusive and tantalizingly vague: "fearing them which were of the circumcision" (2:12 KJ), literally, "the ones of circumcision." The NRSV translates this "the circumcision party," while the SV has "those who were advocating circumcision." Both of these are trying to make the translation less vague. They might be a party but are they an organized party in opposition to Paul? Are they advocating circumcision? Or are they James's friends who agree with his position? And just what is that position?

The aftermath of their arrival clearly indicates the power and authority of James, at least over the Jews among the followers of the Anointed. "The rest of the Jewish followers also began to waffle, with the result that even Barnabas was carried away by their duplicity" (2:13). Barnabas' defection is particularly telling because Barnabas had been Paul's fellow envoy. Literally, Paul charges these Jews with hypocrisy. The significance of this charge soon will become evident.

Paul sees this action on Cephas' part as not only hypocritical but a denial of the good news, God's world-transforming message. And so he challenges him to his face.

Conflict over What?
Now the problems start. Just what is the debate about? The most convincing and cogent analysis of this whole confrontation in Antioch is Brigitte Kahl's "Peter's Antiochene Apostasy: Re-Judaizing or Imperial Conformism?" I will be following her lead in analyzing this confrontation. (To avoid confusion, Kahl takes Cephas to be Peter, whereas I have left that issue open and follow Paul's usage. See the cameo essay "Cephas or Peter.")

What is Paul upset about? What is so serious that he thinks the good news/gospel is at stake? Certainly just withdrawing from eating together cannot be that serious? And why is the group from James described as those of the circumcision?

The traditional interpretive model, as we have seen, has juxtaposed Christianity to Judaism, Gentile to Jew, faith to works, uncircumcision to circumcision, and freedom to slavery. This model has been used to understand Paul's accusation against Cephas: "If you, though a Jew, live like a Gentile and not like a Jew, how can you compel the Gentiles to live like Jews?" (2:14 NRSV) Hans Deiter Betz's analysis of this passage in his Hermeneia commentary *Galatians* is typical of the traditional understanding.

> By changing back to the observance of Jewish custom and law, the Jewish Christians have only reversed their emancipation from Judaism. When they gave up the observance of the Torah, they also admitted that as a Christian one can be saved without the Torah. Returning to the Torah cannot simply eliminate that first step of denying the existence of Torah observance. (112)

As Kahl shrewdly notes about Betz's analysis, "to live like a Gentile" means "to live like a Christian." Cephas' hypocrisy lies in asking Gentiles to live like Jews. Betz's interpretation keeps the traditional model firmly in place, equating Gentile with Christian and understanding it to be opposed to Judaism. Betz clearly sees Cephas and Paul at the meeting in Jerusalem abandoning Judaism in favor of Christianity, but then at Antioch Cephas reneges. However we have seen that model is an inappropriate, anachronistic misreading of Paul. Paul did not convert from Judaism to Christianity, nor did Christianity even exist in this period.

Moreover Kahl notes that this reading destroys the rhetoric of Paul's argument. Since Paul is confronting Cephas face to face, we expect a strong rhetorical attack. Instead as Kahl remarks, "Paul all of a sudden becomes exceedingly polite, diplomatic, and pussyfooted." Instead of confronting Cephas, Paul gives him "a limp and very strangely worded applause for being a good Christian." This misreading results from misunderstanding the Greek *ethnikōs* as "Gentile," that is, Christian, not Jewish.

The rhetoric of Paul's argument would suggest that *ethnikōs* should be understood in a negative sense as an insult to Cephas. Actually this Greek word root does have a negative sense in the New Testament. We have already examined the related word *ethnos*, which illustrates the problem in this case. That noun traditionally has been translated "Gentile," non-Jew, and we have argued that a better translation is "nations." *Ethnik-* belongs to the same family root.

The Greek *ethnikōs* is an adverb and the *-ōs* ending is an adverbial ending, like "-ly" in English. The root *ethnik-* is used four times in the New Testament, always in a negative sense, which illustrates Paul's usage.

> And if you greet only your friends (*lit:* brothers) what have you done that is exceptional? Even the pagans (*ethnikoi*) do as much, don't they? (Matt 5:47)

The contrast between brothers and pagans makes it clear this is a contrast between insiders and outsiders or, as we might say colloquially, between "us and them."

> And when you pray, you should not babble on as the pagans (*ethnikoi*) do. They imagine that the more they say, the more attention they get. (Matt 6:7)

> Then if he or she refuses to listen to them, report it to the congregation. If he or she refuses to listen even to the congregation, treat that companion like you would a pagan (*ethnikos*) or toll collector. (Matt 18:17)

In each of these cases the *ethnikoi* are those outside, foreigners, and they are viewed as negative examples, definitely lower in status from the perspective of honor. One should do more or better than these foreigners, the pagans or nations, do. The implication: we are better. In Matthew's gospel this negative view of the nations/*ethnikoi* leads directly to the gospel's conclusion: "make all the nations (*ethnē*) your disciples" (Matt 28:19 BBS). Thus Matthew's community/readers who have seen the nations as their inferiors are now told that their fate lies among them—they are to make them their disciples. Even though Matthew's gospel was written considerably later than Paul's letter, his usage helps us understand how this *ethnik* word group is employed.

When Paul says that Cephas is living like one of the nations and not as a Jew (*ethnikōs kai ouchi Ioudaikōs*) he is not commending Cephas but condemning him. The next verse exposes the Jewish presupposition: "We may be Jews by birth and we may look at people of the nations as ignorant and corrupt" (2:15). From the Jewish point of view, the nations are natural-born sinners, and literally in the Greek Paul refers to them as sinners. Kahl draws what is the "natural interpretation" of Paul's condemnation of Cephas:

> You, Peter, have made a big public show of being a Jew, but in fact I, Paul, tell you, you live like a Gentile sinner, a *goy*: *ethnikōs*. And as a Jew, as you and I know, you should not. You should live *Ioudaikōs*, **not** *ethnikōs*. (31)

In Kahl's reconstruction of events, Cephas (and I would add James) have become concerned about the ramifications of these mixed meals in Antioch. How will the imperial officials judge them? Kahl catches the claustrophobic atmosphere of life in the Roman Empire.

> In a situation where everything is over-determined and colonized by civic religion and most of all imperial religion, nothing, not even Jewish law, Jewish identity, and the Jewish God can escape the omnipresent grip of the Roman empire and its idols: *Sin*, in Paul's terminology. (31–32)

The perspective from Jerusalem may have to shift when confronted with the realities of Antioch. Eating together in Antioch in Syria, in the period after the meeting in Jerusalem, sometime in 47–48 CE, is a very different situation than in the Jewish homeland where Judaism is the dominant religion. The young movement is still experimenting. In Antioch, the Roman imperial presence is much more prominent than in Judaea and Galilee. As James and then Cephas see the situation, the mixed meals in Antioch are too dangerous. They are apparently withdrawing from the meals to minimize the danger. They are proposing that those of the nations have three choices.

1. They can perform some of the rituals that are required by the imperial religion as part of one's civic duties. Judaism had long worked out an accommodation on this issue.
2. They can become fully Jewish by accepting circumcision.

The first option does not appear to have been seriously considered. For Cephas and James the second solution, circumcision, is a pragmatic solution to a dangerous situation, a solution that has the advantage of fitting with established tradition. If neither one of these options is accepted, then third choice would be obvious:

3. Cephas and the Jews must withdraw from table fellowship.

Paul rejects this offer from a Jewish perspective and accuses Cephas of behaving not as a Jew but as *goyim, ethnikōs,* a heathen. Ironically both Paul and Cephas see themselves as acting from a Jewish perspective. For Paul the proposal of Cephas is idolatry; it violates the oneness of God. For Jews the defining characteristic of the nations is that they worship idols. In Paul's earliest letter he commends his converts as having "turned to God from idols, to serve a living and true God" (1 Thess 1:9 NRSV). Or again in the debate about food offered to idols, we see clearly Paul's position:

> What is my point? That meat sacrificed to a pseudo-divinity really is what it is alleged to be, or that an idol is what it is alleged to be? Not at all. My point is that such sacrifices are actually offerings to demons and not to God. I don't want you to become involved with demons. (1 Cor 10:19–20)

Paul argues that the solutions offered by Cephas and James return the nations back to the worship of idols. Their solutions acknowledge the primacy of the idol Caesar against the call of the one true God. God has called the nations from the worship of idols to the worship of the one true God in the name of the Anointed. Any backtracking on this call is a violation of God's oneness, an act of idolatry.

It is not clear who won this debate. From this point forward, no evidence supports Barnabas as a fellow-envoy with Paul (so Meier in Brown, 39). Had that been the case surely Paul would have mentioned it in the letter to the Galatians, for it would have been the linchpin in his narrative of the events: "Barnabas agreed with me," he could claim. Moreover the similarity between the situation in Antioch and that in Galatia, which is why he tells the story, points to a continuing issue in this regard. This controversy would continue to plague Paul.

The Acts of the Apostles is silent on the Antioch episode, perhaps because of Acts's harmonizing tendency. For the author of Acts, all is peaceful in the church. Yet Ignatius of Antioch (martyred about 110 CE) refers to conflict with Jewish Christians in his letters (Ign. *Mag.* 8–11; *Phld.* 6:1–2; *Smyrn.* 2:4–7). We do not know the final outcome, although I would think that if Cephas and Barnabas had been reconciled to Paul's position, he would have mentioned it. Most likely the breech was never healed. Paul never returned to Antioch, and in essence became a freelancer.

Kahl's thesis matches perfectly with what we saw in the call/revelation model, whereas the traditional understanding does not. The traditional model demands Paul's conversion to Christianity and opposition between Christianity and Judaism. In that model Paul is a Christian who converts from Judaism. The assumptions of that model mislead us in understanding what is happening in Antioch. Kahl assumes that Paul, in Antioch, is still operating within the Jewish model but with the important difference that now God has called the nations to the worship of the one true God and liberated, saved them, from the enslaving worship of idols. This coheres perfectly with what we learned from our analysis of Paul's call. The puzzle is beginning to fit together, to form a coherent image of what Paul was about.

We should be clear about our gains. We have now examined the two major traumas in Paul's life and have found the same model underlies both. The traditional model views Christianity in opposition to Judaism and does not explain Paul's two experiences but distorts them. Paul sees himself as still a Jew and acting within Judaism. His real opponent, in his judgment, is God's opponent, the Roman Empire, with its most divine leader Caesar Augustus. God has called the nations to turn away from idols, the greatest idol of which is the imperial religion of Rome, and turn to the God of Israel.

We must not lose sight of this gain as we turn now to examine what Paul means by *pistis*, faith in Christ or faith of Christ.

Readings

Betz, Hans Dieter. *Galatians: A Commentary on Paul's Letter to the Churches in Galatia.* Hermeneia. Philadelphia: Fortress Press, 1979.

Brown, Raymond Edward, and John P. Meier. *Antioch and Rome: New Testament Cradles of Catholic Christianity.* New York: Paulist Press, 1983.

Elliott, Neil, and Mark Reasoner, eds. *Documents and Images for the Study of Paul.* Minneapolis: Fortress Press, 2011.

Goodman, Martin. *The Roman World, 44 BC–AD 180.* London/New York: Routledge, 2012.

Jewett, Robert. *A Chronology of Paul's Life.* Philadelphia: Fortress Press, 1979.

Kahl, Brigitte. "Peter's Antiochene Apostasy: Re-Judaizing or Imperial Conformism?" *Forum* Third Series 3,1 (April 2014) 27–38.

Knox, John. *Chapters in a Life of Paul.* Nashville: Abingdon Press, 1950.

Murphy-O'Connor, Jerome. *St. Paul's Corinth: Texts and Archaeology.* Wilmington, DE: Michael Glazier, 1983.

Smith, Dennis Edwin. *From Symposium to Eucharist: The Banquet in the Early Christian World.* Minneapolis: Fortress Press, 2003.

Smith, Dennis Edwin, and Hal Taussig, eds. *Meals in the Early Christian World: Social Formation, Experimentation, and Conflict at the Table.* New York: Palgrave Macmillan, 2012.

Smith, Dennis Edwin, Joseph B. Tyson, and the Acts Seminar. *Acts and Christian Beginnings: The Acts Seminar Report.* Salem, OR: Polebridge Press, 2013.

Tacitus, Cornelius. *Annals.* Trans. Cynthia Damon. London: Penguin Books, 2012.

Zetterholm, Magnus. *The Formation of Christianity in Antioch: A Social-Scientific Approach to the Separation between Judaism and Christianity.* London/New York: Routledge, 2003.

CHAPTER 8

FAITH OR FAITHFUL

While a first major new turn in the understanding of Paul began with Krister Stendhal's famous essay on "The Apostle Paul and the Introspective Conscience of the West," a second major turn occurred in the debate over the meaning of the phrase *pistis tou christou*. This debate was initiated by Richard Hays (*The Faith of Jesus*) and Sam K. Williams (*Jesus' Death*). New Testament scholarship usually moves at what I would describe as a glacial pace. Seldom are issues solved in a short period of time. But in this case scholarship has reached a consensus in a matter of a few years. Not that everyone agrees (Dunn, "Once More"; Jewett, 276–79), but major scholars have shifted their positions (Keck, 105) and translations are taking note (NRSV has recognized the shift in a footnote).

The debate can be explained rather easily. It involves an issue of translation based on a distinction of Greek grammar. Not surprised? In the Greek phrase *pistis tou christou* (*lit:* faith of the Anointed) how is the genitive (*tou christou*, of the Anointed) modifier to be understood and translated? The King James translates it "faith of Jesus Christ" (Rom 3:22), while the NRSV has "faith in Jesus Christ." Both are possible translations. The question:

- Is the modifier objective, in which case faith has as its object Jesus? If so, the translation would be "faith in Jesus."
- Is the modifier subjective, in which case faith has as its subject Jesus, i.e., possessive, it belongs to Jesus, it is Jesus' faith? If so, the translation would be "the faith of Jesus" or "Jesus' faithfulness."

As you can guess, much depends on a small point of Greek grammar. How do we resolve this issue? By observing Paul's usage.

Pistis in Greek

Greek has a verb, *pisteuein*, a noun, *pistis*, and adjective, *pistos*, all based on the stem *pist-*. This word group has a range of meanings in Greek and in the New Testament, as well as in Paul. A single English gloss as a translation almost always is a mistake. The word's dominant sense in Greek is "*trust in* others" or "that which gives *confidence*" (LSJ). Standard English glosses would be trust, faith, persuasion, confidence, proof, belief. It can be used in a commercial sense for "good credit" or "good faith," or concerning business dealings, honesty.

Paul basically uses four forms listed below with their traditional English translations:

pisteuein (verb)	to have faith, to believe
pistis (noun)	faith
hoi pisteuontes (participle)	those who have faith or those who believe, i.e., believers
pistos (adjective)	faithful or trustworthy

A problem in translating this word group in English is that faith in the sense of belief as an intellectual act has become dominant in English, an aspect almost absent in Greek. The creeds, seen as expressions of faith and belief, enable one to list what one believes, and this list then becomes the object of faith. The notion of creedal faith emerged later in fourth-century Christianity. Moreover because of the creeds, in western Christianity faith becomes a synonym for religion, so that a religion is a faith, a notion we take as universal, but which is unique to western Christianity. Judaism, Islam, and Buddhism, for example, are practices. So once again there is a lot to sort out in order to begin to recover Paul's understanding of *pistis*.

Paul can and does use the *pist-* family of words in a normal sense. "First of all, I hear that when you meet as a community there are divisions among you and to some extent I believe it" (1 Cor 11:18). This use of *pisteuō* is identical to the common English usage "I believe," that is, "I have confidence or trust in the report I have heard." This is a good example of the basic sense of *pistis* which we should keep in mind as we move forward. We should beware of special pleading for a unique theological sense for a word.

Objective or Subjective Genitive?

To cut the Gordian Knot I will present what I take to be the compelling piece of evidence in this matter. The final verse of Rom 3:21–26, probably the most famous passage on faith in Paul, presents the decisive example.

> it was to prove at the present time that he himself is righteous and that he justifies *the one who has faith in Jesus.*
> (Rom 3:26 NRSV)

The NRSV has unambiguously rendered the phrase as an objective genitive. A parallel passage occurs in the very next chapter dealing with Abraham's faith. Again in the translation of the NRSV:

> For this reason it depends on faith, in order that the promise may rest on grace and be guaranteed to all his descendants, not only to the adherents of the law but also to those *who share the faith of Abraham* for he is the father of all of us. (Rom 4:16 NRSV)

The Greek in the two italicized phrases is parallel.

Ton ek pisteōs Iēsou (Rom 3:26)
Tō ek pisteōs Abraam (Rom 4:16)

Now the compelling issue. Since these two phrases are parallel, should they not be translated in a parallel fashion? Their placement in two different chapters should not obscure their obvious parallelism. Chapter divisions are not original and in this case mask the evident continuity between chapters 3 and 4, both of which are part of a rhetorical structure called a diatribe, an imagined debate. If the first example is translated "he justifies *the one who has faith in Jesus,*" why not translate the second one, "*who have faith in Abraham*"? Why not? Because it makes theological nonsense. No one would argue that "faith in Abraham" is the correct translation. And that is the point. The issue has been decided on theological grounds. The NRSV and the rest of the theological tradition want to translate the first example as an objective genitive (faith in Jesus) and the second one as a subjective genitive (Abraham's faith or the faith that belongs to Abraham).

If we translate both as subjective genitives the problem goes away, but a very different understanding of Paul begins to emerge. Just making this simple change in the NRSV translation opens up the text.

it was to prove at the present time that he himself is righteous
and that he justifies *the one who shares in the faith of Jesus*

Jesus' *faith* does not refer to what he believes, but his *faithfulness*
to God, his trust or confidence in God, the normal meaning in
Greek of *pistis*. Just as in the parallel with Abraham, Abraham's
faithfulness to God's promise is the point. "The faithfulness of
Jesus" is a clearer translation. The SV catches this sense well:

> This shows God's reliability at this decisive time, namely, that
> God is reliable and approves the one who lives on the basis of
> Jesus' unconditional confidence in God. (Rom 3:26 SV)

"Unconditional" is an interpretive addition that clarifies and in-
tensifies "confidence." It is not necessary.

A second reason for preferring the subjective over the objective genitive translation I find less compelling, but still interesting:
If one is justified by faith in Christ, why then is faith not a work?
Would that not make faith something one does? Would Paul not
be logically inconsistent?

A final and more important reason is that understanding
pistis as faithful makes more sense of Paul's argument. We will be
testing that hypothesis in the remainder of this chapter. "Faith"
is not a wrong translation, but I will employ "faithfulness" as the
gloss for *pistis*. If we keep the traditional gloss "faith," we may be
seduced back into the traditional meaning.

ROMANS 3:22

Now that we have resolved the basic grammatical and translation
issue concerning the faithfulness of the Anointed, we need to see
what the payout is in understanding Paul. The *locus classicus* for
the discussion of faith is Rom 3:22 and its context 3:21–26. This
passage raises a host of issues, and we will tackle them in a logical
and sequential order. But first, let's begin with a sample of translations of 3:22.

KJ   Even the righteousness of God *which is* by faith of Jesus
        Christ unto all and upon all them that believe: for there is
        no difference.

NRSV   The righteousness of God through faith in Jesus Christ for
        all who believe. For there is no distinction.

SV   God's reliability has now been made clear through the un-
       conditional confidence in God of Jesus, God's Anointed, for
       the benefit of all who come to have such confidence—no
       exceptions!
Stowers It is God's [own] righteousness [effected] by means of Jesus
       Christ's faithfulness for who are faithful. For there is no dif-
       ference. (223)

Both the SV and Stowers' translations verge on becoming para-
phrases, because of how dense and concise Paul's language is. The
tradition's use and elaboration of this language has obscured the
concise nature of Paul's language, thus further confusing what an
already difficult passage is trying to communicate. Both the SV
and Stowers' translations are unpacking that dense language by
spelling it out, filling in the blanks.

Context in the Letter

The traditional interpretation of Paul's letter to the Romans has
trained us to read it as a generalized and universal theological
treatment. Stanley Stowers in his important book *A Rereading of
Romans* states the problem well. "The tradition and its translations
have conditioned moderns to read Romans in a flat, universalistic
way as an answer to the question, 'How can the sinner be saved?'"
(202). The problem, to which Paul supposedly has the answer, is
how to save the individual sinner. The individual and sin are the
two critical focal points. What gets missed in this generalized and
universalistic reading is the particularity of Paul's actual context.
Paul is the envoy to the nations and the fate of the nations is what
concerned him. The envoy/apostle to the nations is quite different
from Apostle to the Gentiles. Gentile implies "not Jew" and implicitly "a Christian." In addition to Stowers' point concerning how
can the sinner be saved, the traditional interpretation of Romans
also assumes supersessionism, that Christianity or the church supersedes and replaces Israel. That is not Paul's assumption. This is
the old model in which the opposition between Christianity and
Judaism is the primary polarity by which Paul is understood. As
we saw in our analysis of Paul's call and his conflict with Cephas
at Antioch, that opposition is not supportable.

The Greeting

The specificity of the context of Rom 3:22 should determine its meaning. The generalized, universalistic understanding of the passage rips it out of its context. The question is, how does it fit into its context within the letter, and where does it come in the flow of Paul's argument? The letter's salutation, always a good guide to Paul's intentions, stresses that Paul is the envoy to the nations.

> Paul
>> *slave* of Anointed Jesus
>> called to be an envoy
>> set apart for the good news of God
>>> which he promised beforehand through his prophets and
>>> holy writings
>>> concerning his son
>>>> who was begotten out of the seed of David according to
>>>> the flesh
>>>> who was designated son of God in power according to
>>>>> the spirit of holiness out of the resurrection of the dead
>>>>> Jesus anointed our *master*
>>>>>> through whom we have received grace and envoyship
>>>>>> for bringing about obedience based on faithfulness
>>>>>> among all the nations on behalf of his name
>>>>>> among whom you also are called to belong to Jesus
>>>>>> Anointed
> to all who are in Rome
>> beloved of God,
>> called to be the holy ones
> grace and peace to you from God our father and *master* Jesus
> Anointed.
>> (Rom 1:1–5 BBS; emphasis added)

This is the most elaborate greeting/salutation in any extant Pauline letter. My translation attempts to exhibit in graphic form, even if inelegantly, its careful construction, balance and elegance. The vocabulary sets up echoes that will ring throughout the letter. "Slave" (servant in most translations) contrasts with "master" (Lord in traditional translations). An organizing pattern emerges around slave and master:

- at the beginning, slave is the first descriptor of Paul
- at the salutation's midpoint, where Jesus' name first appears, he is *Jesus Anointed our master*
- at the salutation's conclusion, he is *master Jesus Anointed*

The slave/master relationship, a primary social structure of the Roman Empire, contains and constrains the whole salutation.

Slave of Anointed Jesus almost surely invokes an implicit reference to the Roman situation. It contrasts with the slaves of Caesar, members of Caesar's household and important administrators of the empire. This was a large and extremely prestigious group of slaves. Slave and master define the relationship between Paul and Jesus, and starting off with the descriptor slave situates Paul in the lowest social status. The humiliating nature of slavery is unavoidable, as pointed out in Glancy's excellent study.

Called to be an envoy implies "envoy to the nations" and this phrase combined with the next phrase, "set apart for the good news of God" recalls the formulaic description in Galatians of Paul's call (Gal 1:15–16, see also 1 Cor 15:8–9). Following the naming of Jesus Anointed our master, Paul returns immediately to the theme of his envoyship and elaborates on it: "By whom we have received grace and apostleship, for obedience to the faith among all nations, for his name" (Rom 1:5 KJ). What then does obedience to the faith mean?

Obedience

Obedience fits right in with slave/master. A slave must obey his or her master. Even more, the nations have been disobedient to God, and now are being offered a way to obedience. But what does faith have to do with this? In the King James translation it sounds like "to the faith" means to a body of doctrine or to Christianity. Any such meaning would be anachronistic for Paul. The NRSV slightly shifts the translation: "to bring about the obedience of faith." The sense would be the obedience that consists in faith. The classic 1902 commentary on Romans by William Sanday and Arthur C. Headlam catches this traditional sense perfectly:

> *pistis* is still, what it is predominantly to St. Paul, the lively act or impulse of adhesion to Christ. . . . Faith is the act of assent by which the Gospel is appropriated. (11)

While this is a possible meaning, it is not probable, because it does not cohere with what we have seen is the meaning of *pistis* for Paul. Moreover it detaches the phrase from the specific context of the salutation, namely his envoyship to the nations. Paul's apocalyptic scenario helps make sense of this cryptic phrase. In Paul's Jewish story, the nations disobeyed God and deserve God's punishment. The good news for the nations, according to Paul, is that now that disobedience has been dealt with by the faithfulness of Jesus. The theme of the disobedience of the nations is explored in the first two chapters of Romans. "Although they know full well

Apocalyptic Scenario

Paul does not spell out in detail his apocalyptic scenario, but it is implied in what he writes. We have to ferret it out and reconstruct it from clues he has left behind.

His apocalyptic scenario clearly involves the overthrow of Rome. This is an unavoidable conclusion. This is no spiritual kingdom coexisting with Rome. Separation of church and state is not a possibility in the ancient world. Rome is itself making religious claims that at times are similar to and conflict with those of the early Jesus movement.

But Paul is not fomenting direct revolution, rousing the masses to attack the barricades. In his scenario, the overthrow of Rome will be accomplished by God with the return (*parousia*) of Jesus the Anointed. Then all will be subjected to God.

This anti-Rome, anti-imperial aspect of Paul's good news must not be neglected. It is implicit throughout his message. Even his preaching on celibacy, which seems odd or even obnoxious to us, would be viewed as a threat to the empire and a rejection of the imperial policy requiring marriage.

In early Christianity's conflict with the Roman Empire we tend to view Christianity as innocent, the victim of a cruel empire. The Christians were no threat. But it all depends upon your point of view. From that of the empire, the Jesus movement was a threat, and Paul's preaching was clearly bad news for the empire.

God's judgment that those who do such things deserve to die, they not only do these evil deeds themselves, but even support those who do them" (Rom 1:32). In chapters 5–8 Paul returns to this theme to show how the Anointed's faithfulness solves the problem of the disobedience of the nations. Therefore I would tentatively suggest that we translate the phrase, "for bringing about obedience based on faithfulness among all the nations on behalf of his name" (Rom 1:5). This obedience reverses the disobedience of the nations.

At the conclusion to the thanksgiving in Romans Paul turns yet again to the theme of his relation to the nations.

> I think you ought to know, my friends, how often I planned to visit you—but have been prevented until now—in the hope that I may work as fruitfully among you, as in the rest of the world (*ethnesin*, *lit*: the nations). [By virtue of my calling] I am under obligation both to Greeks and barbarians, both to the wise and the foolish; that's why I'm eager to proclaim God's world-changing news also to you in Rome. (Rom 1:13–15)

Significantly Paul speaks of Greeks and barbarians, wise and foolish (see the cameo essay "Greek and Barbarians" in chapter 5), not Jew and Greek as in the programmatic statement in 1:16. This elaborates who the nations are and he closes by writing, "that's why I'm eager to proclaim God's world-changing news also to *you* in Rome." The "you" (plural) refers not only to the nations, but to the nations in Rome. Paul's addressee is the nations, not a universal human. Those nations have been subjugated to the idol Rome. Paul is proclaiming liberation from that subjugation by the faithfulness of the Anointed.

How Does It Go Together?

Two problems obscure Rom 3:21–26 in translations.

- The grammar of this passage is a bit unclear and ambiguous.

This is one of those passages whose structure is easier to see (and in the ancient world to *hear*) than it is to read silently in a printed text (which no one in the ancient world was doing).

- The division into verses obscures the underlying pattern both in Greek and English translations.

As Leander Keck has said, "Paul's Greek is not as clear as translations try to make it" (110). This is one of the tradeoffs in translation and makes using a standard translation for our purposes difficult.

Douglas Campbell in his study *The Rhetoric of Righteousness in Romans 3.21–26* (83–101) offers a convincing way through this twisted grammar. The passage offers a number of clear structural clues, often obscured by translations and versification. So I will employ my own translation that clarifies the structural clues and ignores the versification.

1. The word "righteousness" (*dikaiosynē*) occurs four times, and in the concluding verse 26 two more words, "righteous" and "makes-righteous" (with the *dikai-* stem), appear.
2. "Faithfulness" (*pistis*) occurs three times and "one who is faithful" (*pisteuontas*) once.
3. Three clauses introduced with the preposition "through" (*dia*) occur in rapid succession.
4. Two clauses of demonstration conclude the passage.
5. Finally, the passage begins and ends with a reference to the present time.

If we lay all this out in a visual, graphic translation, it quickly appears that the passage's grammar is interrupted by a parenthesis.

> *Now* apart from the law the **righteousness** of God is made manifest, having been born witness by the law and the prophets
> that is, God's **righteousness**
> *through* the <u>faithfulness</u> of Jesus Anointed for all who are <u>faithful</u>
> (for there is no distinction, all have sinned and fallen short of the glory of God, being made **right** as a gift of his graciousness)
> *through* the deliverance which is in the Anointed Jesus whom God has put forward as a means of propitiation
> *through* the <u>faithfulness</u> in his blood
> <u>to demonstrate</u> his **righteousness** through the passing over of previously committed sins in the forbearance of God,
> <u>to demonstrate</u> his **righteousness** in the *now time* so that he might be **righteous** and make **righteous** the one who lives out of the <u>faithfulness</u> of Jesus. (BBS)

The grammar unsnarls itself once we see that Paul is stacking phrases together in an effort to build up an impression of God's righteousness, which is the passage's theme as clearly announced in the first line (3:21) and by frequent repetition. After the initial statement, "Now apart from the law . . ." Paul repeats "God's righteousness" in apposition to the first statement, as though he wants to emphasize the passage's topic for his audience. Then three through-clauses appear, followed by two demonstration clauses drawing a final conclusion. That makes the structure clear, but the meaning still appears to be tied in knots. With our newly gained understanding of the faithfulness of Jesus and with a clearer understanding of the passage's rhetorical structure, we can now analyze the passage. We will move through it phrase by phrase.

RiGHTEOUSNESS

Since righteousness is the passage's theme, we should be clear about its meaning. As a translation of *dikaiosynē* it is perfectly adequate, except for that worrying feature that in English, righteousness has an overtone of self-righteousness, which is a negative term. Some of that negatively washes into a contemporary English translation. What is a positive word in Greek has in the English translation a potentially negative overtone. The fundamental sense of the Greek root *dik-* is custom, usage, order, what is right, judgment or lawsuit (LSJ). It concerns justice. The goddess Dike is the goddess of justice, identified with the daughter of Zeus. So the underlying sense of *dikaiosynē* as righteousness is justice, rightness, rectitude. God's justice comes about by setting matters aright.

Psalm 97 LXX (Psalm 98 in Hebrew and English translations) provides a helpful background for understanding Paul's usage.

> The Lord has made known his deliverance (*lit:* salvation);
> before the nations he revealed his righteousness.
> He remembered his mercy to Iakob
> and his truth to the house of Israel.
> All the ends of the earth saw
> the deliverance (*lit:* salvation) of our God. . . .
> Let the sea shake, and all that fills it,
> the whole world and those who live in it.
> Streams will together clap their hands;
> the mountains will rejoice

because he has come
to judge the earth.
He will judge the world with righteousness
and the peoples with uprightness.
   (Ps 97:2–3; 7–9 LXX)

Paul associates God's righteousness with God's faithfulness. This is very clear in Rom 3:1–9. Paul is engaging with an imaginary dialogue partner envisioned as a fellow Jew. This literary convention, called a diatribe, is common in the ancient world. In order to understand this section of Romans it helps to differentiate when Paul or his dialogue partner is speaking.

> *Interlocutor:* What's the advantage in being a Jew? Or what's the benefit of circumcision?
> *Paul:* A great advantage with many benefits. Above all, the Jews were entrusted with the words of God.
> *Interlocutor:* So what if some of them were unreliable (*lit:* unfaithful)? Surely, their unreliability (*lit:* unfaithfulness) doesn't invalidate God's reliability (*lit:* faithfulness), does it?
>   (Rom 3:1–3)

Verse three contrasts the faithfulness or reliability of God with the unfaithfulness of the Jews. This is a good example of where *pistis* could not be translated faith in the sense of belief. The belief of God simply does not make any sense. God's faithfulness is at question. Paul responds to his questioner as follows:

> *Paul:* Absolutely not! Surely God must be true even if everyone else is false, so that, as scripture says, "in all you say your justice shows and when you are accused you win your case." (Rom 3:4)

Paul completely agrees with the logic of his questioner and equates God's faithfulness with God's justice, but he makes this equation by quoting the scriptures, the very words of God (Ps 51:4). God's faithfulness and his justice, which are now intertwined, cannot be invalidated by any human treachery.

> *Interlocutor:* [Well, Paul,] if our misdeeds (*adikia*) highlight God's reliability (*dikaiosynē*), dare one conclude that God who punishes us is unjust—if one may speak irreverently?
> *Paul:* Absolutely not! If that were so, how could God judge the world?
>   (Rom 3:5–6)

The SV translators in my judgment have cleaned up verse 5 a little too much and in the process have hidden an important aspect of Paul's apocalyptic scenario. More literally, the interlocutor's question could be translated:

> But if our unrighteousness commend the righteousness of God, what shall we say? *Is* God unrighteous who taketh vengeance? (I speak as a man.) (KJ)

The unrighteous or wicked have earned God's vengeance or anger (*orgē*). His righteousness or justice could demand such a punishment, but his righteousness is merciful. Stowers explains this sense of *dikaiosynē* in this fashion:

> Thus, righteousness here does not signify strict justice but quite specifically a redeeming merciful justice. In some places, the phrase could be translated as "the merciful justice of God." Romans associates this merciful justice with a promise to Abraham and the good news. (195)

The reference to Abraham reminds us of the scenario that backs up Paul's understanding. In that apocalyptic story the promise God made to Abraham that he should be the father of all nations is now being redeemed in the faithfulness of his Anointed one. Paul is willing to allow a sense of God as unjust to creep into his argument. Not strict justice but merciful justice (righteousness) characterizes God for Paul.

Robert Jewett in his Hermeneia commentary on *Romans* has accented a missional facet to the righteousness of God. The good news of the Anointed "equalizes the status of Greeks and barbarians, wise and uneducated, Jews and Gentiles, which offers new relationships in communal settings to all on precisely the same terms" (142). This re-enforces the point that we have seen over and over again, that Paul's concern is not the individual but the nations and the community (*ekklēsia*) as the way in which the nations are redeemed. "This missional context makes it highly likely that *dikaiosunē tou theou* should be taken as a subjective genitive referring to God's activity in this process of global transformation, rather than as an objective genitive that would refer to the human righteousness bestowed by God" (Jewett, 142).

> Now apart from the law the *righteousness* of God is made mani-
> fest, having been born witness by the law and the prophets.
> (3:21, emphasis added)

In Rom 3:20 Paul concludes the discussion begun at the letter's
beginning (1:16–3:20). He has shown that both the nations and
Israel have disobeyed and have found no way, by their own efforts, to rectify the situation. He concludes: "Therefore, no human
being will be acceptable in God's sight on the basis of traditional
religious observances" (Rom 3:20). All humans deserve divine
judgment, but "only now" (3:21) God's righteousness or God's
setting matters aright has been made manifest "apart from law"
(NRSV) or "independent of the tradition from the law" (SV). It
is not quite clear whether the phrase "apart from law" refers to
law in general or to the Jewish law. It ought not to be viewed as
shorthand for "works of the law" which had been mentioned in
the previous verse (Rom 3:20). Since there is no article used in the
Greek, many commentators see it as a reference to law in general,
and not to the Torah of Israel. This is reinforced by the immediate reference that "the law (with an article) and the prophets have
borne witness" (BBS) to God's righteousness. Law in this case
equals Torah, since the law and the prophets is referring to the
twofold division of the Jewish scriptures.

God's solution to the problem of human sin is to set the world
aright, which Paul says is happening now in the preaching of the
good news. This good news is set in the context of the problem
facing the nations, their status as conquered. Both Rome and God
have a gospel with the same promise—peace and liberty—but
with radically different outcomes and values.

Having stated his thesis about God's righteousness, Paul
begins, in disjointed grammar, stacking up phrases. He relates
how God's righteousness comes about with three "through" (*dia*)
clauses, almost like three bullet points:

- Through the faithfulness of Jesus Anointed for all who are
  faithful
- Through the deliverance which is in the Anointed Jesus whom
  God has put forward as a means of propitiation

- Through the faithfulness in his blood
  (Rom 3:22, 24 BBS)

Moving from the general to the specific, all three clauses elaborate how righteousness comes to be.

Through the Faithfulness of Jesus

through the *faithfulness* of Jesus Anointed for all who are *faithful* (3:22a, emphasis added)

First, God's righteousness, God's making things right, is made evident through the faithfulness of Jesus for all who are faithful. Jesus' faithfulness is the model for the faithfulness of others. This is where our analysis of the meaning of faithfulness of the Anointed (*pistis tou Christou*) pays off. The King James translation makes little sense: "by faith of Jesus Christ unto all and upon all them that believe." The NRSV takes the genitive as objective: "through faith in Jesus Christ for all who believe." In both these translations the repetitive word play in the Greek gets lost since the translation must switch from "faith" to "believe." But more seriously "faith in Jesus" tends to mean belief, so that faith or belief in Jesus, with Jesus as the object, is the prior act, clearly against Paul's intentions. As Richard Hays in his pioneering study, *The Faith of Jesus Christ,* argues,

> It is very difficult to see what possible sense this could make if the phrase is translated as "through believing in Jesus Christ." On the other hand, it makes very good sense to say that the righteousness of God is manifested "through the faithfulness of Jesus Christ." (172)

The subjective genitive makes much more sense. "Through the faithfulness of Jesus Anointed for all who are faithful" (BBS) or in the more expansive translation of the SV: "through the unconditional confidence in God of Jesus, God's Anointed, for the benefit of *all* who come to have such confidence."

The objective genitive, faith in, implies a creedal understanding, even though there is no creed in Paul's time. In the traditional understanding belief about Jesus matters. But the shift from objective genitive to subjective, from faith in to faithfulness of, indicates that for Paul the issue is really behavior. Jesus becomes the model of faithfulness, indicating a new way of living in and resisting the empire. That new way of living is the righteousness of God. God is setting the world aright.

Parenthesis

> (for there is no distinction, all have sinned and fallen short of the glory of God, being made *right* as a gift of his graciousness)
> (3:22b–24a, emphasis added)

As we saw above, Campbell's analysis makes clear that a parenthesis interrupts the careful construction of the three through-clauses. This really helps clarify the grammar and makes the passage much more intelligible. While the parenthesis reiterates Paul's point about righteousness, the question remains, why the insertion of the parenthesis? Why break up this elegant structure?

The parenthesis clarifies the meaning of "all" in the phrase "all who are faithful." Neither Israel nor the nations can claim a special privilege for two reasons.

- all have sinned, picking up on the all who are faithful
- all are made right by a gift of his gracious righteousness

Righteousness is given to those who have fallen short, who have sinned, as a free gift. It is not earned.

Through the Deliverance

> through the deliverance which is in the Anointed Jesus whom God has put forward as a means of propitiation (3:24b–25a)

A number of scholars have argued that embedded in verses 25–26a is an early Jesus movement hymn beginning with "whom God put forward" and ending with "in the forbearance of God." For our purposes we do not need to resolve this issue except to notice that the language used in these verses is not Pauline (for details see Jewett, 270).

This through-clause has had a long and tangled history in the understanding of the death of Jesus as a sacrifice. It has been a linchpin for the doctrine of the sacrificial and vicarious substitutionary atonement. That understanding of this verse has been

Ransom

Ransom language comes from the world of commerce and denotes the price to buy back a slave or pawned object. In the New Testament, it is used metaphorically. The Anointed makes the payment to buy back humankind from the slavery of sin. The New Testament neither asks to whom the price is paid nor enquires into the mechanism. It remains within the bounds of the metaphor. Bruce Vawter shrewdly remarked in *This Man Jesus,* "Unfortunately, it is an observable law of human life that succeeding generations tend to reify the poetry of their fathers, betraying thereby the demise of imagination and ushering in all manner of confusion" (75).

After the New Testament the notion of Satan's rights over the soul pushed the metaphor into a mythology, and even later, the price was understood as being paid to God, whereas in the Pauline metaphor, God pays the price (Rom 3:24).

severely challenged in recent years to the point that I think it is no longer sustainable. The Greek words *apolytrōsis* and *hilastērion* lie at the heart of the issue. The former is dealt with more easily than the latter.

Apolytrōsis is translated as redemption (KJ, NRSV, NIV, NAB). This translation is adequate except that it makes Paul's statement sound more theological than it sounded originally. Redemption in English is primarily a theological term, whereas in Greek the word is associated with the slave trade. It denotes the ransom or payment for the freedom of the slave. A modern reader needs to remember the ubiquitous character of slavery in the ancient world. In his authentic letters Paul does not use the technical term for ransom (*lytron*) to apply to the death of Jesus, although it does occur in the gospel of Mark (10:45, parallel Matt 20:28) and in 1 Tim 2:6.

The Greek root *apoluein* means to loose from or set free, and the noun form *apolytrōsis* used here has the primary sense of release or deliverance, by extension the payment that buys back a slave. Deliverance would be a good English translation, but it is important to remember that Paul is using this term metaphorically, not realistically. He does not ask to whom a payment is paid. He is only interested in the redemption of a slave as a metaphor for understanding what has happened in the crucifixion of Jesus. He does not think it is a literal ransom.

Means of Propitiation

The second term *hilastērion* presents a more complicated problem. This word occurs only here in the New Testament and is not a common word in Greek, although its Greek root is easily understood. The word is variously translated:

propitiation (KJ)
expiation (RSV and NAB)
a sacrifice of atonement (NRSV and NIV)
the means of expiating sin (REB)
as the one who conciliates (SV)

Quite a range of proposed translations! These variations indicate the level of difficulty or range of disagreement over this word. Perhaps it is appropriate to quote Keck once again, "Paul's Greek is not as clear as translations try to make it" (110).

To get at the meaning of this word we must first undo an old misunderstanding and tackle a false identification of this word with the Christian doctrine of Jesus' death as a sacrificial substitutionary atonement.

A Mistranslation

The Hebrew *kapporeth*, translated in the LXX by *hilastērion*, referred to the gold cover of the ark, the place where the high priest sprinkled blood on the Day of Atonement. Traditionally in English this was translated as the mercy seat. "And thou shalt make a mercy seat *of* pure gold: two cubits and a half *shall be* the length thereof, and a cubit and a half the breadth thereof" (Exod 25:17 KJ). William Tyndale (1494–1536) was the first to employ this translation. He in turn was influenced by Luther's translation of the Hebrew word into German as *Gnadenstuhl* which literally means "seat of grace."

The mercy seat interpretation still has its modern defenders (e.g., Jewett, 284–86, strongly in support of this position). As Stowers summarizes, "those who favor this interpretation of *hilastērion* have imagined [Romans] 3:25 saying that God put forth Christ as a once-and-for-all place where atonement is made: Christ replaces the temple cult" (209). Robert Jewett in his Hermeneia commentary *Romans* supports such an interpretation:

> Prior to the cross event, God had merely shown forbearance for sins not covered by Temple rites, which would have included all transgressions outside Israel's ethnic boundaries. The situation was finally overcome by Christ's death, which replaced the Temple as a means of conciliation with God. (290)

There are several convincing objections to this interpretation. First, this understanding of the death of Jesus as a sacrifice replacing the Temple does not fit with the Jewish understanding of what happens in Temple sacrifice. Christians have forced their later understanding of the sacrificial death of Jesus onto the sacrificial system of Second Temple Judaism. The sprinkling of the blood had to do not with atonement, but with cleansing and purifying the Temple. Atonement was more closely associated with the scapegoat. Secondly, Paul is living while the Jewish Temple is still in force. There is no evidence that he envisions its replacement. To view the death of Jesus as a replacement for the Temple requires a perspective only available after the Temple's destruction in 70 CE. Such a position assumes Christian supersessionism. Not only does this position demand Christian supersessionism, but, if this were really Paul's position, would he not have mentioned it somewhere else in his letters?

This understanding of *hilastērion* demands a Christian typological understanding of the Septuagint which views Jewish Temple ritual foreshadowing Christian understandings that we find nowhere else in Paul. And finally, such an interpretation would have demanded that Paul's readers make a reference to an obscure text in Exod 25:17 referring to a ritual no longer practiced in the Second Temple. All of this seems highly problematic. The modern translations of "a sacrifice of atonement" in the NRSV and NIV are a direct descendent of this mercy seat interpretation, and attempt to maintain, in a modern translation, the doctrine of substitutionary atonement. These translations should be rejected as going well beyond Paul and projecting a later doctrine into Paul.

CORRECT TRANSLATION

This Greek word group *hilas-* is easily understood. BAGD defines the verb *hilasomai* as "to cause to be favorably inclined or disposed," with the glosses to propitiate or conciliate, while defining the noun *hilastērion* as "means of expiation" or "place of propitiation." Here the sense would seem to be "means of expiation or propitiation."

4 Maccabees 17:22 presents a striking parallel to Paul's language in this verse. The narrator is describing the effects of the martyrdom of the seven sons.

> These then, having consecrated themselves for the sake of God,
> I now honored not only with this distinction but also by the fact
> that through them our enemies did not prevail against our na-
> tion, and the tyrant was punished and our land purified, since
> they became, as it were, a ransom for the sin of our nation.
> *Through the blood* of these righteous ones and to the *propitiation*
> of their death the divine providence rescued Israel, which had
> been shamefully treated.
> (4 Macc 17:20–22; translation from Charlesworth, 563)

The Greek of 4 Macc 17:22 shows a clear resemblance to that of Rom 3:24. I have italicized the similar phrases in the above English translation.

A second passage from 4 Maccabees bears scrutiny. As Eleazar is dying under torture, he prays:

> "Be merciful to your people and let our punishment be a satisfac-
> tion on their behalf. Make my blood their purification and my
> life as a ransom for theirs."
> (4 Macc 6:28–29; translation from Charlesworth, 552)

The view in these two passages of the death of the Maccabean martyrs parallels that of the death of Jesus. The death of Jesus is interpreted within the same tradition. Sam K. Williams concludes, "No more probable background to *hon proetheto ho theos hilastērion* [whom God has put forward as a means of propitia-tion] can be discovered in pre-Christian literature than IV Mac. 17:21a read in light of [4 Macc] 6:29" (248). There is no doubt that the parallel to 4 Maccabees is very strong, suggestive, and con-vincing, but the dating of 4 Maccabees remains controversial. It may be contemporary with Paul or even a little later. Nevertheless Williams' basic point is correct—the tradition of the suffering noble death as exemplified in 4 Maccabees is the context for this language in Romans.

While the language is not Paul's, its sense fits well with his understanding. In other places Paul speaks of reconciliation in a way that strongly parallels the sense of this clause:

> For if while we were living as if we were rebels against God's rule, our relationship with God was changed through the death of God's son, now that we have been reconciled we can be even more assured that we will be spared [from, facing condemnation] through his life [as the risen lord]. (Rom 5:10)

We have reached an important conclusion. Contrary to the traditional understanding of Rom 3:25 as seen in the NRSV or NIV, Paul does not view the death of Jesus as sacrifice of substitutionary atonement. Rather he views the death of Jesus within the tradition of suffering noble death as seen in 4 Maccabees. After all, Paul was a Jew and we would expect him to view Jesus' death with the martyr tradition of Judaism, not a later Christian context developed only after the destruction of the Temple.

Through the Faithfulness in His Blood

> through the *faithfulness* in his blood
> (3:25a, emphasis added)

Once again Campbell's rhetorical analysis helps clarify the structure. The traditional versification lumps this through-clause with the previous phrase, and most translations follow suit. Tying together expiation (*hilastērion*) and the phrase "in his blood" supports the doctrine of substitutionary atonement. For example, the NRSV takes verse 24 through 25a as part of a single sentence.

> They are now justified by his grace as a gift, through the redemption that is in Christ Jesus, whom God put forward as a sacrifice of atonement by his blood, effective through faith.
> (3:24–25 NRSV)

Campbell's analysis indicates that this final through-clause parallels the other two and is yet another explanation of how the righteousness of God is manifest:

- Through the faithfulness of Jesus Anointed for all who are faithful
- Through the deliverance which is in the Anointed Jesus whom God has put forward as a means of propitiation
- Through the faithfulness in his blood.
  (Rom 3:22, 24 BBS)

His blood is not the point but is rather a metonym employing a part (blood) for the whole (death). In sacrificial systems the shedding of an animal's blood serves to purify the sacred space. The animal's death is an unintended consequence. In this case "in his blood" signifies the manner of his death, a bloody death, a shameful death on the cross (Rom 1:16). The final through-clause indicates that in his death Jesus was faithful. Jesus' death, his crucifixion, is the manifestation of God's righteousness; it is how God is setting the world aright.

Demonstrations

to demonstrate his righteousness through the passing over of previously committed sins in the forbearance of God,
to demonstrate his righteousness in the now time so that he might be righteous and make righteous the one who lives out of the faithfulness of Jesus.
(3:25b–26)

Paul concludes with two demonstrations of God's righteousness. The first demonstration indicates that God demonstrates his righteousness by passing over previously committed sins. This is not a matter of forgiveness, but rather God has been holding back his punishment. This implies Paul's apocalyptic scenario. The nations deserve God's wrath, but God has been withholding that wrath. Now he has passed over or foregone his wrath.

The final demonstration returns to language that is strongly Paul's and marks his summary for the passage.

This shows God's reliability at this decisive time, namely, that God is reliable and approves the one who lives on the basis of Jesus' unconditional confidence in God. (Rom 3:26)

To demonstrate his righteousness in the now time so that he might be righteous and make righteous the one who lives out of the faithfulness of Jesus. (3:26 BBS)

"The now time" echoes the reference to the present time with which this passage began, while turning attention back to righteousness and faithfulness, which is described by the preposition *ek* in the sense of "out of" or "from," even in the sense of "born from." The one who is made righteous is the one who is out of, comes out of, or born out of Jesus' faithfulness. His faithfulness is the source of the righteousness or the being made right of the one who lives by that faithfulness.

This has been a long and convoluted explanation of a relatively short passage, but it clearly demonstrates the importance of understanding what the phrase faithfulness of the Anointed (*pistis tou Christou*) means. It ties back to our discussion of Paul's call to be an envoy to the nations. At the heart of that experience was the recognition that the crucified one was God's son, the Anointed. Out of that experience came the conviction that what led to Jesus' death was his faithfulness to God's desire to make the nations righteous. God's desire to set the nations aright inevitably brought God's Anointed into conflict with Rome, "even to death by crucifixion" (Phil 2:8). So the notion of the faithfulness of Jesus coheres with and derives from Paul's initial experience of *apocalypsis/* revelation. From that experience came his *apocalypsis*/insight into the meaning of Jesus' death—how that death, a great shame in the eyes of the Roman gospel, is in reality the redemption of all the nations because it brings life and destroys slavery.

READINGS

Campbell, Douglas A. *The Rhetoric of Righteousness in Romans 3.21–26*. Journal for the Study of the New Testament Supplement, 65. Sheffield: JSOT Press, 1992.

Charlesworth, James H., ed. "4 Maccabees." Pp 531-64 in *The Old Testament Pseudepigrapha, Vol. 2: Expansions of the "Old Testament" and Legends, Wisdom and Philosophical Literature, Prayers, Psalms, and Odes, Fragments of Lost Judeo-Hellenistic Works*. Garden City, NY: Doubleday, 1985.

Dunn, James D. G. "Once More, PISTIS CHRISTOU." Pp. 730–44 in *Society of Biblical Literature 1991 Seminar Papers*. Society of Biblical Literature Seminar Paper Series 30. Atlanta: Scholars Press, 1991.

_____. *Romans 1–8*. Word Biblical Commentary, vol. 38a. Dallas: Word Books, 1988.

Glancy, Jennifer A. *Slavery in Early Christianity*. Oxford: Oxford University Press, 2002.

Hays, Richard B. "Justification." Vol. 3, pp. 1129–33 in *Anchor Bible Dictionary*. Ed. David Noel. Editor-in-Chief David Noel Freedman. New York: Doubleday, 1992.

Hays, Richard B. "PISTIS and Pauline Christology: What Is at Stake?" Pp. 714–29 in *Society of Biblical Literature 1991 Seminar Papers*. Atlanta: Scholars Press, 1991.

_____. *The Faith of Jesus Christ: An Investigation of the Narrative Substructure of Galatians 3:1–4:11*. Chico, CA: Scholars Press, 1983.

Jewett, Robert. *Romans: A Commentary*. Hermeneia. Ed. Roy David Kotansky and Eldon Jay Epp. Minneapolis: Fortress Press, 2007.

Keck, Leander E. *Romans*. Abingdon New Testament Commentaries. Nashville: Abingdon Press, 2005.

Sanday, William, and Arthur C. Headlam. *A Critical and Exegetical Commentary on the Epistle to the Romans*. Edinburgh: T & T Clark, 1902.

Stendahl, Krister. *Paul Among Jews and Gentiles*. Philadelphia: Fortress Press, 1976.

Stowers, Stanley K. *A Rereading of Romans: Justice, Jews, and Gentiles*. New Haven/London: Yale University Press, 1994.

Vawter, Bruce. *This Man Jesus: An Essay toward a New Testament Christology*. Garden City, NY: Doubleday, 1973.

Williams, Sam K. *Jesus' Death as Saving Event*. Harvard Dissertations in Religion. Missoula: Scholars Press, 1975.

_____. "The 'Righteousness of God' in Romans." *Journal of Biblical Literature* 99 (1980) 241–90.

_____. "Again Pistis Christou." *Catholic Biblical Quarterly* 49 (1987) 431–47.

CHAPTER 9

FATHER of Us All

Paul invokes the figure of Abraham in his letters to the Galatians and Romans. While strong similarities exist in how he plays with the figure of Abraham in these two letters, important differences are apparent. Abraham's story provides the figurative elements with which to work out an exegetical solution as to how the nations can partake in the benefits of God's blessing, without following the requirements of the Torah and being circumcised. Abraham provides a *post factum* solution to a position Paul had already arrived at, namely that God was now calling the nations to the obedience of faithfulness apart from circumcision, a conclusion he had reached as a result of his *apocalypsis*/insight. In the previous chapter we saw how God's righteousness was manifest in Jesus' faithfulness. Now Abraham's story provides a narrative to show how faithfulness is at the heart of God's action.

ABRAHAM'S STORY

Abraham's story is told in Genesis 12–25, and out of this cycle of stories Judaism expanded an even greater stock of stories. Samuel Sandmel in his study *Philo's Place in Judaism: A Study of Conceptions of Abraham in Jewish Literature* (30–95) has conveniently summarized these materials. Abraham is celebrated for

his covenant with God
his faithfulness
his merit
his tests

Nehemiah offers an example of these themes.

You are the LORD, the God who chose Abram and brought him out of Ur of the Chaldeans and gave him the name Abraham;

and you found his heart faithful before you, and made with him a covenant to give to his descendants the land of the Canaanite, the Hittite, the Amorite, the Perizzite, the Jebusite, and the Girgashite; and you have fulfilled your promise, for you are righteous. (Neh 9:7–8)

In regards to the covenant, Abraham's faithfulness is noted and Israel (unnamed) as his descendant will receive the land of the nations. In most retellings of Abraham's story, no real issue is made of the nations as his descendants. Sirach does deal with Abraham as a blessing to the nations, but does not refer explicitly to them as his descendants.

Abraham was the great father of a multitude of nations, and no one has been found like him in glory. He kept the law of the Most High, and entered into a covenant with him; he certified the covenant in his flesh, and when he was tested he proved faithful. Therefore the Lord assured him with an oath that the nations would be blessed through his offspring; that he would make him as numerous as the dust of the earth, and exalt his offspring like the stars, and give them an inheritance from sea to sea and from the Euphrates to the ends of the earth.
(Sir 44:19–21 NRSV)

The binding of Isaac (*Akedah*) is the great example of Abraham's testing, although later traditions frequently note that he was tested often. According to the rabbis, he was tested ten times and always found righteous (Sandmel, 87). Jubilees, which was written about 150 BCE, has an extensive section on Abraham. Sandmel notes:

The Abraham portrayed in Jubilees is greatly concerned with the encroaching Hellenism of the period in which the book was written. There is the ever-present enticement of idolatry. Gentiles are in the immediate vicinity, and it is necessary that one should not eat with them and surely not intermarry with them. (49)

Paul's Jewish contemporaries assumed that Abraham gained God's favor through his virtuous acts. Jubilees 23:10 is typical: "Abraham was perfect in all his deeds with the Lord, and well pleasing in righteousness all the days of this life" (translation in Charlesworth, *The Old Testament Pseudepigrapha*, 2: 100). Claiming the lineage of Abraham gave one a competitive advantage over others, such as the nations.

Descendants

While there are many elements to the Abraham story, Paul seizes on the promise in Gen 17:5 that he will be the father of many nations. This promise allows Paul to solve, exegetically, the problem of how the nations can become recipients of God's blessing, enabling them to participate in the benefits of God's covenant. At the risk of oversimplifying, in Paul's day the mainstream solution to this problem was to join the people of Israel, which meant circumcision for the males: not an attractive option. As we have seen, this was the solution of the James/Cephas party in the conflict in Antioch and apparently also those in Galatia who were agitating for circumcision. Paul advocates for another option, what might be called a heterodox option: free grace. As part of his *apocalypsis*/insight, the good news is that the nations have available now the blessings of the covenant through the faithfulness of Jesus the Anointed. This awareness or insight is part of his originating *apocalypsis*/revelation.

Why is the Abraham story so important as a solution to his problem? In the ancient world family is critical. It is the central organizing principle. Religion is not a separate existing reality or institution, as in modern, Western societies, but is embedded in the family. With family comes religion. Bruce Malina, a pioneer in the use of social world categories to understand the New Testament, underlined the importance of family. "First-century Judaism, of course, put great stress on family tradition and continuity, the traditions of 'the house of Israel'" (140). All Israel is viewed as one family. Lineage is important, which is why genealogies abound. They establish who one is.

We can see the importance of lineage in the case of the Roman emperors. Octavian (Augustus) was an adopted son of Julius Caesar, and on the basis of that adoption he claimed the mantle of Caesar after his adopted father's assassination. On the same basis he also claimed the title of *Divi Filius*, son of god, which was often stamped on his coins. Tiberius was his adopted son and was called "son of the divine Augustus." Most of the emperors of the Julio-Claudian house were adopted. These claims on the part of the emperor were part of the way in which power was handed on and legitimated. An inscription from Nero is instructive:

[Dedicated] to Nero, son of the Divine Claudius,
   Descendent of Tiberius Caesar Augustus
      And Germanicus Caesar,
   [themselves] sons of the divine Augustus.
      (Elliot, 144)

Rome even traces back its lineage to Aeneas. As Zanker in *The Power of Images in the Age of Augustus* noted, Virgil in the *Aeneid* "imbued the myth of Venus, the Fall of Troy, and the wanderings of Aeneas with new meaning, in which not only the future rule of the Julian house, but the whole history of Rome was portrayed as one of predestined triumph and salvation" (193).

In the *Aeneid*, Jupiter promises, "the toga-bearing Romans will be Lords of the world" (1:281). The god also tells Venus,

No need to be afraid, Cytherea [Venus].
Your children's destiny has not been changed.
As promised, you shall see Lavinium's walls
And take up, then, amid the stars of heaven
Great-souled Aeneas. . . .
In Italy he will fight a massive war,
Beat down fierce armies, then for the people there
Establish city walls and a way of life. . . .
Afterwards, happy in the tawny pelt
His nurse, the she-wolf, wears, young Romulus
Will take the leadership, build walls of Mars,
And call by his own name his people Romans.
For these I set no limits, world or time,
But make the gift of empire without end.
      (*Aeneid* 1.257–79, Fitzgerald, 12–13)

The imperial model demonstrates the importance and seriousness with which lineage and adoption were taken. The model follows the male line, since seed is from the male, while the female is viewed as the receptacle. Agriculture furnishes the analogy. A man plants his seed in the field of the woman's womb, which is fertile or infertile. In this model, descent from the man is decisive. Hence genealogies trace the male lineage, as in the gospel of Matthew where the genealogy is Joseph's (Matt 1:16).

The model of patrilineal descent allows Paul to take elements of the Abraham story and assemble them into a schema that explains how the nations can partake in the blessings of the God of Israel without having to formally join the people of Israel by means of circumcision.

Abraham in Galatia

The letter to the Galatians in all probability was written in the early 50s, but surely before the letter to the Romans. In Galatians Paul engages in a struggle with a group that is advocating circumcision for his converts. Their model seems to require two steps:

baptism
then circumcision

This could be interpreted as incorporation into Christ and then incorporation into the Jewish people. To be clear about the issue: in Galatia Paul confronts a group of agitators, a felicitous description coined by Williams in his commentary on *Galatians* (25–26). These agitators insist that, for the nations to fully benefit from the covenant, they must be incorporated into the Jewish people by circumcision. But Paul thinks that incorporation into the Anointed suffices for the nations to receive the benefits of the covenant. This is similar to the controversy with James and Cephas in Antioch, which is why Paul had retold that story as part of his argument in his letter to the Galatians. Significantly, both Paul and the agitators agree about the end point: the blessings of the covenant for the nations. They disagree about how the nations obtain access to these blessings or benefits of God. The debate, by the way, concerns the nations, not what Israel is to do.

Faithfulness

For Paul, Abraham's story resolves this debate.

Abraham's story marks the second part of Paul's response to the position of the agitators. In the first part, which was autobiographical, he related his call (Gal 1:13–24), his meetings with those in Jerusalem (Gal 2:1–10), and the conflict with Cephas in Antioch (Gal 2:11–21). The Abraham exposition marks a shift in Paul's style of discourse, from autobiographical narrative to scriptural argument.

But before he launches into this different type of argument he assaults the Galatians.

> You clueless Galatians! Who has cast an evil eye on you, putting you under a spell? Your own eyes saw Jesus, God's Anointed, graphically portrayed on a cross. Tell me this: Did you experience God's presence and power (*lit:* spirit) by relying on traditional religious practices (*lit:* works of the law) or by being convinced (*lit:* faith) by what you heard? (Gal 3:1–2)

"Traditional religious practice" or "works of the law" refers to circumcision, not the whole of ethical practices. Having detailed his own experience, Paul appeals to the experience of the Galatians. How "did you experience God's presence and power (*lit:* spirit)?" he asks. The logic of appealing to their experience is clear, but one does have to ask about his people skills when he begins with such a frontal assault, "You clueless Galatians" or "foolish Galatians" (KJ, NRSV), and then asks if someone has given them the evil eye or bewitched them. As Alan Dundes remarks in his study of this topic, the evil eye is an ancient Mediterranean symbol, "remarkably pervasive and persistent" both then and now (ix).

Paul states that their situation is just like Abraham's (Gal 3:6). And the situation of Abraham to which he points is Abraham's concern about not having a son, an heir. Paul quotes a verse of Genesis, "Abraham put his trust in God, and God counted that the right thing to do" (Gal 3:6, quoting Gen 15:6 LXX). Surely this quotation triggers a train of associations for his audience, invoking at least the gist of the story of which it is a part. The Lord appears to Abraham in a vision: "Do not be afraid, Abram, I am your shield; your reward shall be very great" (Gen 15:1 LXX). But Abraham pleads that he is still childless. God promises him that "your very own issue shall be your heir." Then the Lord took him outside and showed him the heavens. "Look toward heaven and count the stars, if you are able to count them." Then he said to him, "So shall your descendants (*lit:* seed) be" (Gen 15:5 LXX).

Now comes the verse Paul quotes: "Abraham put his trust in God, and God counted that the right thing to do." Paul's interest is in the verb, "put his trust" (*pisteusin*), and the noun, "the right thing" (*diakaiosynē*, righteousness). As we have had occasion to observe before in chapter 8, these are key theological terms for Paul. In Romans Paul in addition will play on the other verb "counted" (λογίζομαι; see below, "Abraham in Rome").

Trust and righteousness tie into Paul's theological program, but the nations as Abraham's progeny fuels his case. "From this you ought to draw the conclusion that Abraham's heirs are those born of confidence in God" (Gal 3:7). The Greek is worth paying attention to. "The ones out of (*ek*) faithfulness, these ones are the sons of Abraham." "Out of" (*ek*) includes the sense of those whose origin is "born out of"; that is, these are out of (*ek*) Abraham's lineage. "Sons" is also important because sons are heirs. While this represents the patriarchal world in which Paul lived, for him this applies equally to men and women, because as he will soon state, there is "no longer 'male and female'" (Gal 3:28).

Paul sets up a lineage of those who are faithful, with Abraham first, and then Jesus as his descendant, whose faithfulness in the cross, sets the nations free. This is a kind of spiritual patrimony or lineage that he takes seriously, that for him is real. The concern for lineage taps into a deep value in the Mediterranean world.

So central is this to Paul's understanding of the gospel that he personifies scripture as saying, "the scripture announced-the-gospel-beforehand (all one word in Greek, *proeuēggelisato*) to Abraham" (Gal 3:8 BBS). The content of that gospel is then quoted: "Because of you all the nations will be blessed." As Betz notes in his commentary *Galatians*, "The words are clearly marked as a quotation, although they cannot precisely be identified with any LXX passage in which the blessing is found" (142). Paul maintains that this means the same thing as "the nations are right to put their confidence in God" or more literally, "God would make the nations right out of faithfulness" (BBS).

The Curse

Paul now reverses the argument and contends that if the blessings of Abraham come out of faithfulness, then from works of the law come a curse. We must be careful with this argument (for elaboration see chapter 12, "The Law"). It is easy to generalize or universalize Paul's language. "For all who rely on the works of the law are under a curse" (3:10 NRSV). While this translation is technically correct, it sounds as though Paul is speaking of everyone, all humans, both gentiles and Jews alike, for all time. But that ignores the specific context in Galatians. Paul is clearly speaking to and about the nations. The particular problem of the nations concerns him, not the problem of the abstract universal human. As long as the old model of Christianity versus Judaism controls understanding, then this will be read in a universalistic fashion. But once we realize that is not Paul's model, the particularity of the context exposes Paul's contest with Rome for the allegiance of the nations. With that contest as hermeneutical horizon, we will read the letters in quite different fashion. Context determines meaning and so we must be careful to construct the proper context.

That Paul's topic is the nations is made clear when he concludes:

> God's Anointed freed us from the curse of subjection to the Law, by becoming a curse for us, since it is written, "Anyone who is crucified is accursed." This was done so that Abraham's blessing might come to the nations by belonging to the Anointed Jesus, and so that we might receive the promise of God's presence and power through putting our unconditional trust in God.
> (Gal 3:13–4)

The "us" is the dialogical us, Paul the speaker is speaking for and identifying with his readers who are among the nations, not "we" in the sense of "us Jews and you gentiles." The Anointed bears the curse destroying the curse the nations were under. Why did he bear this curse? "So that Abraham's blessing might come to the nations." How are the nations removed from the curse? By being "in the Anointed." In the final purpose clause ("so that"), Paul moves back to the dialogical we. The blessing comes to the nations "so that we might receive the promise." The topic all along is the nations, not universal humanity.

Finally, to whom belongs the "unconditional trust"? I think the SV translators have over-translated the Greek, once again falling victim to the translator's dilemma and making Paul clearer than he is. The Greek only says, "so that we may receive the promise of the spirit (breath) through faithfulness" (Gal 3:14 BBS). It makes more sense to interpret this as "through the faithfulness of the Anointed," especially since Paul is talking about the Anointed bearing the curse. Paul is making a distinction here that will emerge more clearly in Romans:

out of (*ek*) Abraham
through (*dia*) the Anointed

The Anointed's Faithfulness

Paul pulls these themes together at his argument's conclusion (Gal 3:26–9). "Indeed you are all now God's adult offspring (*lit:* sons) through (*dia*) the kind of confidence exemplified by God's Anointed, Jesus." This whole argument has built on the starting point of being heirs of Abraham, because the heir receives the inheritance, namely the promise. The Greek once again makes this clear: "through (*dia*) the faithfulness in the Anointed Jesus" (BBS). To make the connection clearer, I am tempted to translate this sentence: "For you are all sons of God through the faithfulness of the Anointed that makes you part of Jesus Anointed." Paul is drawing upon the notion of coming from (*ek*) the loins of one's ancestor. The nations are now out of (*ek*) Abraham through (by means of) the Anointed's faithfulness, which makes the nations a part of the Anointed, not a part of Rome.

This means that the nations are part of a new reality. Paul does not refer to it here, as kingdom or empire of God, a phrase he only uses fourteen times, but that is what he means. In Gal 5:21 he will speak of what one must do to inherit the kingdom of God. Paul draws the conclusion as to what this new reality of being in the Anointed looks like and it is in radical contradistinction to the Roman Empire: "You are no longer Jew or Greek, no longer slave or freeborn, no longer 'male and female'" (Gal 3:28a). The Roman Empire is emphatically hierarchical from the emperor on down. Everyone has their place. In the counterworld/kingdom in the Anointed, there is no hierarchy; all are one. Elisabeth Schüssler Fiorenza in her classic book *In Memory of Her* maintains:

> Gal 3:28 is therefore best understood as communal Christian self-definition rather than a statement about the baptized individual. It proclaims that in the Christian community all distinctions of religions, race, class, nationality, and gender are insignificant. (213)

As the Galatians counter-statement has it, "Instead, you all have the same status in the service of God's Anointed, Jesus" (3:28b). The Greek says this line more simply: "You are one in the Anointed Jesus," and "one" recalls the oneness of God. God's oneness stands against the idolatry of the nations—the chief complaint against the nations in the tradition of Israel. Idols are in opposition to the one God.

With the new reality in place, Paul returns to Abraham as the progenitor of the new race: "Moreover, if you now belong to God's Anointed, that also makes you Abraham's offspring (*lit:* seed) and—as promised—his heirs" (Gal 3:29). From Abraham's seed come these new children of God.

Abraham in Rome

Unlike the situation in Galatia, there is no mention in the letter to the Romans of a party of the circumcision nor, so far as we can tell, is anyone calling for the male non-Jewish members of that community to be circumcised. Yet in defending his gospel to those in Rome, his good news that the nations need not be circumcised, but are redeemed on the basis of Jesus' faithfulness, Paul turns again to the Abraham story.

The version of this discussion in Romans draws on the same type of argument as in Galatians but is more elegant and polished. Paul has clearly learned between the writing of these two letters.

The Ungodly

The discussion about Abraham occurs in a part of the letter that employs the diatribe style; Paul engages an imaginary (that is, Paul made him up) Jewish teacher. In Romans the interlocutor, the imaginary Jewish teacher, raises Abraham as a counterargument to Paul's position. The Jewish teacher had maintained that Paul's teaching concerning God's faithfulness nullifies the law. This Paul vigorously denies.

> *Interlocutor:* Are we then nullifying the law through this so-called confidence in God?
> *Paul:* Certainly not! We are affirming the law.
>   (Rom 3:31)

As an aside, the traditional chapter division between Romans 3 and 4 is particularly egregious, because it not only breaks up and obscures the dialogue between Paul and his questioner, but it also separates redemption in the Anointed from the story of Abraham. The chapter division masks the parallel between Jesus and Abraham.

After Paul denies that he has nullified the law but rather has affirmed it, the interlocutor counters with the example of Abraham:

> *Interlocutor:* What, then, shall we say? That we have found Abraham to be our forefather by virtue of his religious credentials? If Abraham became a righteous man by virtue of his admirable deeds, then he does have something to boast about, doesn't he? (Rom 4:1)

By allowing the interlocutor to raise the example of Abraham as a counterargument, Paul appears not to be cherry picking his evidence but responding to an example, and the evidence selected by his opponent. The interlocutor has a good argument, because fellow Jews viewed Abraham as a paragon of virtue (see above, "Abraham's Story").

Paul does not seek to deny or minimize Abraham's achievements, but argues that they mean nothing "in the sight of God." To prove this becomes the task of the rest of the argument. As in Galatians, Paul turns to Gen 15:6 for his counterargument. "Abraham put his trust in God, and God counted that the right thing to do" (Rom 4:3). The same reasons that fitted Paul's argument in Galatians still apply—his interest in faithfulness (*pisteusin*) and righteousness (*diakaiosynē*)—so we will not repeat that discussion. But now he adds an important twist by seizing on the verb "counted" (*elogisthē*, "reckoned" in the NRSV) which is repeated ten times in this chapter of Romans like a mantra.

"Counted" (*elogisthē*) in Greek means "to determine by mathematical process," with the glosses "reckon," "calculate" (BDAG) or "count." With his proof text in place Paul draws upon an everyday analogy.

> Now, the wage paid to a worker is not *counted* as a gift, but as what he has earned; and to the one who does no work but who puts his unconditional trust in the One who accepts the non-religious, his confidence in and total reliance upon God is *counted* as doing the right thing. (Rom 4:4–5, emphasis added)

What the SV translates as "non-religious" in the Greek is *asebēs*, which more literally means "ungodly." As Keck notes in his commentary on *Romans*: "This astounding statement is offensive because it implies that Abraham is ungodly!" (121). Keck is correct.

The Greek is economical in its insult: "to the one who works not but trusts in the one [God] who makes right the ungodly, his trust [faithfulness] is counted for righteousness" (Rom 4:5 BBS). Keck goes on to note:

> Contrary to a common reading of 4:3, Paul does *not* say that Abraham's faith *made* him righteous (then he would have had something to boast about), but says that God "reckons" (considers, counts) as rightness Abraham's trusting in God as the rectifier of the ungodly. Paul sees that only the *un*godly trust such a God; the godly trust the God who counts their godliness as righteousness. (121)

Keck's comment on this passage brilliantly cuts right to the heart of Paul's insight/*apocalypsis*. Only the ungodly can trust God and God rectifies only the ungodly. This also ties to Paul's view of the crucified Anointed of God. Such a one is cursed and is surely according to the flesh—that is, by human standards, the standard of the law and Rome—ungodly. The *apocalypsis*/revelation/insight unveils the oxymoronic nature of God's making right.

Abraham's ungodliness harks back to Rom 1:18: "For the wrath of God is revealed from heaven against all ungodliness" (NRSV), which inaugurated Paul's discussion of the nations. Referring to Abraham as ungodly places him among the nations, as one of the nations. Just as Rom 4:5 looks back to Rom 1:18, it anticipates Paul's dealing with Israel in Romans 11. While in chapter 4 Abraham is the model for the nations, in Romans 11 he is the implied model for Israel. In dealing with how Israel will be brought to God, Paul creates a quotation made up of Isa 27:9 and 59:20.

> "The liberator will come from Mount Zion,
> he will eliminate godless behavior from Jacob.
> And this will be my covenant with them
> when I do away with their waywardness."
> (Rom 11:26–27)

Paul describes their current state as "godless," recalling the inaugural description of the nations in 1:18 and his description of Abraham in 4:5. This indeed demonstrates that God shows no partiality (Rom 2:11 NRSV). All are godless, both the nations and

Israel. But in Rom 11:28 Paul indicates that Israel's ungodliness is for the benefit of the nations.

> So far as God's world-changing news is concerned, their hostile opposition has turned out for your benefit, but as far as [God's] free selection is concerned, they are loved, because of their ancestors (*lit:* fathers). (Rom 11:28)

The mention of the fathers (ancestors, SV) is telling, because that too recalls the Abraham story, the father of the nation of Israel.

A natural reference in this discussion would be Rom 5:6: "For while we were still helpless, at the appointed time, God's Anointed died for the ungodly." This verse would make such a nice bow to tie this all together. Unfortunately many think Rom 5:6–7 is a later interpolation into Paul's letter (Keck, 139–40; SV 253). In keeping with our decision to use only the best evidence, I set this verse aside as non-Pauline, a later interpretation of Paul.

Abraham's Erection

To follow out the ancestor theme—when was Abraham counted or reckoned as right? Before he was circumcised? Or after? According to the order in which the stories occur in Genesis, the answer is "before." "This was so that he would be the proto-typical 'father' of all of the uncircumcised who put their trust in and rely upon God and they too would be counted as getting this right" (Rom 4:11). Once again Paul picks up on the counting motif. But he also returns to the theme of Abraham as *the* ancestor, father of all the uncircumcised. "Prototypical" is a correct interpretation on the part of the SV, implied but not present in Paul's Greek. Once again to make his point, Paul quotes verbatim Gen 17:5 LXX.

> He is the father of us all, just as it is written, "I have appointed you to be the father of many nations." [Thus Abraham is the father of us all] in the sight of the God in whom he put his trust—the God who has the power to bring the dead to life, and to call into existence things that did not exist. (Rom 4:16b–17)

In Paul's argument Abraham's faithfulness to God's promise that he shall be the father of many nations makes him the father of both the circumcised and the uncircumcised. This God is described as one "who has the power to bring the dead to life." The language is close to the second Benediction, prayed by many Jews on a daily basis: "Blessed be you, Lord who gives life to the dead" (see Jewett, 333). Many think Paul is quoting a Jewish liturgical text, and that may be so, but it also is a reference to the resurrection of Jesus. The phrase "to call into existence things that did not exist" almost exactly parallels a phrase in Philo (Jewett, 334). This is the closest any New Testament author comes to *creatio ex nihilo*, creation out of nothing.

Although Paul retells the story from Genesis 21 of the conception of Isaac, the point of view of Genesis differs from that of Paul's retelling. Genesis only says, "When Sarra had conceived, she bore Abraam a son in his old age at the appointed time, as the Lord had spoken to him" (Gen 21:2 LXX). The note about Abraham's age comes in verse 5. Other than Abraham naming and circumcising Isaac, the remaining Genesis story is about Sarah and her jealousy of Hagar. Paul, on the other hand, omits all this and tells the story from Abraham's point of view. His situation was desperate. "Who beyond hope in hope he was faithful so that he might become the father of many nations as he had been told: so will your seed be" (Rom 4:18 BBS). The physical reason there was no hope is described vividly—Abraham was impotent and Sarah's womb was dead. "And not being weak in faithfulness he considered his own body as good as dead, being about a hundred years old, and the deadness of Sarah's womb" (Rom 4:19 BBS). How will his seed become numerous? "For the promise of God he did not hesitate by faithlessness but he grew strong in faithfulness, giving glory to God and being fully convinced that what he was promised he was able also to do" (Rom 4:20–21 BBS). Paul is describing Abraham's erection, and the verbs accent this underlying image. It begins with seed, being weak, grew strong, fully convinced, was able to do. Finally, "it was counted to him as righteousness" (Rom 4:22 BBS), that is, set aright.

Paul sets Jesus, the Anointed, and Abraham, the father of many nations, in parallel. Both faced a shameful situation, Abraham's lack of a son and Jesus' death by crucifixion. Both despite that shame were faithful to God's promise. Both are life giving: Abraham by the birth of Isaac and Jesus by the resurrection.

Both stand in a line of spiritual paternity. Abraham is the father of the nation of Israel through Isaac and of all the nations through Jesus. As John White in his study of Paul's use of Abraham notes, "Faith is only an appropriate response to what is the true source of Paul's theology, his recognition of God's benevolent power as creator to procreate life out of negative situations, even out of death itself" (xxvi).

Paul concludes by tying Abraham and Jesus together: That "God counted" was not written in scripture only for Abraham's benefit, but for ours also. We are destined to be counted right who put our confidence in the one who raised Jesus our lord from among the dead, who was given up to death because of our wayward offenses and raised so that we could be counted right in the sight of God (Rom 4:23–25).

Akedah

The binding of Isaac, in Hebrew *Akedah* and recorded in Genesis 22, is a major story in the Abraham cycle. It exemplifies his faithfulness when put to the test by God. But that story never appears in Paul's retelling of Abraham's story. This is particularly telling in light of the parallel Paul draws between Jesus the Anointed in Romans 3 and Abraham in Romans 4. If Paul were referring to the death of Jesus in Rom 3:25 as a vicarious substitutionary atonement or as the NRSV and NIV have it, "a sacrifice of atonement," one would expect Paul in Romans 4 to refer to the binding of Isaac. He does not. Instead the aspect of the Abraham story he draws on is the conception of Isaac, accenting the shame of Abraham's impotency and God's life-giving power in Abraham's erection and Sarah's conception. Out of impossible circumstances, God draws life. This use of the Abraham story confirms our analysis of Rom 3:25. It demonstrates a consistent picture in Paul's thought, deriving from his *apocalypsis*/revelation. Later Christian theology saw the binding of Isaac not as a test of Abraham but as prefiguring the sacrifice of Jesus, thus obscuring Paul's original parallel between Abraham and Jesus and substituting a new parallel. The loss for understanding Paul was considerable, but the new parallel, based on sacrifice, had tragic results for the relationship between Judaism and Christianity.

Readings

Betz, Hans Dieter. *Galatians: A Commentary on Paul's Letter to the Churches in Galatia*. Hermeneia. Philadelphia: Fortress Press, 1979.

Charlesworth, James H. *The Old Testament Pseudepigrapha, Vol. 2: Expansions of the "Old Testament" and Legends, Wisdom and Philosophical Literature, Prayers, Psalms, and Odes, Fragments of Lost Judeo-Hellenistic Works*. Garden City, NY: Doubleday, 1985.

Dundes, Alan. *The Evil Eye: A Casebook*. Madison, WI: The University of Wisconsin Press, 1981.

Elliott, Neil, and Mark Reasoner, eds. *Documents and Images for the Study of Paul*. Minneapolis: Fortress Press, 2011.

Jewett, Robert. *Romans: A Commentary*. Hermeneia. Ed. Roy David Kotansky and Eldon Jay Epp. Minneapolis: Fortress Press, 2007.

Keck, Leander E. *Romans*. Abingdon New Testament Commentaries. Nashville: Abingdon Press, 2005.

Malina, B. J. *The New Testament World: Insights from Cultural Anthropology*. Louisville, KY: Westminster/Knox, 2001.

Sandmel, Samuel. *Philo's Place in Judaism: A Study of Conceptions of Abraham in Jewish Literature*. Cincinnati: Hebrew Union College Press, 1956.

Schüssler Fiorenza, Elisabeth. *In Memory of Her: A Feminist Theological Reconstruction of Christian Origins*. New York: Crossroad Press, 1983.

Virgil. *The Aeneid*. Trans. Robert Fitzgerald. New York: Vintage Books, 1990.

White, John L. *The Apostle of God: Paul and the Promise of Abraham*. Peabody, MA: Hendrickson, 1999.

Williams, Sam K. *Galatians*. Abingdon New Testament Commentaries. Nashville: Abingdon, 1997.

Zanker, Paul. *The Power of Images in the Age of Augustus*. Reprint edition. Ann Arbor: University of Michigan Press, 1990.

Chapter 10

In the Anointed

We often assume a progression:

faith
then baptism
then church membership

Since we have no evidence that Paul thought this way, we should be careful not to implicitly project our model onto Paul. In all probability the relation between faith, baptism, and the body of the Anointed were not worked out in detail. Paul works it out as he proceeds, responding to specific circumstances. He is not working from a pre-established theological or ecclesial model, but trying to understand his present circumstances in light of his experience, the experience of his communities, and the traditions of Israel. From that a theology might emerge, but even then we construct it.

Wise and Foolish

In this chapter and the following one, the focus is on Paul's use of the phrase "in the Anointed" (chapter 10) and "body of the Anointed" (chapter 11). These two phrases are clearly related and occur most prominently in the Corinthian correspondence. But before exploring Paul's usage, we must determine the letter's context. What issue is Paul trying to solve by invoking this metaphor?

As usual important clues lay at hand in the letter's beginning, in this case the thanksgiving. The prominent words in the discussion between Paul and the community are emphasized:

> I thank God all the time for the generous favor God has shown to you through the Anointed Jesus. You have been richly en- dowed with *speech* and *knowledge* of every kind. . . . You do not

131

lack any *gift* as you wait for the coming of our lord, Jesus the Anointed. . . . God is faithful and is the one who has called you into *fellowship* with God's "son," Jesus the Anointed, our lord.
(1 Cor 1:4–9, emphasis added)

Power in speech and knowledge (*gnōsis*) and spiritual gifts (*charisma*) are highly valued by the Corinthians. These are perhaps their code words for demonstrating their power in the spirit of the Anointed. For Paul they are called "into fellowship (*koinōnia*) with God's 'son,' Jesus the Anointed, our lord."

Fellowship is precisely what Paul sees at risk in the Corinthian community. He has heard from Chloe's people that there are divisions or breakups (*schisma*) among them. Paul sees fellowship (*koinōnia*) and divisions (*schisma*) as opposites. The Corinthians have divided into groups by claiming, "I follow Paul," or "I follow Apollo," or "I follow Cephas," or "I follow the Anointed" (1 Cor 1:12). I have to admit that I have never understood why, given these four options, everyone would not choose, "I follow the Anointed"? Paul challenges these identifications by rhetorically

Chloe

Chloe is a female householder in whose house the Corinthian church meets. In such a position, she is a patron and leader of the community. This is an indication of women being in significant positions in the Pauline churches. How many house churches there were in Corinth and how many were headed by women we do not know. Fitzmyer (141) is dismissive of Schüssler Fiorenza's argument (219) that Chloe was an "outstanding" leader in the Corinthian community. But why would Paul mention her if her name did not carry weight. The fact that she has "people" (*lit:* those who belong to Chloe), indicates slaves or freemen, and since no husband is mentioned, she may well be a widow. Most likely, while her people were in Ephesus on business, they reported on the situation about which Paul is writing to Corinth. Fitzmyer seems too minimalist. Her naming is more suggestive than he is willing to admit.

Corinthian Correspondence

Paul's correspondence with the church in Corinth has survived in a highly edited form—how edited, of course, is conjectural and debated. What appears in the New Testament canon as 1 Corinthians was preceded by another letter, now lost (see 1 Cor 5:9). Considerable debate surrounds chapter 13, the famous love hymn. Is it part of the original letter? If it is, did Paul compose it? Was it added later? No consensus obtains on this issue. Many have suspected that in the editing and copying of 1 Corinthians, the scribes slipped in interpolations. After all, the time gaps between the writing of the letter in the mid-50s, its editing and collection around 100 and the earliest extant manuscript, no earlier than 200 CE, is considerable.

The correspondence with the Corinthian community offers us a rare opportunity to see how Paul related to a community he had founded over a period of time.

1 Corinthians shows Paul challenging a community that understands the gospel differently from him. He struggles to help them understand what the good news means. Even the resurrection is vigorously debated. 1 Corinthians 15 is not only the earliest detailed discussion of the resurrection in the New Testament, but also the most extensive. Paul and his converts appear to be at loggerheads on this topic. At times I think they are ships passing in the night, hardly able to understand each other (for more detail, see my *The Trouble with Resurrection*, 124–28).

That relationship was not always easy and at times painful. In 2 Cor 7:8–9, Paul refers to what is now apparently a lost letter:

> I'm not altogether sorry if my letter upset you. Even if I were sorry, I see that the letter distressed you only for a while. I rejoice now, not that you were offended, but that your remorse led to a change of heart. Your pain was so profoundly transformative that you were in no way damaged by us.

asking: "The Anointed is not divided, is he? Paul was not crucified for you, was he? Nor were you baptized in the name of Paul,
were you?" (1 Cor 1:12–13). In each case the rhetorical question
demands "no" as an answer, so therefore their claim is voided,
including even the claim "I belong to the Anointed."

Paul undercuts these claims in an important way: "The
Anointed did not send me out to conduct baptisms, but to proclaim God's world-transforming message not, however, by means
of pretentious speech that would rob the Anointed's cross of its
significance" (1 Cor 1:17). Paul provides two important clues.
The Corinthians are claiming to be baptized in the name of Paul
or Apollo or Cephas, etc., which is why it is important for Paul to
claim "none of you can say that you were baptized in my name" (1
Cor 1:15). They are apparently claiming a type of spiritual paternity as the result of baptism.

Paul's second clue tells what he thinks is important: "pretentious speech . . . would rob the Anointed's cross of its significance." The foundation is the cross. So he launches into a contrast
between the cross on the one hand, and on the other, wisdom and
power, as normally constructed in the culture at large. He boldly
states, "The message about the cross is utter nonsense to those
who are heading for ruin, but to us who are bound for salvation
it is the effective power of God" (1 Cor 1:18). "Heading for ruin"
should not mislead us into a pietistic interpretation. Rather "ruin"
and "salvation" invoke Paul's apocalyptic scenario. Ruin is what is
going to happen to those who are exposed to God's wrath, including the Roman Empire. In stating that the message of the cross
is "utter nonsense" or "foolishness" (NRSV), Paul is stating the
obvious truth. Paul has played this card before, but it is important
to take it seriously. For him the crucifixion, with its obviously
anti-imperial message, is the oxymoronic heart of the good news.

> Where does that leave the expert? Where does that leave the
> scholar? Where does that leave the pundit of this age? Has not
> God shown the world's wisdom to be foolish? Since in the larger
> scheme of God's wisdom the world did not come to acknowledge
> God through its own wisdom, God decided to save those who
> embrace God's world-transforming news through the "nonsense"
> that we preach. (1 Cor 1:20–21)

Because the world's wisdom has chosen idols and Caesar, not the true God, it evidentially has failed. Therefore God decided to save by means of nonsense, the crucifixion of Jesus. This nonsense runs counter to everything Jews and Greeks expect:

> At a time when Jews expect a miracle (*lit:* a sign) and Greeks seek enlightenment (*lit:* wisdom), we speak about God's Anointed *crucified!* This is an offense to Jews, nonsense (*lit:* foolishness) to the nations. (1 Cor 1:22–23)

Paul continues to drive his point home—the absolute contrast between God's wisdom and that of the world, as viewed by both Jews and Greeks.

> But to those who have heard God's call, both Jews and Greeks, the Anointed represents God's power and God's wisdom; because the folly of God is wiser than humans are and the weakness of God is stronger than humans are. (1 Cor 1:24–25)

The wisdom and strength of God is the nonsense of the cross. The good news, the nonsense of the cross that Paul preaches, is a radically deconstructive agent that undoes the world's hierarchy. Pointedly for Paul, this radical overturning of the world's standards is not simply turning the world upside down so that God's folly is on top and the world's wisdom is on the bottom. That would be maintaining the world's hierarchy only in reverse. For Paul a new order is being created that does away with hierarchy. In 2 Cor 5:17 he restates this same idea: "So if anyone is in Christ, there is a new creation: everything old has passed away; see, everything has become new!" (NRSV). He reminds the Corinthians that they were for the most part people of no status—and so they still are. They have nothing in themselves of which to boast.

> God has chosen people who have no status in the world and even those who are held in contempt, people who count for nothing, in order to bring to nothing those who are thought to be really something, so that no human beings might be full of themselves in the presence of God. It is God's doing that you belong to the people of the Anointed Jesus (*lit:* you are in the Anointed Jesus). God has made him our wisdom and the source of our goodness and integrity and liberation. (1 Cor 1:28–30)

In the Anointed

"You are in the Anointed Jesus" is Paul's phrase for the incorporation into the Anointed. But what exactly does he mean by this phrase? Albert Schweitzer, before he became a famous humanitarian doctor in Africa, was a New Testament scholar. One of his important books was *The Mysticism of Paul the Apostle* (first published in German, 1930). He viewed "in Christ" as a type of Christ mysticism, what he described as a "mystical doctrine of redemption through the being-in-Christ." He famously declared,

> The doctrine of righteousness by faith is therefore a subsidiary crater, which has formed within the rim of the main crater—the mystical doctrine of redemption through being-in-Christ. (225)

For Schweitzer, Christ mysticism was the key that unlocked the whole of Paul.

> In Paul there is no God-mysticism; only a Christ-mysticism by means of which man comes into relation to God. The fundamental thought of Pauline mysticism runs thus: I am in Christ; in Him I know myself as a being who is raised above this sensuous, sinful, and transient world and already belongs to the transcendent; in Him I am assured of resurrection; in Him I am a child of God. (3)

Schweitzer deserves credit for proposing a new, even comprehensive, way to look at Paul. He was really one of the first scholars to break out of the stranglehold that the Augustinian/Lutheran tradition had on Pauline interpretation. He should be applauded for seeing the importance of eschatology (apocalyptic) for understanding Paul, but he rejected Adolf Deissmann's effort to see Paul as under the influence of Hellenistic culture. His Christ-mysticism, while influential, has not held up well.

The British scholar C. H. Dodd probably represents the majority opinion. While rejecting Christ-mysticism, he redefines in Christ:

> It is the baptized person who *is in Christ*. He has been baptized into the Church, into the body of Christ, and so *into Christ*. He has become of that company of people who embody the new humanity of which Christ is the inclusive Representative.
> (87–88, emphasis in original)

For Dodd "in the Anointed" is Paul's way of saying "Christian." It becomes a boundary marker, setting off those who belong to the community from those who do not, thus delimiting the church from those outside. Besides the obvious anachronistic understanding that simply equates all these phrases as a boundary marker, it reduces "in the Anointed" to a matter of Christian identity. In contradistinction I would argue that for Paul it was a way to make the reality of the good news present.

In 1 Corinthians 4 when Paul is attacking the "wise in the Anointed" (4:10), he contrasts himself with them:

> We are made to look like fools for the sake of the Anointed, but you are the Anointed's wise men (*lit*: the wise in the Anointed); we are weak, but you are strong; you are well thought of, we get no respect. (1 Cor 4:10)

In this contrast Paul assumes the place of the cross, while the "wise in the Anointed," clearly said in a sarcastic voice, represent the wisdom of the world—wise, strong, and well thought of.

> Right up to this very moment we are hungry and thirsty and poorly clothed, cuffed around, have no place to call home, and are worn out by the hard work we do with our own hands. When we are abused, we bless; when we are harassed, we put up with it; when we are slandered, we are conciliatory. We have been treated as if we were the scum of the earth, the filth everyone wants to get rid of, and still are. (1 Cor 4:11–13)

The cross empowers Paul and those in the Anointed to be nonsense to the world. This very nonsense breaks down the barriers that the wise, the strong and well thought of are trying to erect in the community.

After warning them that he is coming for a visit, Paul urges them to take him as a model (4:16 SV) or to be an imitator of him (NRSV) because he is their father in the Anointed Jesus through the preaching of the good news (4:15). Having laid out his behavior, to be an imitator of him is to imitate the crucified one. After all, the good news is the nonsense that one who died on the cross was not defeated but defeats. Timothy is to remind them of "my ways which are in the Anointed"—or more elegantly, "my views on our life as people who belong to the Anointed Jesus" (SV)—"just as I always teach in every church/community" (4:17

BBS). This indicates that "in the Anointed" and "church" are not same thing. "My ways which are in the Anointed" means living in such a way that the power of Jesus' death is exemplified. This "way in the Anointed" is explicated in Gal 2:19–20:

> I was crucified with the Anointed. The person I used to be no longer lives. God's Anointed lives in me; and the bodily life I now live, I live by the same confident trust in God that the "son of God" had. He loved me and gave up his life for my benefit.

And in 1 Cor 15:31 Paul claims that he faces death every day. Yung Suk Kim in his important book on this topic, *Christ's Body in Corinth,* catches the social sense perfectly:

> For Paul to die with Christ . . . has to do with sharing the experience of the one who suffers the death of a slave, who experiences the extreme limits of human suffering and rejection. In other words, when Paul talks about Christ crucified ([1 Cor] 1:23; 2:2), he probably thinks of the slave's death, too, and of the slave's life, which is a daily shame and a liminal experience between life and death. (37)

Paul does refer to himself as a slave of the Anointed (Rom 1:1), as the scum of the earth (1 Cor 4:13). Living by a standard that the wise, the strong, and well thought of judge as shameful is living in the Anointed crucified.

Body of the Anointed

The body of the Anointed, or the body of Christ, in more traditional translations, oftentimes has struck me as an anomaly. Although frequently considered an important, maybe even central Pauline term, it only occurs four times in all the authentic Pauline letters: Rom 7:4; 12:5; 1 Cor 12:12, 27. Rather than functioning as a central term, is it an occasional usage in a rhetorical argument to make a point? Is it an expanded way of saying "in the Anointed"?

Spiritual Things

The situation that provokes the discussion in 1 Corinthians 12 is the same one that has run throughout the whole letter. Paul is dealing with an elite group within the community who claim to be wise, strong, and well thought of. While valuing knowledge (*gnōsis*), wisdom, and spiritual gifts (*charisma*), their elitism according to Paul threatens the community's fellowship (*koinōnia*) or cohesion. These concerns come to a head in chapter 12 in Paul's analysis of spiritual gifts, the chief of which for them is speaking in tongues (1 Cor 14:2).

This section of the letter has the title, "And concerning spiritual things" (1 Cor 12:1 BBS). The Corinthians in a letter now lost has written Paul about several issues. Beginning in 1 Cor 7:1 he refers to the topics they raised: "Now about the matters you raised in your letter." Then in 7:25, 8:1, and now 12:1 he takes up other topics from their letter. While the Greek says literally "spiritual things," the KJ and NRSV render the Greek as "spiritual gifts" in anticipation of Paul's later use of *charisma* (1 Cor 12:4). The discussion moves from the general topic, spiritual things, to the more specific, spiritual gifts.

Breath and Spirit

The fundamental sense of the Greek *pneuma* is wind or breath. Wind or breath is a metaphor for God's activity or presence or "spirit." The first creation story in Genesis exemplifies this usage.

> At the beginning of God's creating of the heavens and the earth,
> when the earth was wild and waste,
> darkness over the face of Ocean,
> rushing-spirit of God hovering over the face of the waters.
> (Gen 1:1–2, Fox translation)

Wind or breath makes a good metaphor for God's activity, power or presence, because they have power, force and presence, but from a naïve perspective are not physical. Furthermore breath is life. Deprive a body of breath and it dies. In the creation of Adam, God breathes life into the lifeless human.

> And YHWH, God, formed the human, of dust from the soil,
> he blew into his nostrils the breath of life
> and the human became a living being.
> (Gen 2:7, Fox translation)

When capitalized, Spirit quickly and unconsciously is equated with the third person of the Trinity, something altogether foreign to Paul and the Jewish heritage from which his use of *pneuma* derives. The NRSV's capitalization "Holy Spirit" (1 Cor 12:3) is quite egregious and the SV attempts to solve the problem by using a workaround like "the authentic power of God." The SV eliminates the metaphor and translates that to which the metaphor points. I do not have a good solution to this problem. Sometimes divine breath works well, but when spirit is used, it should not be capitalized. Paul's usage is in no sense Trinitarian, neither implicitly nor anticipatory. It is standard Jewish usage.

Paul begins his discussion of spiritual matters by reminding the Corinthians that when they were among the nations, they engaged in ecstasy before dumb or soundless idols, idol worship always being the standard Jewish characterization of the nations' disobedience. As Paul frequently does, he begins a discussion with an appeal to experience. We saw this move in his disagreement with the Galatians and when discussing the status of the Corinthians before their conversion (1 Cor 1:26).

His first example strikes many as very strange. "No one speaking by the Spirit of God ever says 'Let Jesus be cursed!'" (1 Cor 12:3 NRSV). The NRSV over-translates, in my opinion, while the SV under-translates: "no one whose speech is inspired by God says, 'Jesus be damned'" (SV). In this example if we just translate the metaphor, it makes beautiful sense. "No one speaking with God's breath says, 'Jesus be cursed.'" The breath metaphor works wonderfully and one immediately gets Paul's point. But to entitle this chapter "Windy or breathily matters" just does not sound right.

More to the point, what is going on? What is Paul describing? While engaged in ecstatic speech, the strong and wise Corinthians imagine themselves or are actually crying out, "Jesus be cursed." And because nothing happens to them, because they are not struck down, that demonstrates their spiritual or God-like power.

A Holy Breath

Paul says the opposite is true: "no one can say, 'Jesus is the master,' except by a holy breath" (1 Cor 12:3 BBS). The community's confession that Jesus is the lord is really God speaking.

This counterpoint is more complex than it first appears. The wise and strong Corinthians are attempting to demonstrate their divine power by saying "Jesus *anathema* (cursed)!" But that is precisely what Rome said; it cursed Jesus by crucifying him. The

Corinthians are still led astray by voiceless idols. But Paul says, God is speaking when one confesses, "Jesus is the master/lord." Master or lord translates the Greek *kurios*, an important imperial title. The Latin equivalent is *dominus*, which is why Vito Corleone is called "Dom Corleone!" In this exchange Paul summarizes the paradoxical and oxymoronic heart of the gospel.

Paul then lays out a triptych in parallel phrases:

> There are
> different spiritual gifts,   but the same breath of God,
> and there are
> different kinds of service,   but the same master,
> and there are
> different activities,   but the same God activates them
>   all in all.
>
> (1 Cor 12:4–6 BBS)

The different "spiritual" gifts (*charismata*) all come from the same breath of God, service (*diakonia*) contrasts with master, and God activates all activities. The A and B sides of the triptych are carefully balanced. The A elements are human while the B elements are divine. The triptych indicates that God is always the active agent.

Following the triptych as introduction, Paul lists a number of "spiritual" gifts.

> The ability to speak wisely is given to one through God's power, the ability to speak knowledgeably to another in accordance with the same divine power, to another deeds of faith by the same divine power, to another gifts of healing by the one divine power, to another the ability to do powerful deeds, to another prophecy, to another the ability to distinguish the gifts that are inspired by God's power from those that are not, to another different forms of ecstatic speech, to another the ability to interpret ecstatic speech. (1 Cor 12:8–10)

The rhetoric of the list in 1 Corinthians 12 depends upon the oneness of God. The conclusion in 1 Cor 12:11 underlines and highlights the point: "The one and same [divine] breath makes active the differences for each to his own as he [God] wishes" (1 Cor 12:11 BBS). This concluding verse picks up the vocabulary with which the section began: same, breath, active, and differences, thus forming an *inclusio*, a wraparound, for the section. The conclusion makes an argument that Paul has consistently made—the reader has nothing about which to boast.

The list of spiritual gifts in 1 Cor 12:7–12 differs from the one in Rom 12:6–8, indicating that the lists are constructed to meet different rhetorical situations. In Rom 12:4–5 he begins with the analogy of the oneness of the body instead of the oneness of God.

> Just as each of us has one body with many parts that do not all have the same function, so although there are many of us, we are the Anointed's body, interrelated with one another. (Rom 12:4–6)

Then follows the lists of spiritual gifts.

> We have different capabilities according to the gifts with which God has endowed us. If your gift is prophecy, then prophesy in a way that reflects your confidence in and reliance upon God. If your gift is providing service, then serve. If you can teach, then teach. If you are good at exhortation, you should offer encouragement. The one who is able to contribute money should do so generously. The one who gives aid should do so willingly. The one who does deeds of compassion should do so cheerfully.
> (Rom 12:6–8)

The Body

Verse 12 marks a shift in Paul's discussion of spiritual gifts.

> For just as the body is one and has many members, and all the members of the body, though many, are one body, so it is with Christ. (1 Cor 12:12 NRSV)

At the beginning of this sentence Paul introduces an analogy based on the human body. While a body has many parts or members, it remains one body. To which he concludes, so is the

---

baptizō

Baptizō—"to baptize" and "baptism"—is another example, like "apostle," of a word that is not translated but transliterated. In Greek the word means "to put or go under water in a variety of senses" (BDAG). In the New Testament it always refers to the ritual.

Anointed. So is the Anointed a body? Well, yes, but in what sense? The Anointed has a body, but is a body? How so?

> For we were all baptized by the same power of God into one body, whether we were Jews or Greeks, slaves or free, and we were all invited to imbibe the same divine power. (1 Cor 12:13)

The SV catches the sense of Paul's image at the expense of the literal wording. So let's take a minute to parse his description. "By one divine breath we were all baptized [immersed] into one body [i.e., the Anointed's]." For Paul, baptism, which literally means to dunk, is dying with Christ. Romans 6:3–4 makes this clear.

> Or do you not grasp the fact that all of us who were immersed in baptism as a way of identifying with the Anointed Jesus were symbolically immersed into his death? What that means is that we were buried with him when we were symbolically immersed into his death so that, just as the Anointed was raised from the dead by the power and splendor of God, we also might live a new kind of life. (Rom 6:3–4)

"Symbolically" in the SV might be a bit over the edge, but it moves in the right direction. The line between translation and interpretation is always fine. The KJ is closer to the literal Greek: "Know ye not, that so many of us as were baptized into Jesus Christ were baptized into his death?" (Rom 6:3 KJ) Symbols are stronger when they are in contact with real experience and lose their power when the connection to the physical experience is broken. Being immersed in water so that one begins to experience drowning, brings one close experimentally to death. Dunking/baptism ritualizes death, in this case Jesus' death. How is one brought back to life? Through breath, breathing, gasping for air. So having died in the ritual act of baptism, one breathes life back in. So even though "symbolically" is not present in the Greek, the SV correctly interprets the Greek. But let us not be so naïve as to equate symbolic with unreal. What is symbolic is real, but only in a different way.

Moreover, Jesus' death is not just any death, but death by crucifixion and all that means for Paul. It is the death of a cursed one, the poor and marginalized, a slave. Such a death calls into question the pretentions of the wise, strong, and well regarded Corinthians. By baptism they have become part of a body of the cursed one.

New Life

From this death Paul draws two types of conclusions. In Romans he says, "we were buried . . . so that, just as the Anointed was raised from the dead, . . . we also might live (*lit:* walk) a new kind of life" (Rom 6:4). What Paul does not say is as important to notice as what he does say. He does not say that having been buried with the Anointed we are raised with him. Rather, "so that we might (or should) walk in new life" (BBS). *Walk* is often a metonym for *life*, but in this image it is especially appropriate, for it pictures the dead, after the divine breath is breathed into them, walking about alive with new life. Paul once again draws not a creedal or belief conclusion, but an ethical or behavioral conclusion.

The second conclusion that Paul draws from his being crucified with the Anointed is made evident in Gal 3:27–28.

> So, everyone of you who has been baptized into solidarity with God's Anointed has become invested with the status of God's Anointed. You are no longer Jew or Greek, no longer slave or freeborn, no longer "male and female." Instead, you all have the same status in the service of God's Anointed, Jesus. Moreover, if you now belong to God's Anointed, that also makes you Abraham's offspring and—as promised—his heirs.

Many have argued that Paul is quoting an early Jesus movement baptismal formula (Betz, 186–89). He clearly introduces it in the context of baptism. The SV translation encloses "male and female" in quotes because this is most likely a quotation from Gen 1:27 (LXX): "Male and female he created them." Wayne Meeks, in exploring the social implications of this language, maintains that this baptismal formula is performative language. "As perceived within that community's accepted norms of order, it does what it says" (182). Within the community these distinctions no longer matter.

In Gal 3:28 Paul draws a conclusion very similar to the one he draws in 1 Cor 12:13. The differences or distinctions of this world, Jew or Greek, slave or free, are abolished. In Galatians the argument is moving towards the conclusion that all are heirs of Abraham, while in 1 Corinthians the conclusion is that all are members of the body of the Anointed. Why is the reference to "male and female" which is present in Galatians absent in 1 Corinthians? Several reasons have been suggested. Antoinette

Wire suggests that since Paul is dealing with women's behavior in Corinth, he omits the troubling aspect from the formula (118–28). I am not sure I think that is correct. Since all are part of one body, sexual differentiation is not important.

Fable of the Body

Beginning in 1 Cor 12:14 Paul explores his analogy of the body, which he restates as the ancient Greek problem of the one and the many. How one thing can be the source of many is a problem that has plagued philosophy since the pre-Socratics until today. Paul's statement of this problem leads to a variation on the theme. "The body does not consist of only one part, but of many" (1 Cor 12:14). Paul then engages in a personification of the body parts arguing with each other. "And if the ear were to say, 'Because I am not an eye, I am not part of the body,' that's no reason for thinking it isn't part of the body, is it?" (1 Cor 12:16). The image of the body parts arguing with each other is meant to be funny, but the next part of the personification verges on the ridiculous. "If the whole body consisted of an eye, how would it hear?" (1 Cor 12:17). This *reductio ad absurdum* proceeds even to the point of being slightly off-color.

> And the parts of the body that we think are undignified we treat with more respect, and we clothe our private parts with a greater degree of propriety than our more presentable parts require. But God unified the body by giving the inferior part greater value, so that there would be no division in the body, but that the parts would care about each other. (1 Cor 12:23–25)

The inferior parts, the genitals, have great value because from them come life.

Paul draws, from a humorous and ridiculous personification, a practical conclusion: "If one part is in pain, all parts suffer; if one part is honored, all parts celebrate" (1 Cor 12:26). His analogy of the body as a unity implies the elimination of the individual as the most important part. There are parts, but the whole is what counts.

The analogy of the body is a famous trope in the ancient world. A well known example is reported by the Roman historian Livy (59 BCE– 17 CE). This story involves military pay. The plebs, the ordinary Roman soldiers, having not been paid, were on the verge of rebellion against the patricians. The senate sent a senior member, Menenius Agrippa, to negotiate with the soldiers:

> The Senate decided, therefore, to send as their spokesman Menenius Agrippa, an eloquent man, and acceptable to the plebs as being himself of plebeian origin. He was admitted into the camp, and it is reported that he simply told them the following fable in a primitive earthy style.
>
> "In the days when man's members did not agree amongst themselves, as is now the case, but had each its own ideas and a voice of its own, the other parts thought it unfair that they should have the worry and the trouble and the labor of providing everything for the belly, while the belly remained quietly in their midst with nothing to do but to enjoy the good things which they bestowed upon it; they therefore conspired together that the hand should carry no food to the mouth, nor the mouth accept anything that was given it, nor the teeth grind up what they received. While they sought in this angry spirit to starve the belly into submission, the members themselves and the whole body were reduced to the utmost weakness. Hence it had become clear that even the belly had no idle task to perform, and was no more nourished than it nourished the rest, by giving out to all parts of the body that by which we live and thrive, when it has been divided equally amongst the veins and is enriched with digested food—that is, the blood." Drawing a parallel from this to show how like was the internal dissension of the bodily members to the anger of the plebs against the fathers, he prevailed upon the minds of his hearers. (Livy 2.32.9–12)

In Menenius' fable the belly is the aristocrats, while the other lesser parts are the plebs. The point of his fable is the other parts need the belly, even if they do have to serve it. So his fable justifies and defends the existing social order. Therefore the plebs should be happy with their lot. After all, it is fixed and to the benefit of the whole body.

Paul draws a different conclusion from his fable. Yes, the parts need each other, but no one part is better or superior to the other parts. His fable is explicitly anti-hierarchical. In Paul's solution to the problem of the one and many, he sees difference and recognizes that some will scale difference as superior and inferior. But he reverses the evaluation: "in many respects the parts of the body that seem to be less important are the most necessary" (1 Cor 12:22). Why does he not take Menenius' hierarchical solution? Because the crucifixion has taught him that the cursed, the least in the eyes of the world, is what God has raised up. Hierarchy has no claim.

Directly addressing his readers, Paul announces: "All of you together are the body of the Anointed and individually you are members of it" (1 Cor 12:27). This has moved beyond the analogy of the body to envisioning the community as the Anointed's body. What is the relation of the Anointed to the body? Does the body belong to the Anointed, so is it a possessive genitive? That does not seem right. It makes more sense as an attributive or descriptive genitive. Anointed describes the body. So one might translate the phrase, "all of you together are the Anointed-like body." The body is the Anointed. The body, then, is in the world like the Anointed. The crucified Anointed one would describe how the body is in the world. Yung Kim in his recent study of the body language in 1 Corinthians maintains:

> Paul's point is to exhort his hearers to live like Christ. In this way, we might take the genitive "body of Christ" as an attributive genitive (which I represent with the phrase *christic* body), not a possessive genitive (i.e., the body *belonging to Christ*). (67)

Just as God has ordered the body in a particular way, the community is ordered in a particular way. Paul lists these members, beginning with envoys/apostles in the first place. This list is not hierarchical, although it is often interpreted that way. For Paul an envoy of the Anointed is also a slave of the Anointed, therefore being both first on the list and at the bottom of the social order. The later successors to the apostles forgot the slave part.

Readings:

Betz, Hans Dieter. *Galatians: A Commentary on Paul's Letter to the Churches in Galatia*. Hermeneia. Philadelphia: Fortress Press, 1979.

Dodd, Charles Harold. *The Epistle of Paul to the Romans*. The Moffatt New Testament Commentary, vol. 6. London: Hodden, 1932.

Fiorenza, Elisabeth Schüssler. *In Memory of Her: A Feminist Theological Reconstruction of Christian Origins*. New York: Crossroad Press, 1983.

Fitzmyer, Joseph A. *First Corinthians*. The Anchor Yale Bible, vol. 32. New Haven/London: Yale University Press, 2008.

Fox, Everett, trans. *The Five Books of Moses: Genesis, Exodus, Leviticus, Numbers, Deuteronomy*. The Schocken Bible, vol. 1. New York: Schocken, 2000.

Kim, Yung Suk. *Christ's Body in Corinth: The Politics of a Metaphor*. Paul in Critical Contexts. Minneapolis: Fortress, 2008.

Livy. *History of Rome*. Vol. 1. 14 vols. Trans. B. O. Foster. Loeb Classical Library. Cambridge: Harvard University Press, 1919.

Meeks, Wayne. "The Image of the Androgyne: Some Uses of a Symbol in Earliest Christianity." *History of Religions* 13 (1974) 165–79.

Schweitzer, Albert. *The Mysticism of Paul the Apostle*. Trans. William Montgomery. New York: Seabury Press, 1931.

Wire, Antoinette Clark. *The Corinthian Women Prophets: A Reconstruction through Paul's Rhetoric*. Minneapolis: Fortress Press, 1990.

CHAPTER 11

THE MATTERS
YOU RAISEd

The discussions of "in the Anointed" and "the body of the Anointed" are not just theoretical analyses or the working out of a theological system. As we have noted, Paul often appeals to experience, both his own and that of the community, and he concludes with behavior or ethics, not belief or creedal statements. So it behooves us to take a look at one of these concrete behavioral situations.

1 Corinthians 7 initiates Paul's response to the issues about which the Corinthians had written: "Now about the matters you raised in your letter" (1 Cor 7:1). The first issue he takes up concerns marriage.

ON TouchiNG A WOMAN

We do not know exactly what the questions were about which the Corinthians inquired. Like listening in on a telephone conversation, we are left guessing, filling in the blanks. Many commentators think that "It is well for a man not to touch a woman" (1 Cor 7:1 NRSV) is a Corinthian slogan to which Paul responds. While the NRSV encloses it in quotation marks for this reason, the SV does not. Joseph Fitzmyer in his Anchor Bible Commentary *First Corinthians* surveys the evidence on both sides, but remains unsure (278). It is hard to know whether it is a Corinthian slogan or the starting principle in Paul's discussion. As will become evident in our discussion, I think it is a Corinthian slogan that Paul quotes. But I do not think it makes much difference in any case.

Most contemporary readers considered this first statement as a prudish or pleasure-denying statement: "I do think it is better for a man to abstain from sexual intercourse with a woman" (1 Cor 7:1). "Touch," the more literal translation of NRSV, is a euphemism for sexual intercourse. Once again the SV replaces the metaphor with what it stands for, making for a clearer and somewhat bolder statement. Before deciding that it is prudish, consider it in context. Paul as always operates with an apocalyptic mindset. In that scenario, the end is close and that very closeness determines the focus. "Except for this case, each of you should continue to live the life the lord has apportioned to you as you were when God called you. This is the rule I follow in all the communities of the Anointed" (1 Cor 7:17). This is often called interim ethics, ethics for the time before the end. At the conclusion of this chapter dealing with sexual relationships, he draws his discussion to an end with a summary of this position and provides a good statement of his interim ethics.

> This is what I mean, friends: this period of opportunity <for our mission> is coming to an end. In what is left of it those who have wives should live as if they did not have them, and those who mourn as if they have nothing to be sad about, and those who rejoice as if they have nothing to celebrate, and those who buy things as if they have no possessions, and those who deal with the world as if they have no use for it; because the world in its present form is passing away. (1 Cor 7:29–31)

The sense of the end's closeness, its impending nearness, determines Paul's schema. He is not laying out a universal ethics, a theoretical position good for all time. This should be kept in mind as Paul plays out from the slogan or general principle at the discussion's beginning. "I do think it is better for a man to abstain from sexual intercourse (*lit:* touch) with a woman" (1 Cor 7:1).

Furthermore in the early Jesus movement baptismal formula as expressed in Gal 3:28, the notion that there is "no longer 'male or female'" could easily lead to a position in which celibacy is mandatory. Setting aside our modern notions of equality, the statement or baptismal confession that there is "no longer 'male or female'" would mean, not that the sexes were equal, but there was no sexual differentiation and if no sexual differentiation, then no need for sex! Celibacy was widely practiced and admired in early Christianity and is certainly Paul's preferred option. As

Sandra Polaski in her excellent summary of scholarship on Paul and women, *A Feminist Introduction to Paul*, observes, "to commend celibacy itself . . . would almost certainly have risked Paul running afoul of the Roman authorities" (50).

Paul turns first to a specific situation: a man and his wife. "Nevertheless, *to avoid* fornication, let every man have his own wife" (1 Cor 7:2 KJ). The Greek is a bit elliptical, saying only "because of fornication," so "to avoid fornication" or "because of the temptation to fornication" (NRSV) or "because sexual immorality is so prevalent" (SV) must be supplied. Both the NRSV and the SV have over translated. What Paul has in mind is what we sometimes call sexual urges. Because of these sexual urges he says, "each man should have one wife (*lit:* woman)." Greek, like many languages, but unlike English, does not have a specific word for wife, the generic "woman" has to suffice. The word "have" is a bit tricky. It could have the sense of "to marry," but more likely it means "to possess." The wife is literally the possession of the husband, just as a slave is the possession of the master. This statement repeats the cultural assumption of that world.

But then he continues: "and let every woman have her own husband" (1 Cor 7:2 KJ). The two parts of the statement are simple and set in a carefully balanced parallel.

| Let each man | have | his own | wife |
| Let each woman | have | her own | husband. |

As noted, the first line is the cultural presupposition of patriarchy. But as far as I can tell, the second line is unattested anywhere else in Greek literature. For a woman to possess or own her husband undoes the assumptions of patriarchy.

Lest you think I am over-interpreting Paul's simple language, especially given Paul's well known supposed dislike of women, if not misogynist views, consider his next statement.

> To the wife the husband should give what is due,
> And likewise also the wife to the husband.
> (1 Cor 7:3 BBS)

The economy of the Greek is striking, especially the second line: "the wife to the husband," with "should give what is due" in ellipsis supplied from the first line. The NRSV spells out what is owed, namely "conjugal rights." In verse 2 the two lines were set in exact parallel, stressing their parallelism, equality, and mutuality. In these two lines wife and husband stay in the same word order, but their grammatical relationship reverses. Also the ellipsis in the second line makes it much more succinct. The relation between husband and wife is mutual, or in the vernacular, Paul says the wife can ask for sex! And the wife is mentioned first.

Verse 4 continues this line of mutuality but with an interesting twist. "The wife does not have authority over her body, her husband does; and the husband does not have authority over his body, his wife does" (1 Cor 7:4). Again the first part of the verse repeats the assumptions of patriarchy and I suspect that the men in Corinth upon hearing this part of the letter said the Greek equivalent of, "Finally, he's getting it right." But the second part of the verse reiterates the pattern we have been observing. Paul states that the wife has authority over her husband's body, an authority reserved in the culture exclusively for the man. Paul throughout stresses mutuality—what is true of the husband is true of the wife. Polaski notes how Paul handles gender issues in an even-handed fashion throughout 1 Corinthians 7:

> Again, the text is remarkable in the predominance of an even-handed tone as regards gender. Through most of the chapter, Paul instructs his readers as if women had the same freedom to choose their sexual and marital status as men. (49)

This mutuality emerges from his sense of what it means to be in the Anointed or part of the body of the Anointed. This shows what it means that there is "no longer 'male or female'" The hierarchy of male/female relationships is set aside. The man is not the master of the woman; both have authority over the other. Paul replaces hierarchy with mutuality.

While Paul sets up the relation between the wife and husband as a relationship of mutuality, matters are not equal on both sides of the relation. For, as the feminist scholar Elizabeth Castelli correctly points out (228), a woman is at considerably more risk in engaging in sex than a man. Childbirth for a woman in the ancient world was dangerous, and this should not be overlooked. Paul's point of view remains androcentric in 1 Corinthians 7, although not as extremely androcentric as in Galatians, where the good news is almost reduced to the male sexual organ.

Having laid out what can only be revolutionary principles, he concludes by offering practical advice.

> Don't withhold yourselves from each other, except perhaps for a little while by mutual consent so that you may have the leisure you need to pray; then come together again so that Satan will find no opportunity to tempt you because of your lack of self-control. But I offer this advice as a concession, not as a command. I wish that everyone were like me in this regard; but we all have our own special gift (*charisma*) from God, one has a gift of this kind, another has a gift of that kind. (1 Cor 7:5–7)

Paul is easily misread, if we forget his apocalyptic scenario. He views each person as blessed with a "special gift," a *charisma*, which we dealt with in chapter 10. Rather than being opposed to marriage or having a negative attitude, he claims it is a spiritual gift. Nor does he view the body or sex as unclean. In verses 12–14 he deals with the case of a husband or wife whose partner is not part of the community, literally "one who does not trust" (1 Cor 7:12 BBS). There should be no divorce because that one "member is consecrated through his wife and the wife who is not a member is consecrated through her husband" (1 Cor 7:14). The physical connection makes the nonbeliever holy. And there is no word here about converting the other one—that is not a requirement. Living in peace is the requirement (1 Cor 7:15). Paul's proof of the holy connection in marriage is the children who are its product. How does he know that the unbelieving partner is sanctified? Look at the children, he says: "your children would be unclean, but as it is, they are holy" (1 Cor 7:14 NRSV).

The Body in Ephesians

Because we decided at the beginning to use only the best evidence in our search for Paul, we have set aside Ephesians as not belonging to Paul's authentic letters. But in this case the contrast with Paul helps clarify matters. The language can sound very Pauline and it certainly belongs to a later Pauline school or tradition. But subtle and important differences crop up.

There is one body and one Spirit, just as you were called to the one hope of your calling, one Lord, one faith, one baptism, one God and Father of all, who is above all and through all and in all. (Eph 4:4–5 NRSV)

The language sounds very much like 1 Corinthians 12 with the accent on "one." "One" is accented by a too-clever wordplay. The thrice repetition of one in Greek shifts from the masculine, to the feminine and finally the neuter genders: *heis—mia—hen*, thus declining the adjective. Yet the accent is stronger because there is no counterbalancing accent on difference. "One faith" is a very un-Paul like usage. *Pistis* (faith) is never used in such an absolute sense in the authentic Pauline letters and, as Margaret MacDonald in her commentary maintains, may well "be a warning against false teaching" (288). It is not such a stretch as to be unimaginable as Pauline, but the move in describing Christ's relationship to the body moves in a direction very different from Paul's.

But speaking the truth in love, we must grow up in every way into him who is the head, into Christ, from whom the whole body, joined and knit together by every ligament with which it is equipped, as each part is working properly, promotes the body's growth in building itself up in love. (Eph 4:15–16 NRSV)

In 1 Cor 12:27, the community is the body of the Anointed. The two are equated. Not in Ephesians. The community is the body, but Christ is the head. The body has now become a hierarchical model, with Christ the head in heaven, and the body, the church, here on earth. The model is hierarchical, metaphysical, and ontological. The apocalyptic scenario is absent. The shift to Christ as the head seems subtle, but the difference is huge. Paul's usage is anti-hierarchical and implicitly anti-imperial. The model in Ephesians is clearly hierarchical and the church is a new empire in waiting.

Wives, Be Subject

Just as Paul's model of the body of the Anointed has practical outcomes in behavior, the same is true for the Ephesians model. The views of the author of Ephesians on marriage are well known, even if they are often mistaken as Paul's views, because folks fail to recognize that Paul is not the author.

Wives, be subject to your husbands. (Eph 5:22)

"Be subject" is not present in the Greek but is carried over as an ellipsis from verse 21: "Be subject to one another out of reverence (*lit:* fear) for Christ." Just as verse 21 has two parts, be subject/ for Christ, so also does verse 22: "Wives, be subject to your husbands as you are to the Lord." The shift from Christ (Anointed) to Lord (master) is significant. Lord/master automatically implies one who is subject to the lord as a subject or to the master as a slave. The guiding metaphor will be lord/master. This is important to notice because a metaphor works as a system, playing out the implications of that system. In this case the fundamental metaphor is *Jesus is the lord/master.* What is true of the system lord/ master is true of Jesus. Jesus is then a ruler, dominant, in charge, the head; implied are slaves or servants or subjects. Whatever the culture has determined is true of lord/master is potentially true of Jesus and insofar as lord/master implies a relationship, also true of those in that relationship.

George Lakoff and Mark Johnson in their groundbreaking *Metaphors We Live By* provide the following definition of a

Letter to the Ephesians

Paul was imprisoned for several years in Ephesus, and wrote several of his letters while there. While written in Paul's name, this letter is not Paul's. It shows a literary dependence on Colossians, and the apocalyptic scenario of Paul's authentic letters is missing. It is not so much a real letter, but a treatise on the church, which has become an army fighting the devil (Eph 6:10). It takes a very different view than Paul on the status of Israel. "He has abolished the law with its commandments and ordinances, that he might create in himself one new humanity in place of the two, thus making peace" (Eph 2:15).

The letter was possibly written as early as the late first century, or more probably in the first quarter of the second century. Because of similarity of ideas with the Acts of the Apostles, dating it around the same time is feasible (circa 125 CE).

metaphor: "The essence of metaphor is understanding and experiencing one kind of thing in terms of another" (5). They stress the systematic character of metaphor so that the system affects

> perception
> consciousness
> behavior

Metaphors are not neutral, but they determine what one can perceive and see and at the same time hide other things from sight. Jesus as lord/master lets one see the subordinate relation to him, his dominance of the world. But it hides that he is a friend. Friend is not part of the metaphorical system of lord/master. Metaphors affect consciousness. One will understand oneself in a way conditioned by the metaphor, in this case as subordinate or subject or slave. In such a metaphorical system only with difficulty can one see oneself as equal to Jesus. Such a system reinforces a hierarchical worldview, so those operating with such a metaphorical system will take that hierarchical world for granted. Finally, metaphors affect behavior. The metaphor conditions behavior. The metaphor instructs us so that in this case one will behave as a subject.

The dominant metaphor in Ephesians for determining the husband/wife relationship is the metaphorical system *Jesus is the lord/master*. So the statement "wives, be subject to your husbands as you are to the Lord," lays out the assumption of the metaphorical system. Jesus is the lord/master and all are subject to him, but the husband is the lord/master of the wife, just as *Jesus is the lord/master*. With the system in place, the implications can be elaborated.

"For the husband is the head of the wife, even as Christ is the head of the church: and he is the saviour of the body" (Eph 5:23 KJ). This is the first implication drawn from the metaphorical system. Christ as head of the church implies not just authority over, but separation from. Christ as the head in heaven and the church on earth implies an ontological difference between Christ and church and likewise an ontological difference between male and female. This is the cultural assumption of the Greco-Roman world. Men are different in kind of being from women; women are deviant men, somehow less in being than men. All this is part of Aristotle's chain of being. The metaphor can also reverse itself. If the male/female relationship is part of the lord/servant metaphor, then the church becomes metaphorically female, thus mother church, and the congregants become children. There is a richness in the metaphorical system that allows it to expand in several directions.

"He is savior of the body" is ambiguous in the Greek. Who is "he"? Christ? Or the husband? Or both? Commentators are divided (See MacDonald, 327). The NRSV eliminates the ambiguity: "For the husband is the head of the wife just as Christ is the head of the church, the body of which he is the Savior." But the ambiguity should probably be allowed to stand.

The husband's status derives from the lord/master and the wife's from the church. "Just as the church is subject to Christ, so also wives ought to be, in everything, to their husbands" (Eph 5:24 NRSV). The wife is solely defined by her subject status to her lord/master husband. The husband's responsibility is then elaborated:

> Husbands, love your wives, just as Christ loved the church and gave himself up for her, in order to make her holy by cleansing her with the washing of water by the word, so as to present the church to himself in splendor, without a spot or wrinkle or anything of the kind—yes, so that she may be holy and without blemish. (Eph 5:25–27)

The author begins to lose control of the metaphor and switches from the husband and wife to Christ and the church. But eventually regaining control, he returns to the husband's care of the wife. The author's logic is interesting: "In the same way, husbands should love their wives as they do their own bodies. He who loves his wife loves himself" (Eph 5:28). The man's possession of the woman is so total that it becomes a form of self-love.

The concluding sentence tells it all: "Each of you, however, should love his wife as himself, and a wife should respect her husband" (Eph 5:33). The point of view and one to whom this is addressed is the male. The woman is clearly an impersonal object. Her role is to be subject and show respect. The topic of being subject was introduced in Eph 5:21: "Be subject to one another out of reverence for Christ." As we noted above, the Greek word's primary meaning is "fear," a word of strong emotions. But when used in a positive sense, awe or respect is an appropriate gloss. Respect is not an incorrect translation, but a little weak as a translation of *phobētai*. A more correct translation would be: "a wife should show awe for her husband," since awe is the positive side of fear, which is the intention. A lord and master deserves awe.

This view of the husband and wife relationship not only flows from the *Jesus is the Lord* metaphorical system but also is very far from Paul's understanding in 1 Corinthians 7. Paul stresses mutuality, not subjection. His notion of mutuality flows out of his understanding of the body of the Anointed, the crucified one. He does not build on the lord/master model. In his model, the Anointed is not the head of the body, the Anointed *is* the body; the Anointed describes the body. Most importantly, the body of the Anointed is a crucified body, a slave body. So domination is an abomination. The way one works out the model has direct and important consequences and ought not to be ignored and dismissed as just theological theory.

The Real Paul

Why is the real Paul, as seen in this chapter, so invisible? This is an intriguing question. Most people, if not most scholars, view Paul as authoritarian and as one who does not like women. How did this view become so dominant? There are a variety of reasons. How many weddings include as a reading the Eph 5:22–33 passage? Until recently it was the standard reading. The public use of this text has set a tone and context for viewing Paul.

Only in the last generation of scholarship has the pseudonymity of Ephesians become the dominant position. It has been challenged for a long time, but there have always been strong defenders. That has begun to fade in the past thirty years. As long as it was strongly debated, for many, Ephesians remained one of Paul's letters. Even though there is a consensus among scholars on this issue, that view is hardly well known among the general public. The canon and printed bibles continue to reinforce the view of Paul as author of Ephesians.

The patriarchal character of the Christian tradition has only been challenged in the past thirty years. Elisabeth Schüssler

House Church

In a number of his letters, Paul sends greetings to those meeting in a house community or church (1 Cor 16:19; Rom 16:3, 5; Phlm 2). How many people made up a house church community, and how many house churches make up the whole church in a city? Given the size of ancient houses, the number cannot have been large, 10 to 15 people.

On other occasions, Paul mentions the whole church gathering for the lord's supper (1 Cor 11:17) and in another case he reports, "If then the whole community of the Anointed has come together in one place and everyone is speaking in ecstatic languages and outsiders or non-members come in, will they not say that you are mad?" (1 Cor 14:23). So how many people are attending such a larger gathering? Vincent Branick has worked out the details based upon villa sizes in Pompei and Corinth.

> If we averaged out these sizes, we would arrive at a villa with a *triclinium* [dining room] of some 36 square meters and an *atrium* of 55 square meters. If we removed all the couches from the *triclinium*, we would end up with space for perhaps 20 persons. If we included the *atrium*, minus any large decorative urns, we could expand the group to 50 persons, provided people did not move around, and some did not mind getting shoved into the shallow pool. The maximum comfortable group such a villa could accommodate would most likely be in the range of 30–40 persons. (39–42)

This would indicate that the total number of Paul's converts in Corinth would be thirty to fifty people.

Fiorenza's *In Memory of Her: A Feminist Theological Reconstruction of Christian Origins* was published in 1983. That groundbreaking feminist analysis put feminism on the agenda of New Testament studies. The churches have been highly invested in seeing Paul as a supporter of patriarchy. Actually Ephesians is at the beginning of that tradition. The Pastorals, 1 and 2 Timothy and Titus, continued re-inventing Paul in the patriarchal tradition that is only now being undone. Even Paul's letters were edited in such a way as to bring him into agreement with the later canonical Pauline tradition.

The command in 1 Cor 14:33b–38 provides an example of a later interpolation designed to bring the real Paul into alignment with the Pastorals: "As in all the churches of God, the women should be silent during the meetings. They are not permitted to speak, but must be subordinate, just as scripture says." When read in the context of 1 Corinthians 14, these verses interrupt the flow of a discussion about prophecy. First come verses 31–33a:

> All of you can prophesy if you speak one at a time, so that all may learn and be encouraged. When and how prophets speak is under the control of the prophets, because God is not a God of disorder but of peace.

Then the command about women being silent, verses 33b–38, and finally the discussion of prophecy resumes in verse 39:

> So, my friends, be eager to prophesy and don't forbid ecstatic utterance, but everything should be done appropriately and in an orderly way. (1 Cor 14:39–40)

Clearly verses 33b–38 interrupt the flow of a discussion on prophecy in chapter 14. But does that prove they are an interpolation? It depends upon how much evidence you demand. To me, this looks compelling. It is re-enforced by Gal 3:26–28 where Paul says the distinction between male and female is abolished in the Anointed and in 1 Corinthians 7 where, as we have seen, Paul advocates for a mutual relationship between women and men. Furthermore no such "command of the lord" is known and the passage sounds more like something from 1 Tim 2:11–12, a second-century writing. The passage also occurs in some manuscripts after 14:40. On the principle of only using the best evidence, this should be judged an interpolation and excised from the text. It looks like a scribe added it sometime in the second century.

Yet as obvious as it appears to me that 1 Cor 14:33–38 is an interpolation, some scholars continue to argue that it is from Paul. Their strongest piece of evidence is that every extant manuscript of 1 Corinthians has the passage, especially the most important manuscripts. But this evidence is not as strong as it appears. Consider the following.

- The Corinthian correspondence is highly edited.
- Paul's letters were edited once again when they were collected.
- They may well have been edited yet again when incorporated into the canon of the New Testament.
- There is more than a hundred years between the original letters and the earliest manuscripts of Paul's letters.

All of this indicated ample opportunity for the interpolation concerning the command for women to be silent (1 Cor 14:33b–38) to occur. We know that Colossians, Ephesians and the Pastorals are much more socially conservative than Paul. While scholars are willing to grant, in theory, that Paul's letters have been edited, they are reluctant in practice to admit the extent of the editing. It opens up a can of worms they just do not want to take on. Antoinette Clark Wire in her *The Corinthian Women Prophets* (229–33) has argued that Paul is engaged in trying to control a group of ecstatic women prophets, that all of 1 Corinthians is directed toward discrediting these women and that 14:33b–38 fits into this rhetoric. I have presented both sides of the argument because in the end one must make a judgment on the basis of how one interprets that evidence. It is always a matter of judgment. Seldom is there a smoking gun.

1 Corinthians 11:2–16 is another interpolation that brings Paul's letters into even stronger agreement with the later Pauline tradition. "Now I want you to know that the Anointed is the head of every man, a man is the head of every woman, and God is the head of the Anointed" (1 Cor 11:3). The language is strongly reminiscent of Eph 5:23–4.

The same basic arguments advanced above concerning the command for women to be silent are applicable to this interpolation.

- It interrupts the flow of the letter's discussion. 1 Corinthians 10 deals with meals and 11:17 continues that discussion.
- It undercuts Paul's anti-hierarchical position, clearly subordinating women to men.
- It bring Paul into alignment with Colossians, Ephesians and the Pastorals.
  (For a detailed argument see Walker, 91–123.)

The domesticating of Paul so that he lines up with the standard Greco-Roman view is a long tradition, going back to every stage of the handing on and editing of Paul's letters.

Finally, we have had blinders on when reading Paul. The inherited model has viewed Paul as anti-Jewish and anti-women. These are even linked together in ways. In the traditional model both Jews and women were seen as fleshly, in need of control, and not to be trusted.

With blinders in place, a passage like 1 Cor 7:1–7 can be read as anti-women. The very first statement is easily understood in this vein: "It is well for a man not to touch a woman" (1 Cor 7:1 NRSV). Ripped out of context and understood with the traditional suspicion of women, this verse is understood as denying sexuality, whereas it leads into practical and caring advice for the couple that respects the mutual needs of both partners.

Interpretation is not context-neutral. To understand any text one must understand the appropriate context. In reading contemporary texts, we usually share with the author the same cultural context. In reading foreign works or works written outside our normal cultural context, we have to construct a new and different context to make sense of the work. In dealing with an ancient text, the task is even more difficult because we share so little in common. Modern translations mask the cultural difference; we are not aware in reading a translation that Paul was really writing in Greek. Even more, the tradition provides us with a readymade context in which to make sense of Paul. Deconstructing that traditional context and reconstructing a new one is a major task of this book.

Readings

Castelli, Elizabeth A. "Paul on Women and Gender." Pp. 221–35 in *Women & Christian Origins*. Ed. Mary Rose D'Angelo and Ross Shepard Kraemer. New York: Oxford University Press, 1999.

Fitzmyer, Joseph A. *First Corinthians*. The Anchor Yale Bible, vol. 32. New Haven/London: Yale University Press, 2008.

Lakoff, George, and Mark Johnson. *Metaphors We Live By*. Chicago: University of Chicago Press, 1980.

MacDonald, Margaret Y. *Colossians and Ephesians*. Sacra Pagina Series, vol. 17. Collegeville, MN: Liturgical Press, 2000.

Polaski, Sandra Hack. *A Feminist Introduction to Paul*. St. Louis, MO: Chalice Press, 2005.

Schüssler Fiorenza, Elisabeth. *In Memory of Her: A Feminist Theological Reconstruction of Christian Origins*. New York: Crossroad Press, 1983.

Walker, William O. *Interpolations in the Pauline Letters*. London: Sheffield Academic Press, 2001.

Wire, Antoinette Clark. *The Corinthian Women Prophets: A Reconstruction through Paul's Rhetoric*. Minneapolis: Fortress Press, 1990.

CHAPTER 12

THE LAW

As a topic, Paul and the law has motivated much research in recent years and real progress has been made. In the traditional Augustinian/Lutheran construction, justification by faith and grace was set in opposition to justification by works of the law. This polarization understood justification by faith to represent Christianity and justification by works of the law to represent Judaism. This characterized Judaism as a religion of rigid legalism. The great gain in recent scholarship has been in understanding both how this view caricatures and distorts Judaism and also what Paul's real view of the law is.

THE SCRIPTURES of ISRAEL

Paul uses a variety of terms to refer to the scriptures of Israel. He quotes the Septuagint (LXX), the Greek translation of the Hebrew Bible. At this period, the canon of the Hebrew Bible was not fully set but was in flux; likewise the canon of the Septuagint. Moreover, the canons of the Hebrew Bible and the Septuagint were not in agreement about which books belonged. Eventually the canon of the Septuagint became the canon of the early Christian church and then the Catholic Church, and the Hebrew became the canon of Rabbinic Judaism and the Old Testament of the Protestant reformation.

Paul once mentions the law and the prophets (Rom 3:21), which refers to the twofold division of the scriptures of Israel into the Law (i.e., the Pentateuch, a Greek name) and the Prophets. This twofold division is Jewish and found in other parts of the New Testament (Matt 7:12; 11:13//Luke 16:16//Q 16:16; 22:40; Luke 24:44; John 1:45; Acts 13:15; 28:23). At a later time a third division, the Writings, became traditional, both for Judaism and

Christianity. The New Testament does not employ the threefold division.

Only once, in the address of the letter to the Romans, does Paul refer to the holy scriptures, literally the holy writings: "Paul, slave of God's Anointed, Jesus—summoned as an envoy [and] appointed to announce God's world-changing news, which was anticipated by the prophets in holy scriptures" (Rom 1:1–2). Interestingly he refers to the prophets, not other writings. Also, he once refers to the "words (*logia*) of God" (Rom 3:2 SV, NIV), often translated "oracles of God" (KJ, NRSV). Paul has in mind the oracular, speaking character of God's words through Moses and the prophets (see below chapter 13, "A Jewish Teacher"). This Jewish usage is found in the LXX, Philo, and Josephus.

Several times, when quoting the scriptures of Israel, Paul uses some form of the phrase, "scripture (*lit:* the writing) says," with the verb in the present tense (Rom 4:3; 9:17; 10:11; 11:2; Gal 4:30). Twice in Galatians he personifies scripture (Gal 3:8, "scripture anticipated"; and Gal 3:22, "scripture confined"), although the phrase "scripture says" could also be considered a form of personification. This usage of scripture (*graphē*) views the scriptures (writings) as a whole, as speaking and still speaking with single voice. This usage is well attested in Judaism (BDAG).

Law (*nomos*) is by far the most frequent word used in Paul's letters to refer to the scriptures of Israel, thus marking it out as an extremely important word for him. The statistics are suggestive.

1 Thessalonians	0
Galatians	32
1 Corinthians	9
2 Corinthians	0
Philemon	0
Philippians	3
Romans	68
Total	112

The high total number in Galatians and Romans is not surprising, since in both of these letters the law is a major issue and both quote extensively from the Jewish scriptures. What is surprising is how infrequent or absent is the usage of law in the other letters, and how seldom, in them, the Jewish scriptures are quoted.

Clearly Paul expects his audiences in Galatia and Rome to have a high degree of literacy in the scriptures of Israel.

Paul's use of law (*nomos*) is not always clear and straightforward. One must always ask what is the referent; exactly how is he using the word? Several examples illustrate the problem.

"But now the righteousness of God without the law is manifested, being witnessed by the law and the prophets" (Rom 3:21 KJ). Most commentators take the first occurrence of "law" in this verse to refer to the Jewish law. The important British evangelical scholar James Dunn thinks it is "obviously synonymous" with works of the law (165), while Jewett in his Hermeneia commentary is not so sure because "law" in the Greek is without an article and so it may be law in general (274). Regardless of how this issue is solved, and I do not have a solution, notice that law, in the absolute usage, has a negative connotation, while the law and the prophets has a positive connotation. Do they refer to the same thing, to something different, or different aspects of the same thing?

Consider this passage:

> Friends, if someone is found to have strayed off course in some way, you, who really experienced God's power and presence, must gently get that person back on track. And at the same time look out for yourselves so that you also won't be tempted. Shoulder each other's loads, and in this way you will carry out the "law of God's Anointed." (Gal 6:1–2)

While law in this passage clearly is used in a positive sense, to what law could it be referring? Is the law of the Anointed in contrast with *the* law, that is, the Law (*Torah*) of Israel? Or does it have the sense of principle? Or is it not set in contrast with Torah, but marks the fulfillment of Torah, as Louis Martyn in his important Anchor Bible Commentary on *Galatians* argues (557–58).

Finally one last passage:

> There is therefore now no condemnation for those who are in Christ Jesus. For the law of the Spirit of life in Christ Jesus has set you free from the law of sin and of death. (Rom 8:1–2 NRSV)

The contrast between the law of the Spirit and the law of sin and of death would indicate that law has, here, the sense of principle.

Thus more literally one might render this verse, "for the principle of the breath of life which is from being in the Anointed has set you free from the principle of sin and of death" (BBS). The SV translation tries for this by translating *nomos* as "rule" in this passage:

> So now those who are in solidarity with the Anointed Jesus are no longer under a sentence of death. For the rule of the spirit of life that was in the Anointed Jesus has liberated you from being ruled by seductive corruption and death. (Rom 8:1–2)

But if we do not recognize the multivalent senses of *nomos*/law in Paul's writings, one could easily understand this passage as contrasting the law of the Spirit (positive) with the law of sin and death, that is, the Torah (negative). Such an interpretation would cohere with the traditional Augustinian/Lutheran opposition between Christianity and Judaism.

In the vast majority of cases in Galatians and Romans, the Greek *nomos* (law) is a translation for the Hebrew *torah*. The LXX frequently translated *torah* with *nomos* and so that became the standard translation in Hellenistic Judaism. There is some debate about how accurate a translation *nomos* is for *torah*. C. H. Dodd in an early discussion of the question did not think it was "an exact equivalent" (25), and pointed out that at points the fit between the two words is less than perfect. This is a frequent problem in translations. The Jewish scholar Samuel Sandmel thought the translation caused a real distortion.

> For Hellenistic Judaism, the casualness with which the Hebrew word Torah was translated by the Greek word *nomos*, "law," is apparent on every page of the surviving literature. Greek Jews nowhere raised the question whether Torah really means *nomos*, law! And whenever they defended their Jewish convictions, it was always on the premise, startling to modern Jewish students, that *nomos* did adequately translate *Torah*. To Palestinian Jews, and their spiritual descendants, the word Torah never had a restricted connotation; they equated *Torah* with our word "revelation." (47)

Sandmel's is correct. Torah means "revelation."

Another Jewish scholar, Alan Segal agrees upon recent review of the evidence that "although Torah is partly legal enactment, it is essentially the story of the covenant, hence transcendent and revelatory" (260). But Segal goes on to point out that "law" is a poor translation of *nomos.*

> But nomos does not exactly mean law in our sense of statute or court decision. It is rather a procedure or practice. Greek papyri refer to marriage as a *nomos keimenos,* enduring practice, implying a mutual agreement, which is close to what the Hebrews called a covenant and has, in fact, been translated as covenant. Further, nomos did have many transcendent connotations, especially in stoicism. When the Septuagint translated Torah as nomos it was not mistaken. (260).

The takeaway from this debate is that law in the sense of legal statutes is misleading. The primary sense of *torah* and *nomos* as a translation of *torah* is "revelation." Translating *torah* as *nomos* and then *nomos* as "law" focuses on the legal aspect of the Jewish scriptures, just as the oracles of God focus on the aspect of God speaking in the scriptures and the phrase Law and Prophets focuses on the parts of scripture. These different ways of referring to the scriptures of Israel focus the scriptures in a particular way. Finally, as Dunn observes in regard to Paul's use of law in Romans, "there can be little doubt that the tension between his gospel and the Law and his concern to resolve that tension provide one of Paul's chief motivations in penning the letter" (lxvi). The same can be said of Galatians. This tension between Paul's gospel and the law highlights the rhetorical use of the law in Paul's arguments. Dunn has alerted us to something to which we must pay attention.

A Re-evaluation of Judaism

The most significant study on the topic of the law and Paul in the twentieth century was surely E. P. Sanders' *Paul and Palestinian Judaism* (1977), a book much more about Judaism than Paul—and that is not a critique. Part One, dealing with Palestinian Judaism, is 403 pages, while Part Two on Paul is little more than 100 pages. Sanders changed the way New Testament scholarship had viewed Paul, and made it intellectually difficult, as well as embarrassing, to maintain the traditional Christian view of Judaism at the time of Jesus. If his book was a tremendous success in its study of Judaism, his view of Paul has been less satisfying.

We have been bumping up against this traditional Christian view of Judaism since we decided that Paul was called and not converted. But we have not yet faced it directly. Part of our earlier analysis showed that Paul was not converting to Christianity, so the problem was not Judaism. Paul was not rejecting Judaism, nor was it the opposite of Christianity. His concern was getting the nations into the blessings of the covenant. Jesus the Anointed as God's son became a curse through crucifixion to solve this problem for the nations, thus fulfilling the promise made by God to Abraham that he should be the father of all nations. Now we must face up to the problem with the law and Paul's stance vis-à-vis Judaism. In this chapter we will deal with the law in Galatians, in chapter 13 the law in Romans, and only then with Judaism in chapter 14. But these two issues are tightly tied together and are not easily separated. There will be an inevitable overlap.

Sanders' work is massive and is nearly impossible to summarize without oversimplifying, but summarize we must. His analysis has a twofold thrust:

Negative	to show that the traditional Christian view of Judaism is wrong
Positive	to determine "the overall pattern of Rabbinic religion" (180)

Ironically, the traditional model for understanding Paul demanded that Judaism be the opposite of the Christianity to which Paul was converting. Since Paul's new religion was one of faith and grace, his old religion had to be one of law and works. This theological model determined research, and New Testament scholars delivered up a Judaism that met those requirements. The resulting New Testament handbooks that dealt with the Jewish "background" to the New Testament portrayed such a Judaism by selective editing of rabbinic texts. According to Sanders, the handbooks constructed a set view:

> Rabbinic religion was a religion of legalistic works-righteousness in which a man was saved by fulfilling more commandments than he committed transgressions. I have argued that that view is completely wrong: it proceeds from theological presuppositions and is supported by systematically misunderstanding and misconstruing passages in Rabbinic literature. I do not find such

a view in any stratum of Tannaitic [the rabbis whose views are recorded in the Mishnah] literature or to be held by any Rabbi of the Tannaitic period. (233)

Sanders goes on to say that his goal was "to destroy" this view "which has proved so persistent in New Testament scholarship" (234). He might have added, "and in the preaching of the Christian churches." Such a view of Judaism has provided long-term life-support for anti-Semitism and needs to be destroyed. Such a view of Judaism is all the more insidious because those who employ it are often unaware of it and moreover think it historical.

As indicated, Sanders' project has a positive aspect as well. Positively he set out to determine what was the overall pattern of rabbinic religion. His summary:

The pattern is this: God has chosen Israel and Israel has accepted the election. In his role as King, God gave Israel commandments which they are to obey as best they can. Obedience is rewarded and disobedience punished. In case of failure to obey, however, man [a Jew] has recourse to divinely ordained means of atonement, in all of which repentance is required. As long as he maintains his desire to stay in the covenant, he has a share in God's covenantal promises, including life in the world to come. The intention and effort to be obedient constitute the *condition for remaining in the covenant*, but they do not *earn it*.
    (180, emphasis in original)

Sanders points out that the rabbis were not systematic theologians, so he has worked out the pattern of their religion. He terms this pattern "covenantal nomism," which he defines as follows:

Briefly put, covenantal nomism is the view that one's place in God's plan is established on the basis of the covenant and that the covenant requires as the proper response of man [a Jew] his obedience to its commandments, while providing means of atonement for transgression. (75)

To avoid confusion in the above two quotes, I have inserted in brackets "a Jew." "An Israelite" could also have been inserted. By the use of "man" Sanders does not mean a universal human, but a member of the covenant.

Sanders' view of Judaism has stood the test of scholarly scrutiny and has carried the day—whether or not it has destroyed the opposing view. On that foundation we will move forward with our question: what is Paul's problem with the law? Or as Dunn more delicately phrased it, "there can be little doubt that the tension between his gospel and the Law and his concern to resolve that tension provide one of Paul's chief motivations in penning the letter" (lxvi).

The Law in Galatia

We have already begun to pick up the clues toward solving our problem.

- Paul does not convert to Christianity but remains a Jew.
- Paul is addressing the nations, not the human situation in general.
- As a corollary to this last point, Paul is not addressing Jews.

By keeping these points in mind, Paul's view of the law will appear. John Gager, who has labored on this issue for a long time, states this principle in an engaging way.

> *Any statement that begins with the words, "How could a Jew like Paul say X, Y, Z about the law," must be regarded as misguided. In all likelihood Paul, the apostle to the Gentiles, is not speaking about the law as it relates to Israel but only about the law and Gentile members of the Jesus-movement.* (44, emphasis in original)

Now to the law in Galatians. In chapter 7 we examined the conflict in Antioch; it is important to review our conclusions before proceeding. In the conflict at Antioch, James and Cephas became concerned about the implications of members of the nations eating with Jews. Because they were following the customs of Judaism, no libation to the emperor would have been offered. James thought this was dangerous, which it was, and his delegation convinced the other Jews, including Cephas and Barnabas, to withdraw from table fellowship with the members of the nations. There appear to be three options from the point of view of James and Cephas:

- The nations offer libation to emperor.
- Circumcision, i.e., the nations become Jews.
- The Jews withdraw from table fellowship.

We do not know if the first was even considered, although Jews had worked out this issue previously in other situations dealing with the nations. Perhaps Paul and the members of the nations objected to this solution because it violated faithfulness to the Anointed whom the empire had crucified. Paul violently objected to number two, circumcision, and, as a result, Cephas and the other Jews withdrew from table fellowship.

Why then did Paul object to circumcision? Remember, he is not objecting to circumcision for Jews as members of God's covenant, but to the males of the nations being circumcised. So what is his logic?

Paul's first argument is the example of Abraham, an argument we have already examined in chapter 9.

> You're in the same situation as Abraham. [As scripture says:] "Abraham put his trust in God, and God counted that the right thing to do." From this you ought to draw the conclusion that Abraham's heirs are those born of confidence in God. Indeed, scripture anticipated what is happening right now, namely that God acknowledges that the nations are right to put their confidence in God. (Gal 3:6–9)

For Paul this is the good news, and he even says that scripture "announced-the-good-news-beforehand" to Abraham (Gal 3:8 BBS). Abraham was faithful to God's promise before circumcision, so he became the father of both the circumcised and the uncircumcised, but for both he is father by his faithfulness to God's promise.

Paul's understanding of Abraham's faithfulness is in accord with Sanders' description of covenantal nomism. As Sanders points out, the rabbis do not understand following the commandments as earning the blessings of the covenant, but as part of the obligations required of a member of the covenant. A major difference between Sanders' analysis of the rabbis and Paul, is that Sanders is only dealing with Israel's response to the covenant. Paul is considering both Israel and the nations. For both the response is the same—it is Abraham's response: faithfulness.

After this positive argument, Paul counters with a negative one, again quoting scripture. "Everyone who does not honor all the things written in the book of the law by observing them is accursed" (Gal 3:10 quoting Deut 27:26 LXX). Paul's argument at this point is easily misunderstood and has been misunderstood. Pay attention to the emphasized words in the following quote.

> For *all who* (*lit:* whoever) rely on the works of the law are under a curse; for it is written, "Cursed is *everyone* who does not observe and obey all the things written in the book of the law." Now it is evident that *no one* is justified before God by the law.
> (Gal 3:10–11 NRSV)

These three italicized words sound as though they apply universally to all human beings, and so they traditionally have been understood in that way (for example Martyn, 307). Thus, they would apply to both Jews and gentiles. Moreover, by implication, this is the way Jews understand the law, but as Sanders has shown, such is not the case. Rather Paul is speaking to the nations. So "all who," "everyone" and "no one" in this context refers only to the nations. If they (the nations) "rely on works of the law" they will be cursed because they will be unable to follow all the commandments. Why? Because they are not members of the covenant as Israel is. Israel does not "rely on works of the law" but the works of the law are part of their obedience to God as members of the covenant, and God has provided them a way to deal with failings. The nations have no such benefit. Since Paul is writing to the nations, he does not need to explain how this works for Israel, thus leading to a misreading of the passage.

Paul takes up how the nations have access to the benefits of God's blessings. The explanation involves his paradoxical understanding of the crucifixion of the Anointed.

> God's Anointed freed us from the curse of subjection to the law, by becoming a curse for us, since it is written, "Anyone who is crucified is accursed." (Gal 3:13)

The first person plural voice "us" could again be understood as Paul speaking for all humans, both Jew and Greek, but it is instead the rhetorical "us," the speaker identifying with the audience. That the topic is the nations is made abundantly clear in the next verse.

> This was done so that Abraham's blessing might come to the nations by belonging to the Anointed Jesus, and so that we might receive the promise of God's presence and power (*lit:* breath or spirit) through putting our unconditional trust in God.
> (Gal 3:14)

Verse 14 demonstrates that "we" is a rhetorical usage because it identifies "nations" with "we." So all through this passage Paul is not addressing the universal human, both Jew and gentile, but only the nations.

More precisely, Abraham is the father of all nations, both the circumcised and the uncircumcised. But Israel's access to the benefits promised to Abraham is through the covenant made later, of which circumcision is the sign, while the nations have access to the first covenant made with Abraham, which God has now made active through his Anointed bearing the curse by crucifixion. As Paul states in 2 Cor 3:6, this is a new covenant, but not new in the sense of replacing an older covenant. It is new in that now the nations have access to the blessings of the covenant. For the nations, this new covenant is not in writing but in God's breath or spirit (2 Cor 3:6).

Paul then asks why the law, what is its purpose?

> It was provided to restrain our undisciplined behavior until the arrival of the offspring to whom the inheritance was promised. The law was transmitted by divine messengers through a human mediator. But a mediator implies that more than one was involved. <But God alone made the promise,> since God is one.
> (Gal 3:19–20)

Again I would reiterate, Paul is speaking of the nations. What is the point of the law for the nations? He has not suddenly switched to speaking in general. The law was to restrain undisciplined behavior, literally, transgressions. That Paul is speaking about the nations is made evident with reference to the offspring, which Paul has interpreted as referring to the Anointed. Previously Paul had referred to Gen 13:15: "For all the land that you see, I will give to you and to your offspring (*lit:* seed) forever" (LXX). Paul notes that it reads seed in the singular, not seeds in plural. Therefore, he concludes, seed refers to God's Anointed (Gal 3:16). The Anointed bears the curse that frees the nations.

Generations of scholars have tried to figure out to whom Paul is referring with "The law was transmitted by divine messengers through a human mediator" (Gal 3:19), but without success. No one has found a parallel to this statement. At this point I think guessing is fruitless. Yet his point is clear. The law is somehow less than the covenant with Abraham. Paul appears to distinguish between the law, the law from Moses, and the covenant made with Abraham. He will not make this distinction in the similar discussion in Romans.

Implying that the law was not transmitted by God, of course, leads inevitably to the conclusion that the law is against God's promises, again reinforcing the idea that the law and the covenant (the promises) made with Abraham are different. But Paul protests vehemently that the law is not against God's promises, rather it fits with God's purpose. So what is the point of the law? Paul tries to answer:

> If there were a law that had the power to create life, then our acceptance by God would indeed be based on the law. But the scripture confined everything under the seductive power of corruption (*lit:* sin), in order that the promise that has come to fruition in Jesus the Anointed's complete confidence in God might be extended to those who share the same confidence.
> (Gal 3:21–22)

Once again the distinction between the law and scripture appears. The law lacks the power to create life, while the personified scripture confines all under the power of sin. Again Paul is speaking of the nations, not all humans generally; that is to say, this does not refer to Israel. For him, the sharing in the Anointed's faithfulness grants the nations their own access to the blessing promised to Abraham. That Paul is referring to the nations is clear in verse 23: "Now before this kind of confidence in God arrived, we were under the surveillance of the law, held in bondage until the awaited disclosure of such confidence." Being held in bondage is not an image of Israel in covenant relation with God, but an image of the nations in bondage (*lit:* encircled, like a fishnet) to idols and Rome.

Schoolmaster

Paul now switches to a different image—the Law as *paidagōgos* (Gal 3:25), literally a teacher of children. The KJ translates it "schoolmaster" and for that day and age it was probably the perfect translation. Both the NRSV and the SV have "disciplinarian." Both of these are reflecting the image of the schoolmaster in the ancient world as a harsh teacher with stick in hand. For Paul the law's purpose for the nations was to keep under control the chaos and lawlessness that resulted from idol worship, thereby restraining the just wrath of God. Thus for the nations the purpose of the law is to restrain their lawlessness, while for Israel it is a sign of their covenantal relationship, of their obedience to God in covenant.

Now the nations no longer need a schoolmaster with stick in hand. "Indeed you are all now God's adult offspring (*lit:* sons) through the kind of confidence exemplified by God's Anointed, Jesus" (Gal 3:26). To follow through on Paul's image, when sons reach their majority, they no longer need a schoolmaster. "Sons" also leads into Paul's metaphor of heirs, which follows.

> So, everyone of you who has been baptized into solidarity with God's Anointed has become invested with the status of God's Anointed. You are no longer Jew or Greek, no longer slave or freeborn, no longer "male and female." Instead, you all have the same status in the service of God's Anointed, Jesus. Moreover, if you now belong to God's Anointed, that also makes you Abraham's offspring (*lit:* seed) and—as promised—his heirs.
> (Gal 3:27–29)

SV has chosen to translate "You are no longer Jew or Greek" in the second person plural, whereas in the Greek it is in the third person: "There is no longer Jew or Greek" (NRSV). While being careful not to read into this statement the modern concerns for equal rights, Paul's sweeping statement wipes away major social barriers in the Greco-Roman world. From Paul's, as well as the Jewish point of view, the Jew has an advantage and higher status than a Greek, likewise for freeborn and male over slave and female. Since the Jewish advantage springs from their access to the covenant, that advantage is now eliminated. For Paul, God has finally lived up to the promise made to Abraham, and all can be his children on the same basis—faithfulness. Faithfulness has always been the way that Israel gained access to the covenant blessing; now it is the way the nations also achieve those same blessings.

Paul now picks up on the image of the son as heir.

> An heir who is still a minor, even though destined to inherit the whole estate, is no better off than a menial servant (*lit:* slave) but

remains under the care of overseers and household managers until the time set by the father. (Gal 4:1–2)

This analogy again describes the nations. Before the Anointed, they are heirs-to-be of Abraham, therefore children, therefore slaves. The overseer, under whose care they remained, was the law. But Paul takes a slightly different tactic. Instead of dealing with the law, he turns to why they needed the custodial care of the law.

> It is the same with us; when like children we knew no better, we were dominated by the cosmic powers that controlled human fate. (Gal 4:3)

Or as the NRSV has it "we were enslaved to the elemental spirits of the world."

The cosmic powers include not only the idols but also the divine powers of Rome, which enslave the world. Because of our understanding of governmental powers as secular, we are prone not to include the emperor within the elemental spirits; but, from the ancient point of view, the emperor occupies an important religious, and therefore idolatrous place. Following through with his metaphor, Paul turns to the moment when the nations attained their adulthood.

> And when the fullness of time had come,
> God sent out his Son,
> born of a woman,
> born under the law,
> in order that he might redeem back those under the law,
> so that we might receive adoption.
> (Gal 4:4–5 BBS)

Paul carefully constructs and balances this description of the nations attaining their majority. Paul's use of prepositions offers a guide:

- God sent-out, noting origin (*ek*), and a possible play on the word for envoy (*apostolos*)
- Born out of (*ek*) a woman, and under (*hypo*) the law

The son, not referred to as the Anointed, facilitates the word-play on the nations receiving adoption as sons. The Greek word for adoption (*hyiothesia*) means literally "to set or make one as a son." Both the Greek words for son and adoption share the same sound—*hyio* (son). It could be translated, woodenly but accurately, so as to make the sound evident, "God sent-out his son . . . so that we might receive being-made-as-a-son." "Son" and "being-made-as-a-son" (adoption) draw Jesus and those who share in his faithfulness together. To redeem back invokes the slave model, since the price on a slave is redeemed to free a slave.

Paul brings his description of the nations reaching their majority to a conclusion by recalling the cry of the newly baptized individual.

> And because you are sons, God has sent-out the breath of his son into our hearts, crying out, "Abba! Father!" So you (singular) are no longer a slave but a son. And if a son, also an heir through God. (Gal 4:6–7 BBS)

The supporting metaphor involves a movement from slavery to sonship, from low to high status. It encompasses more than freedom, but also sonship. And, if a son, then also an heir. In the Greco-Roman world, inheritance passes through the son's line, not the daughter's. The metaphor, of course, reflects the assumptions of patriarchy, but Paul has already just indicated that in the Anointed "male and female" do not count, so from Paul's perspective "son" applies to all, both male and female. It is appropriate for modern translations to shift son to child or children, since our inheritance patterns are not patrilineal.

Paul turns this argument to the current situation in Galatia in which the Galatian males are being circumcised. Paul clearly sees what the Galatians are proposing as parallel to the conflict in Antioch between himself and Cephas. He apparently sees what is happening in Galatia in light of his debate with Cephas. Fatally from Paul's perspective, by being circumcised, the Galatians are not becoming Jewish, as they suppose, but subjecting themselves to the power of Rome. Cephas and James had proposed that the nations be circumcised so that they could eat with the Jews without offending Rome. He sees their being circumcised and joining Israel as not claiming their sonship from God and their freedom as sons of God, but becoming yet again slaves to avoid the condemnation of Rome.

> In the past, when you had no knowledge of God, you were dominated by powers that were not really divine (*lit:* gods). Now that

you know God, or rather, God knows you, how can you return to those impotent and impoverished cosmic powers, let alone wish to be their menial servants (*lit:* enslaved) again? For example, you are still involved in observing days and months, seasons and years, as if that determined your fate! I'm afraid my efforts on your behalf have been a waste of time. (Gal 4:8–11)

Once again, Paul is speaking to Galatians as part of the nations. He is not evaluating Israel. Paul apparently maintains that for a member of the nations to be circumcised is to give in to the enslavement of Rome. He does not see it as a religious option for a member of the nations to join the people of Israel. He does not view Judaism and Christianity as two separate religious options. For him, the promise was made to Abraham. Israel has one way to access those blessings, and God has provided another way, other than circumcision, for the nations to partake in the blessings of Abraham.

The Allegory of Hagar

As part of his effort to persuade the Galatians not to circumcise themselves, Paul elaborates on the allegory of Hagar. While we might debate whether Paul remained a Pharisee after his *apocalypsis*/insight, there is no doubt that his exegetical method remained Pharisaic. Like all allegory, this is the twice-told tale. The meaning of an allegory is derived not from the story itself, but from outside the story. The story itself does not lead to the allegorical interpretation, but the outside story leads to the interpretation of the story. In that sense, allegory is always insider knowledge. One cannot get to its meaning from the story itself.

The part of the Genesis 16 story which Paul uses for his allegory, is told rather simply.

> Now Sarai, Abram's wife, bore him no children. She had an Egyptian slave-girl whose name was Hagar, and Sarai said to Abram, "You see that the LORD has prevented me from bearing children; go in to my slave-girl; it may be that I shall obtain children by her." And Abram listened to the voice of Sarai.
> (Gen 16:1–2)

> Abram was eighty-six years old when Hagar bore him Ishmael.
> (Gen 16:16)

What occurs between verses 2 and 16 are not part of his allegory. For his allegory he plays upon the aspect that Hagar was a slave and Sarah, unnamed in Paul's allegory, was free.

> Scripture says that Abraham had two sons, one by a slave woman and the other by a free woman. The difference was that the son of the slave was born naturally, the son of the free woman through God's promise. (Gal 4:22–23)

We have seen this line of argument in connection with Abraham before in chapter 9, "Abraham in Romans." Abraham's blessing is a promise based on both God's faithfulness and Abraham's reliance, or confidence, in God's faithfulness. It is not a wage, something he earned. But Paul goes in a somewhat different direction.

> This is all allegorical: these women represent two covenants. The one from Mount Sinai, who bears slave children, corresponds to Hagar. This Hagar is Mount Sinai in Arabia; but she also corresponds to the present Jerusalem; she is in slavery with her children. In contrast, it's the heavenly Jerusalem that is free—that's the one who is our mother. (Gal 4:24–26)

This is the *locus classicus* proving that Paul rejects and devalues the law. This is a primary text in the arguments in support of supersessionism, that Christianity replaces Judaism. That understanding of this text is supported by two important assumptions.

1. Paul became a Christian and rejected Judaism.
2. Paul is addressing a universal human situation.

We have challenged both of those assumptions as false avenues for interpreting Paul. Paul did not become a Christian, nor did he reject Judaism, and in his understanding, Judaism is not the opposite of Christianity. Moreover, Paul is specifically addressing the Galatians, a member of the nations, in a specific situation, not the universal human situation.

How does a different set of assumptions help us understand this allegory? In maintaining that allegorically Hagar equals both Mount Sinai in Arabia, where Moses received the Torah, and present Jerusalem, Paul is arguing that the Galatians by circumcising themselves will be submitting themselves to slavery and thus become allegorically the children of Hagar and not the children of Sarah as they intended. He is not making a statement about Judaism *per se*. By submitting to circumcision the Galatians are attempting to earn the promise, which for Paul is a contradiction in terms. Thus, for Paul, circumcision has a fundamentally different meaning when applied to a Galatian than when applied to a Jew. For a Jew it is part of the covenant response. For a Galatian, a member of the nations, it is an effort to earn the covenant and thus leads to enslavement.

Paul concludes by returning to the conflict between Ishmael and Isaac:

> Now you, friends, are just like Isaac, you are children born by God's promise. But just as it was back then, so too now: the child conceived naturally tries to harass the one conceived by God's power. Yet, what does scripture say? "Expel the slave woman and her son; because the slave woman's son will not share the inheritance with the free woman's son." The conclusion, my friends, is that we are not children of the slave woman but of the free woman. (Gal 4:28–31)

Interestingly, Paul moves away from the son analogy and moves towards the more generic children (*tekna*). In 4:6 he said "You are sons," while in 4:31 he says, "you are children." The mention of Isaac enables Paul to return to the familiar notion of promise because it invokes Abraham who is faithful to God's promise. But who then is the contemporary Ishmael? It is not Israel, so it surely must be Rome! "The child conceived naturally (*lit:* according to the flesh) tries to harass the one conceived by God's power" (*lit:* according to the breath or spirit). Paul's concern is that the nations will return to submitting to the yoke of slavery, the yoke of the elemental spirits, the yoke of Rome. Paul's apocalyptic scenario proclaims that God is acting now to bring the nations into the blessings of Abraham. That means that the false powers, those who claimed to be gods but were not (4:8), have been overthrown. Formerly they enslaved the Galatians. Now they do not. Hence Paul's plea: "God's Anointed set us free so that we could live free; so stand your ground, and do not be subject again to the yoke of slavery" (Gal 5:1).

Readings

Dodd, Charles Harold. *The Bible and the Greeks*. London: Hodder & Stoughton, 1935.

Dunn, James D. G. *Romans 1–8*. Word Biblical Commentary, vol. 38a. Dallas: Word Books, 1988.

Jewett, Robert. *Romans: A Commentary*. Hermeneia. Ed. Roy David Kotansky and Eldon Jay Epp. Minneapolis: Fortress Press, 2007.

Martyn, J. Louis. *Galatians*. The Anchor Yale Bible, vol. 33a. New Haven/London: Yale University Press, 1997.

Sanders, E. P. *Paul and Palestinian Judaism: A Comparison of Patterns of Religion*. Philadelphia: Fortress Press, 1977.

Sandmel, Samuel. *The Genius of Paul: A Study in History*. Philadelphia: Fortress Press, 1979.

Segal, Alan F. *Paul the Convert: The Apostolate and Apostasy of Saul the Pharisee*. New Haven: Yale University Press, 1990.

CHAPTER 13

THE LAW
IN ROMANS

We are pursuing a strategy of reading Paul based on his own experience in his own words. That strategy has led us to challenge the reigning Augustinian/Lutheran tradition of interpretation that sees Paul as converting to Christianity and rejecting Judaism. That paradigm is incompatible with Paul's own language of prophetic call. He was called to fulfill Israel's divine mission as one of the last of the prophets, inaugurating the final days in which the nations would be brought to the true worship of the one true God, the God of Israel. Finally the promise made to Abraham that he would be the father of all the nations was being fulfilled. That was the good news to the nations. God had acted in Jesus to set right the world. Jesus' faithfulness to God's promise, just like Abraham's faithfulness to God's promise, provided a way of faithfulness. It was Paul's own language that led us to these conclusions.

This strategy provides a new pair of glasses through which to read Paul's letters. This new reading is at times counter-intuitive because it goes so much against the established way of reading Paul in which he converts to Christianity and rejects Judaism. This constitutes a new paradigm, a paradigm shift, to use the phrase of Thomas Kuhn in *The Structure of Scientific Revolutions*. The temptation, of course, is always unknowingly to shift back into the old paradigm.

APART FROM THE LAW

Having dealt with the status of the law in Paul's letter to the Galatians, we now turn to his letter to the Romans. While the argument is at times similar to that in Galatians, it follows a very different path.

In Rom 1:18–2:16 Paul argues that the nations have been radically disobedient and deliberately so.

> What can be known about God is all around them for God has made this clear to them. Indeed, God's invisible qualities—eternal power and divine nature—can be visibly apprehended, ever since creation, through the things God made. As a result, they have no excuse. (Rom 1:19–20)

How the nations should behave did not require a divine revelation. It is manifest in nature itself. The sign of their misjudgment is evident in their idolatry. "They traded the majesty of the immortal God for imitations—a likeness of a mortal man, as well as of birds, cattle, and reptiles" (Rom 1:23). The proof was the breakdown of society symbolized by their sexual chaos, which disables the order of creation.

All of this is standard Jewish propaganda against the nations. The Wisdom of Solomon offers many examples.

> For all people who were ignorant of God were foolish by nature; and they were unable from the good things that are seen to know the one who exists, nor did they recognize the artisan while paying heed to his works; but they supposed that either fire or wind or swift air, or the circle of the stars, or turbulent water, or the luminaries of heaven were the gods that rule the world. If through

Letter to the Romans

This is probably Paul's last extant letter, written around 58 CE from Corinth. Paul is planning to take to Jerusalem the collection, which he has gathered from his communities for the poor in that city. After his trip, he plans to go to Rome on his way to Spain. The Roman community is the only church to which he writes not as the founder. There is some debate as to whether chapter 16 is part of the original letter. Some commentators argue that Rome is made up of Jewish and gentile house churches, but there is no evidence of this in the letter.

delight in the beauty of these things people assumed them to be gods, let them know how much better than these is their Lord, for the author of beauty created them.

    (Wis 13:1–3 NRSV; Elliott, 191–95, provides examples from a range of Jewish texts)

Paul is not innovating some new critique of the behavior of the nations, but is repeating what Jews normally think about the nations. As Paul tells Cephas in the confrontation at Antioch, "We ourselves are Jews by birth and not Gentile sinners" (Gal 2:15 NRSV). This expresses the assumption from the Jewish perspective—the nations are sinners.

Yet in his deriding of the nations, Paul recognizes that the nations are capable of knowing God's will apart from the Torah. "What can be known about God is all around them for God has made this clear to them" (Rom 1:19). Otherwise they could claim an excuse—they didn't know. But they are without excuse and will be subject to judgment.

This leads Paul to recognize that a member of the nations can be as moral as a Jew. So Paul imagines the following hypothetical case.

When the nations who do not have access to the law of Moses do naturally what the law requires, they embody the law in themselves, even though they do not possess the law. They demonstrate that the values engraved in the law of Moses are "written on their hearts." This is confirmed by the witness of their conscience, and by their habit of debating among themselves what is right and what is wrong. This will become clear when God exposes what is hidden of the human condition through the Anointed Jesus, as I understand God's world-changing news.

    (Rom 2:14–16)

"Written on their hearts" may refer to Jer 31:33, although the reference is not exact.

Paul contrasts a written Torah and an unwritten Torah on the hearts of the nations. If they follow that Torah they will be found righteous. As Paul proclaims the good news, the nations can be made right without becoming Jews, without circumcision, and this ability to gain righteousness apart from circumcision anticipates Paul's gospel, just as the good news was preached beforehand to Abraham. This demonstrates that God "has no favorite people" (Rom 2:11) or "shows no partiality" (NRSV), which is the point of this hypothetical case.

In his debate with the Jewish teacher, to which we will turn below, Paul returns to this theme.

> As a result, someone remaining uncircumcised [a member of the nations], who lives by the law ["What can be known about God is all around them for God has made this clear to them" (Rom 1:19)], stands in judgment on you, the law-breaker, who have the written tradition [Torah] and are circumcised [a Jew]. (Rom 2:27)

At the time of judgment the circumcised and uncircumcised will be on equal footing based on Torah, that is, "for God shows no partiality" (Rom 2:11 NRSV).

> To be a Jew, after all, is not just to be one in public, nor is circumcision just something external and physical. To be a Jew is rather to be one inwardly, and true circumcision is a matter of the heart—transformed by God (*lit*: in spirit or by divine breath) not conformed to tradition (*lit*: not written; "not literal," NRSV). Such a person gets praised, not by mortals, but by God.
> (Rom 2:28–29)

Circumcision of the heart is a well-established Jewish notion. While set in contrast with literal circumcision, it does not envision the disappearance of literal circumcision or its lack of importance.

> But if they confess their iniquity and the iniquity of their ancestors, in that they committed treachery against me and, moreover, that they continued hostile to me—so that I, in turn, continued hostile to them and brought them into the land of their enemies; if then their uncircumcised heart is humbled and they make amends for their iniquity, then will I remember my covenant with Jacob; I will remember also my covenant with Isaac and also my covenant with Abraham, and I will remember the land.
> (Lev 26:40–42 NRSV)

> Circumcise yourselves to the LORD, remove the foreskin of your hearts, O people of Judah and inhabitants of Jerusalem, or else my wrath will go forth like fire, and burn with no one to quench it, because of the evil of your doings. (Jer 4:4 NRSV)

Yet the LORD set his heart in love on your ancestors alone and chose you, their descendants after them, out of all the peoples, as it is today. Circumcise, then, the foreskin of your heart, and do not be stubborn any longer. (Deut 10:15–16 NRSV)

To emphasize: the member of the nations whose heart is circumcised and follows the Torah is the exception, not the rule. The nations are for Paul, by definition, sinners, disobedient, and lost. But there are exceptions! Also significantly, Paul's standard is the Jew. The best he can say about the member of the nations who observes the Torah written on his heart is that he is a Jew. There is nothing about being a Christian. To read Christian supersessionism into this text is a travesty.

A Jewish Teacher

Romans 2:17 signals a strong rhetorical shift. The voice shifts from third person to second person and identity shifts as well. Paul to this point in the letter has been addressing the nations, both as the addressee of the letter and their situation. Now there is an abrupt shift: "If you call yourself a Jew" signals a dramatic shift—Paul is now speaking to a Jew. But not a real Jew. This is a caricature, a stock figure of the pretentious teacher. In Paul's construction this is not a Christian view of the self-righteous Pharisee. But since it later contributed to the Christian caricature of the Pharisee, we must be careful not to read the anachronistic Christian caricature into Paul's description.

This stock, fictional, rhetorical figure is not a real person, yet it may represent those Jewish teachers/missionaries with whom Paul is in competition for the favor of the nations. In our mind the differences between Christian, Jew and pagan are sharp. In the mind of Paul and his readers there is no Christian, so the line between a Jewish follower of the Anointed and one who is not may not be as sharp as we imagine. What they share in common—being a fellow Jew—may be stronger than what they do not share, namely, trusting or not trusting in the Anointed. This seems counter-intuitive to us, but the sharp differentiation had not yet occurred. They do not have the categories of Jew and Christian to mark a clear division.

The caricature presents the teacher as pretentious:

> As for you now, you call yourself a Jew, you rest your hopes on the law of Moses, and you boast about your relation with God. Since you are trained in the law, you claim to know God's will and to discern what really matters. You're convinced that you're a guide for the blind, "a light for those in darkness," an instructor of the foolish and a teacher of the young. You appear to embody the knowledge and truth that are in the law. (Rom 2:17–20)

"You call yourself" implies that he is not a true Jew and his characteristics show him to be a proud teacher of the ignorant, the nations. Very much like the caricature Elmer Gantry or the real life preacher Jimmy Swaggert, the teacher does not practice what he preaches. It is important to consider how this caricature works. We are not surprised when things go astray for Swaggert or the televangelist Jim Bakker, yet we would never argue that this caricature is true of all pentecostal preachers. Likewise in this case, this is a caricature of a Jewish teacher; it does not characterize all Jewish teachers or even most and certainly not all Jews themselves.

> When you are teaching others, do you learn anything yourself? When you rant against stealing, are you yourself a thief? When you speak out against adultery, are you an adulterer? As someone who detests idols, have you made an idol of your own religion? You boast about the law; do you then dishonor God by breaking the law? It's just as it is written: "Because of you God's name is held in contempt among the peoples of the world (*lit:* the nations)." (Rom 2:21–24)

By quoting Isa 52:5 Paul turns the acknowledged disobedience and idolatry of the nations back on to the teacher as his fault. In order to make the quote fit its rhetorical purpose, Paul has altered it (Jewett, 230).

Having caricatured his opponent as a pretentious teacher, Paul now constructs a dialogue with him, technically a diatribe. I am following here the careful work of Stanley Stowers, the acknowledged expert on the diatribe literary form (162–65). The diatribe, or imagined conversation, runs from the beginning of chapter 3 through chapter 4. In order to understand the dialogue, the characters need to be marked out. The interlocutor is the Jewish teacher.

Paul's argument, which we saw above—"To be a Jew is rather to be one inwardly, and true circumcision is a matter of the heart" (Rom 2:29)—raises the interlocutor's question.

> *Interlocutor:* What's the advantage in being a Jew? Or what's the benefit of circumcision?
> *Paul:* A great advantage with many benefits. Above all, the Jews were entrusted with the words of God.
>   (Rom 3:1–2)

What are the "words of God," or as the KJ has it, "oracles of God"? Sam K. Williams, in an important article on the righteousness of God, has shown that "words of God" or

> *logia* refers to the promises of God. . . . One set [of promises] dominates and interprets all the rest. . . . Paul makes the Abraham story the center of the Law which illuminates the rest. (267)

Thus Paul's argument with the Jewish teacher is not about the goal, but the method. The Jewish teacher thinks the nations are made right by observing the law; Paul, by the faithfulness of the Anointed, to which Paul will turn after this portion of the dialogue (Rom 3:21–26).

The dialogue continues with the Jewish teacher speaking:

> *Interlocutor:* So what if some of them were unreliable? Surely, their unreliability doesn't invalidate God's reliability, does it?
> *Paul:* Absolutely not! Surely God must be true even if everyone else is false, "so that," as scripture says, "in all you say your justice shows and when you are accused you win your case." (Rom 3:2–4)

This poses the theodicy question: does the justice or righteousness of God depend upon a human response? If God does not remain faithful, God would not be God.

> *Interlocutor:* Wait a minute, [Paul,] if God's truthfulness is made more evident by my lying, so that God is glorified even more, why am I still being condemned as a sinner?
> *Paul:* [To follow your argument,] then why should we not "do evil so that good may come from it," as some people who slander us claim that we say? Such slanderers are rightly condemned.

Interlocutor: Well, [Paul,] are we Jews then better off than other people?
Paul: Not at all! We have already charged that Jews and Greeks alike are all prone to wrongdoing.
(Rom 3:7–9)

Paul is now back to his starting point. The pretentious teacher has nothing to boast in. Both Jews and Greeks "are all prone to wrongdoing." Yet there is a difference to which we will turn in the next chapter: the Jews do have the words of God. But Paul has yet to spell that out.

Self-Mastery

The situations in Rome and Galatia differ greatly. In Galatia Paul thinks he is confronting a situation similar to the conflict in Antioch—therefore the issue revolves around circumcision. But no one is advocating circumcision in Rome. There he is confronting the law's validity for the nations in a different context. The Jewish teacher introduced in Rom 2:17 portrays the law as a set of requirements, commandments, that if followed will lead to self-mastery.

Stanley Stowers in *A Rereading of Romans* (1994) has developed the ancient model of self-mastery as an important cultural code for reading Romans. His study has illuminated Romans, and I will follow his path. We will first examine the notion of self-mastery in general, then how it was applied in the imperial practice and Judaism, before returning to an analysis of Paul and self-mastery.

The Middle Course

The ancient world was what cultural anthropologists term a limited goods society. As the name suggests, all goods were limited. For example, if Hero has 10 denarii and Silvanus has none, it is because Hero is hoarding his 10 denarii. Because everything is limited, greed is such an important notion in the ancient world. "The greedy person stirs up strife, but whoever trusts in the LORD will be enriched" (Prov 28:25). Sharing is therefore the counterpoint to greed and necessary to make sure what limited goods exist are shared for the benefit of all. In a modern Western capitalist society we view goods as unlimited. If Mary has 100 dollars and Jack does not, then Jack should get his own 100 dollars. We see no direct connection between Mary having 100 dollars and Jack not having 100 dollars. In an unlimited goods society, innovation and growth are the goal. Limits are a handicap. This makes it difficult to deal with the fact that oil is a finite commodity, because ultimately we do not believe that, even if it does dangerously warm the climate. As Bruce Malina, who has stressed the importance of limited goods in understanding the ancient world, concludes:

> Thus extensive areas of behavior are patterned in such a way as to suggest to one and all that in society as well as in nature—the total environment—all the desired things in life, such as land, wealth, prestige, blood, health, semen, friendship and love, manliness, honor, respect and status, power and influence, security and safety—literally all good in life—exist in finite, limited quantity and are always in short supply. (89)

In a limited goods society luxury is a problem, so moderation is a form of self-mastery. Seneca the Elder warns, "It is the sign of a great spirit to be moderate in prosperity" (*Suasoriae*, 1.3). But this notion is traditional in Greek thought. In the myth of Daedalus and Icarus as famously retold by Ovid in his *Metamorphoses* (8.183–235), Icarus is warned by his father Daedalus "to fly the middle course"—to fly neither too low towards the sea nor too high towards the sun. Icarus, losing self-control, giving in to the joy of light, flies too high and the sun melts the wax holding his winds together. One of the three inscriptions on the temple of Delphi is "nothing in excess" (*mēden agan*; Plato, *Charmides*, 164d–165a).

Aristotle in *Nicomachean Ethics* associates the middle course with the golden mean, which in turn provides a good introduction to self-mastery.

> Similarly we become just by doing just acts, temperate by doing temperate acts, brave by doing brave acts. This truth is attested by the experience of states: lawgivers make the citizens good by training them in habits of right action—this is the aim of all legislation, and if it fails to do this it is a failure; this is what distinguishes a good form of constitution from a bad one.
> (*Nicomachean Ethics*, 2.1.5, 1103b)

Aristotle sets out his principle that one becomes a skilled doer by doing—or as the proverb has it, "practice makes perfect"—and then appeals to the purpose of law. The purpose of the law is to train a citizen in right behavior. So the purpose of the law is to teach self-mastery.

> Again, the actions from or through which any virtue is produced are the same as those through which it also is destroyed—just as is the case with skill in the arts, for both . . . with builders and all the other craftsmen: as you will become a good builder from building well, so you will become a bad one from building badly. Were this not so, there would be no need for teachers of the arts, but everybody would be born a good or bad craftsman as the case might be. (*Nicomachean Ethics*, 2.1.6–7, 1103b)

Virtue as skill is not innate but learned, and learned by practice and from a teacher.

> The same then is true of the virtues. It is by taking part in transactions with our fellow-men that some of us become just and others unjust; by acting in dangerous situations and forming a habit of fear or of confidence we become courageous or cowardly. And the same holds good of our dispositions with regard to the appetites, and anger; some men become temperate and gentle, others profligate and irascible, by actually comporting themselves in one way or the other in relation to those passions. In a word, our moral dispositions are formed as a result of the corresponding activities. Hence it is incumbent on us to control the character of our activities, since on the quality of these depends the quality of our dispositions. It is therefore not of small moment whether we are trained from childhood in one set of habits or another; on the contrary it is of very great, or rather of supreme, importance. (*Nicomachean Ethics*, 2.1.7–8, 1103b)

Aristotle has laid out the basic understanding of self-mastery in the ancient world. It represents the moderate course, the golden mean. As Daedalus warned Icarus, safety lies in the middle course. Horace repeats the notion:

> Better wilt thou live, Licinius, by neither always pressing out to sea nor too closely hugging the dangerous shore in cautious fear of storms. Whoso cherishes the golden mean, safely avoids the foulness of an ill-kept house and discreetly, too, avoids a hall exciting envy. (*Odes*, 2.10.1–5)

Furthermore as Aristotle indicates, self-mastery is both learned by practice, inculcated from an early age, and must be taught.

Self-mastery partakes in the hierarchical structure of the ancient world. As such it is primarily a male value. Males are supposed to be in control; women are out of control. Therefore it is assumed in the ancient world that women, children, slaves and barbarians are in need of rule because they cannot control themselves. To rule others, the elite must master their own passions. As Democritus remarks, "Immoderate desire is the mark of a child, not a man" (translation Freeman, #70, 101). Xenophon shows this same consideration in selecting a leader.

> But if self-control too is a fair and noble possession, let us now consider whether he led men up to that virtue by discourse like the following:
>
> > My friends, if we were at war and wanted to choose a leader most capable of helping us to save ourselves and conquer the enemy, should we choose one whom we knew to be the slave of the belly, or of wine, or lust, or sleep? How could we expect that such a one would either save us or defeat the enemy? (*Memorabilia*, 1.5.1).

Stowers shrewdly notes how ancient psychology mirrors the organization of the empire. The interior struggle of the individual for self-mastery replicates the empire's effort to control the chaos that threatens.

> Just as intense competition characterizes social life, so a violent competition within characterizes those who aspire to moral excellence and self-mastery. Just as a hierarchy that put everyone in the empire except the emperor under the rule of someone and made a small part of the population masters of others, so the soul was to be master of the body and reason over the passions. (48)

Augustus

Self-mastery was a major aspect of Augustus' imperial propaganda. In the attack on Anthony, his relationship with Cleopatra allowed Augustus to picture Anthony as a non-Roman who had taken on the luxurious and effeminate ways of the East. He was being ruled by a woman. Anthony was identified with Dionysus and Augustus with Apollo. When Plutarch in his *Life of Anthony* reports on the Senate voting for an attack on Anthony and Cleopatra, these themes emerge.

> When Caesar [Octavian] had made sufficient preparations, a vote was passed to wage war against Cleopatra, and to take away from Antony the authority which he had surrendered to a woman. And Caesar said in addition that Antony had been drugged and was not even master of himself, and that the Romans were carrying on war with Mardion the eunuch, and Potheinus and Iras, the tire-woman [lady's maid] of Cleopatra, and Charmion, by whom the principal affairs of the government were managed. (59.60)

Augustus' legislation on marriage and morality was part of a return to traditional Roman values, of which self-mastery was a prime example. Even though this legislation was more observed in the breech than in practice, its propaganda import was considerable. Seutonius' report is intriguing.

> He [Augustus] revised existing law and enacted some new ones, for example on extravagance, on adultery and chastity, on bribery, and on the encouragement of marriage among the various classes of citizens. Having made somewhat more stringent changes in the last of these than in the others, he was unable to carry it out because of an open revolt against its provisions, until he had abolished or mitigated a part of the penalties, besides increasing the rewards and allowing a three years' exemption from the obligation to marry after the death of a husband or wife. When the knights even then persistently called for its repeal at a public show, he sent for the children of Germanicus and exhibited them, some in his own lap and some in their father's, intimating by his gestures and expression that they should not refuse to follow that young man's example. And on finding that the spirit of the law was being evaded by betrothal with immature girls and by frequent changes of wives, he shortened the duration of betrothals and set a limit on divorce. (*Augustus*, 34)

Even Augustus' wife Livia wore homespun clothing as sign of return to the values of those modest and hardy ancient Romans. Ronald Syme in his classic study of the reign of Augustus, *The Roman Revolution*, notes that all of this is clearly propaganda because Augustus' family was hardly an upholder of family values— he himself was a womanizer and his daughter Julia was banished from the capital for immoral living (426).

Jewish Self-Mastery

Jews also were caught up in this Greco-Roman tradition of self-mastery. The Jewish law became a way to contrast the demands of law with the life of pagans. The Wisdom of Solomon, like Paul in Rom 1:18–32, contains a tirade against idolatry.

> Then it was not enough for them to err about the knowledge of God, but though living in great strife due to ignorance, they call such great evils peace. For whether they kill children in their initiations, or celebrate secret mysteries, or hold frenzied revels with strange customs, they no longer keep either their lives or their marriages pure, but they either treacherously kill one another, or grieve one another by adultery, and all is a raging riot of blood and murder, theft and deceit, corruption, faithlessness, tumult, perjury, confusion over what is good, forgetfulness of favors, defiling of souls, sexual perversion, disorder in marriages, adultery, and debauchery. For the worship of idols not to be named is the beginning and cause and end of every evil. For their worshipers either rave in exultation, or prophesy lies, or live unrighteously, or readily commit perjury; for because they trust in lifeless idols they swear wicked oaths and expect to suffer no harm. But just penalties will overtake them on two counts: because they thought wrongly about God in devoting themselves to idols, and because in deceit they swore unrighteously through contempt for holiness. For it is not the power of the things by which people swear, but the just penalty for those who sin, that always pursues the transgression of the unrighteous. (Wis 14:22–31 NRSV)

For the author of the Wisdom of Solomon, the nations are by nature sinners, the same assumption that Paul makes in Gal 2:15—"We ourselves are Jews by birth and not Gentile sinners" (NRSV). They lack the true knowledge of God and as a result their lives are out of control.

Philo casts the Jewish law as a law of self-mastery and as the highest form of that law. "The law holds that all who conform to the sacred constitution laid down by Moses must be exempt from every unreasoning passion and every vice to a higher degree than those who are governed by other laws, and that this particularly applies to those who are appointed to act as judges by lot or election" (*Special Laws*, 4.55). Moses himself is pictured as the ideal of self-mastery.

All these it seems the most holy Moses observed and therefore discarded passion in general and detesting it, as most vile and in its effects, denounced especially desire as a battery of destruction to the soul, which must be done away with or brought into obedience to the governance of reason, and then all things will be permeated through and through with peace and good order, those perfect forms of the good which bring the full perfection of happy living. (*Special Laws,* 4.95)

The high moral code of the Torah provided Judaism with a built-in appeal to those seeking to practice self-mastery, and various Jewish thinkers were ready to exploit it.

Paul's Response

Paul himself exemplifies this same understanding of self-mastery as evidenced in his use of athletic metaphors.

You surely know that all of the runners in the stadium are in the race, but only one wins the prize. So you should run to win. All who engage in athletic competition discipline themselves about everything. They do that to receive a perishable prize, but we for an imperishable one. For that reason I don't run as if I had no goal in mind nor do I box just to punch the air. But I punish my body and make it submit to my aim, so that after I have preached to others I myself do not fail to qualify. (1 Cor 9:24–27)

He shares Hellenistic Judaism's buy-in to the scheme of self-mastery. He agrees with the Wisdom of Solomon on the state of the nations as idolaters. Idolatry is the root of all their problems and as a result their passions and desires have taken control. They are in need of self-mastery.

The imaginary Jewish teacher in Romans is like the real Jewish philosopher Philo in that both think the law is the guide to the nations that will lead them to self-mastery. Paul's description of this imaginary Jewish teacher portrays him as an instructor of the nations in the ways of the law.

Since you are trained in the law, you claim to know God's will and to discern what really matters. You're convinced that you're a guide for the blind, "a light for those in darkness," an instructor of the foolish and a teacher of the young. You appear to embody the knowledge and truth that are in the law. (Rom 2:18–20)

The imaginary teacher's program is teaching the nations the way of the law as a form of self-mastery. Paul accepts that the nations need self-mastery; he agrees that their desires and passions have run amok, because idolatry has darkened their minds. Paul however disagrees that self-mastery can be taught. What he condemns as works of the law is use of the law as self-mastery.

The situation in Rome is very different from that in Galatia. In Galatia, Paul is battling members of the nations who believe they must be circumcised. That is the work of the law that he finds overturns the freedom of the good news. In Romans, his readers, also members of the nations, are not tempted by circumcision, but by the law as a way of self-mastery. They probably see Jesus as a teacher of the law as a way of self-mastery. They may have encountered Jewish teachers, who may or may not have been members of the Jesus movement, who like Philo view the law, especially the Ten Commandments, as the way to teach the nations self-mastery.

Romans 7:7–25 has traditionally been read as part of Paul's autobiography. Reading it this way is almost intuitive for us. Such an autobiographical reading fits perfectly into the Augustinian/Lutheran interpretation since it provides the reason for Paul's conversion to Christianity, namely his guilt at being unable to fulfill the law. But the way to resist this reading is to remind ourselves of our previous conclusions.

- Paul did not convert.
- He was not guilty about his inability to fulfill the law. Rather as he says in Phil 3:6: "In regard to the requirements of the law, I was flawless."

If we remember these two points, then Rom 7:7–25 cannot be Paul's autobiographical comment. So how should we read it? The dramatic shift in the voice of the speaker, from third person in Rom 7:6 to first person in verse 7 signals a shift. Beginning at Rom 7:7 through 7:25 Paul invokes an ancient rhetorical technique called speech-in-character (*prosōpopoiia*). Origen, among other ancient commentators, recognized that Paul was using this rhetorical device (Stowers, 1994: 265). So who is this character that Paul is creating in his speech? It is the voice of a member of the nations who is relating his experience with the law.

My point is that I would not have become aware of what the seductive power of corruption (*lit:* sin) is, were it not for the law.
For example, I would not have been aware of what's wrong with
excessive desire for what others have, if the law had not said,
"You shall not covet." But the power of corruption used this prohibition to deceive me and to arouse all kinds of excessive desire
in me. Without the law the power of corruption (*lit:* sin) is as
good as dead. (Rom 7:7–8)

The character speaking is a member of the nations relating
his experience with the law. The law increases the awareness of
sin and the commandment "You shall not covet" indicates that the
Ten Commandments as a guide to self-mastery is under discussion. It arouses excessive desire, which is what it was supposed to
control.

There was a time when I was living without reference to the
law. But when that prohibition came to my attention, the power
of corruption (*lit:* sin) came to life and my earlier innocent self
"died." I discovered in my own experience that the very commandment whose purpose was to lead me to life led me to death.
For the power of corruption (*lit:* sin) used this moral command
to deceive me and by this means put my naïve self to death.
    (Rom 7:9–11)

The purpose of the Law is life. "It is clear, then, that the law is
grounded in the sacred and that the moral command is pure and
just and good" (Rom 7:12). But this person is led to death. Why?
Because the law is not being used for its sacred purpose. This is
a key point that overturns the traditional autobiographical reading and points us towards its correct rhetorical reading. The law's
sacred purpose is not self-mastery, but as E. P. Sanders argued, for
a Jew its sacred purpose is to fulfill the covenantal obligation (see
chapter 12).

We know that the law has its origin in the divine realm, but I
am a creature of the earth, sold as a slave and in bondage to the
power of corruption. I don't understand what I find myself doing. I do not accomplish what I intend, but what I actually do I
deplore. If what I do is not what I intend, then I am really con-
curring with the law that it is good. In that case it can no longer
be thought that I am the one who is doing this; what's doing

this is the corrupting power (*lit:* sin) that has taken up residence in me. I recognize that the good does not reside in me, I mean my earthly life. I have the capacity to intend what is right, but I cannot make it happen. I do not accomplish the good I intend, the bad I do not intend is what I actually bring about. If I bring about what I do not intend, then it is no longer I who produce this, but the corrupting power (*lit:* sin) that has taken up residence in me. (Rom 7:14–20)

Idolatry has so blinded the person that they can no longer do what they intend. This is the classic Jewish view of the idolatrous state of the nations. Their minds are so obscured by idolatry that they cannot reason and their desires take over. The inner/outer conflict of the self at war is characteristic of the struggle for self-mastery.

So I take it to be a fact of life: that when I intend to do the good, the bad is right there at my side. I rejoice in the law of God so far as my inner self is concerned, but I observe another law in my outward acts at war with the law of my mind and this other law—the law of corrupting power—takes me captive. What a sorry creature am I! Who will rescue me from this earthly self which is captive to death? Thanks be to God, the rescue has come through Jesus, God's Anointed, our lord. So then, left to myself I am mentally devoted to God's law, but in my worldly life I'm enslaved to the law of corruption. (Rom 7:21–25)

Self-mastery has correctly identified the problem, the control of the desires and passions, the illumination of the mind darkened by idolatry.

Just so, my friends, you symbolically died to the jurisdiction of the law when you identified yourselves with the crucified body of the Anointed, so that you could be free to commit yourselves to another, to the one who was raised from the dead, in order that we may be productive in the service of God. (Rom 7:4)

For Paul the only way out of the enslavement caused by idolatry is by identifying with the crucified body of the Anointed. Paul once again returns to the oxymoronic scandal that is at the heart of his good news: the cross and identification with the Anointed crucified that shatters the idolatry by which the elemental powers hold the nations in their sway.

Paul's speech-in-character is not autobiographical nor does it describe Jewish despair in trying to follow the Torah. It is rather the despair of a member of the nations who has been left out of the covenant and tries to use the law, the Ten Commandments, as a guide to self-mastery. This speech-in-character is Paul's construction and represents his take on a member of the nations who tries to overcome sin, to attain self-mastery apart from identification with Jesus the Anointed.

Readings

Aristotle. *Aristotle*. Vol. 19. 23 vols. Trans. H. Rackham. Loeb Classical Library. Cambridge: Harvard University Press, 1934.

Elliott, Neil, and Mark Reasoner, eds. *Documents and Images for the Study of Paul*. Minneapolis: Fortress Press, 2011.

Freeman, Kathleen, trans. *The Pre-Socratic Philosophers: A Companion to Diels, Fragmente Der Vorsokratiker*. 3d ed. Oxford: B. Blackwell, 1953.

Gager, John G. *Reinventing Paul*. New York: Oxford University Press, 2000.

Horace. *Horace, Odes and Epodes*. Trans. C. E. Bennett. Loeb Classical Library. Cambridge: Harvard University Press, 1952.

Jewett, Robert. *Romans: A Commentary*. Hermeneia. Ed. Roy David Kotansky and Eldon Jay Epp. Minneapolis: Fortress Press, 2007.

Kuhn, Thomas S. *The Structure of Scientific Revolutions*. Chicago: University of Chicago Press, 1970.

Malina, Bruce J. *The New Testament World: Insights from Cultural Anthropology*. Louisville, KY: Westminster/Knox, 2001.

Ovid. *Ovid III: Metamorphoses, Books I–VIII*. Trans. Frank Justus Miller and G. P. Goold. 3d ed. Loeb Classical Library. Cambridge, MA/London: Harvard University Press, 1916.

Philo. *Philo*. Vol. 8. 10 vols. Trans. F. H. Colson. Loeb Classical Library, no. 341. Cambridge: Harvard University Press, 1930.

Plutarch. *Plutarch's Lives*. Vol. 9. 11 vols. Trans. Bernadotte Perrin. Loeb Classical Library, no. 103. Cambridge: Harvard University Press, 1920.

Seneca. *Declamations of the Elder Seneca*. Vol. 2. 2 vols. Trans. Michael Winterbottom. Loeb Classical Library, no. 464. London: Heineman, 1974.

Stowers, Stanley K. *A Rereading of Romans: Justice, Jews, and Gentiles*. New Haven/London: Yale University Press, 1994.

Syme, Ronald. *The Roman Revolution*. London: Oxford University Press, 1960.

Williams, Sam K. "The 'Righteousness of God' in Romans." *Journal of Biblical Literature* 99 (1980) 241–90.

Xenophon. *Xenophon.* Vol. 4. 7 vols. Trans. E. C. Marchant. Loeb Classical Library, no. 168. Cambrdge: Harvard University Press, 1923.

Chapter 14

Advantage Israel

In the traditional model, Paul converts to Christianity and rejects Judaism. Christianity actually replaces Judaism. Christianity is about faith and grace; Judaism, works and legalism. We have seen that this model, which has been dominant since the late first century or early second century, is a massive misinterpretation of Paul. Slowly, piece-by-piece, we have built up another interpretation of Paul, one that situates him in the period before 70 CE, before the destruction of the Temple, and in the Roman Empire, preaching an apocalyptic good news in conflict with the good news of Rome. Now we turn to what supposedly Paul had rejected, Judaism, and ask, "what advantage is Israel?"

Ioudaioi

As always, there is a problem of translation. The Greek word *Ioudaioi* has a double meaning. Primarily it has an ethnic-geographic reference, people from Judea, that is, Judeans. The word has an extended sense of those who practice the religion of Judea, in short, Jews. English makes an explicit difference with two words, Judeans and Jews, between the ethnic-geographic identity (Judean) and the religious identity (Jew); Greek did not. Greek used one word, English uses two. In Paul's time the word was used in both senses.

Ioudaioi is used in both senses in the New Testament. John 7:1–2 is a good example of the ambiguity. The NRSV translates as follows:

> After this Jesus went about in Galilee. He did not wish to go about in Judea because the Jews were looking for an opportunity to kill him. Now the Jewish festival of Booths was near.

There are two place names, Galilee and Judea, and in Greek *Ioudaioi* occurs twice. The NRSV translates the first one "Jews" and the second "Jewish." It would appear that the first occurrence refers to people from the place, an ethnic-geographic usage, while the second refers to the religious aspect. So *The Complete Gospels* translates it as follows:

> After this, Jesus moved around in Galilee; he decided not to go into Judea, because the Judeans were looking for a chance to kill him. The Jewish festival of Sukkoth was coming.

Paul does not use the word in the ethnic-geographic sense of Judean. For him, it always has the religious sense.

A number of scholars, translators, and even the authoritative *A Greek-English Lexicon of the New Testament* (BDAG) have argued that in the New Testament and Paul *Ioudaioi* should be translated "Judeans" for several reasons.

- Christianity has freighted the meaning of "The Jews."
- Judaism has evolved since the first century.

The use of Judeans as a translation for *Ioudaioi* has the advantage of warning the contemporary reader of Paul to beware of loading onto the word the over-determined and negative view of Judaism imparted from Christian assumptions, even Christian anti-Semitism. Since Paul does not share those assumptions, it makes it difficult to arrive at a new understanding of Paul and Judaism if we persist in using the same loaded term. Frankly I found this argument persuasive when working on the SV translation of *The Complete Gospels* (1992, revised 2010). Moreover, I have followed this same strategy in dealing with other words that have a loaded or freighted meaning. For example, we have avoided translating *pistis* as "faith" (chapter 8), and we have translated *ethnē* as "nations" and not "gentiles," much less "Gentiles" (chapter 5). These new translations have aided in blocking out the traditional understanding and opening up space for a new understanding of Paul. It has helped to focus on the real issues.

Modern Judaism, in all its varied forms, is different from ancient Judaism in all its different forms. Ancient religions were imbedded throughout a society and culture, while in the modern Western context they are separate and private. Modern religions are an institution; ancient religions were woven into the fabric of society. Mary Beard, John North, and Simon Price in their *Religions of Rome* state this well.

> When we look, therefore, at the way religion and society interacted, we do not find special institutions and activities, set aside from everyday life and designed to pursue religious activities; but rather a situation in which religion and its associated rituals were embedded in all institutions and activities. . . . The whole of the political and constitutional system was conducted within an elaborate network of religious ceremonial and regulation which had the effect of bringing the time, space and hence the validity of political action into the divine sphere. . . . All important areas of life, public or private, had some religious correlates. (43)

Yet while there is considerable discontinuity with ancient Judaism, modern Judaism maintains a historical continuity with ancient Judaism, a stronger continuity than any modern form of Christianity does with the ancient Jesus movement.

Bruce Malina and John Pilch have argued that "the vast majority of modern Jews" are descended from "ninth century Central Asian converts to Talmud based Jewishness, the Khazars (also known as Ashkenazi Jews)" (365). This argument strikes me as strange and puts the accent on the ethnic difference, which seems beside the point. On the other hand, Amy-Jill Levine rightly protests against Malina and Pilch (Levine, 164–65) but I think goes too far when dealing with other scholarly proposals. She says, "The Jew is replaced with the Judean, and thus we have a *Judenrein* ('Jew-free') text, a text purified of Jews" (160). The German Nazi phrase is perhaps rhetorically too strong. Levine knows that these are difficult translation issues, not easily settled.

Shaye Cohen in his *The Beginnings of Jewishness* studied the usage of the Greek *Ioudaios*, Latin *Judaeus*, and Hebrew *Yehudi* and concluded:

> "Jew" (at least in English) is a religious term: a Jew is someone who venerates the God of the Judaeans, the God whose temple is in Jerusalem (the capital of Judaea). "Jew," then, denotes culture, way of life, or "religion," not ethnic or geographic origin.
>
> In the Hellenistic period, virtually all "Judaeans" will have been Jews; that is, virtually all the members of the Judaean *ethnos* will have worshipped the God whose temple is in Jerusalem." (105)

It is important not to import into the words "Judaism" or "Jews" the baggage of Christian anti-Judaism or anti-Semitism. On the other hand, it is equally important not to deprive Judaism of its preferred terminology because of our Christian problem. There is no perfect solution for this issue.

In this book I have employed "Jews" as a translation for *Ioudaioi* with the caveat that Judaism in Paul's usage is not the opposite of Christianity and that Paul did not convert from Judaism to Christianity. He remained a Jew. These assumptions adopted as conclusions from our analysis early on in this book have opened up the understanding of Paul's letters. The translators of *The Authentic Letters of Paul* also have employed "Jews" as the translation for *Ioudaioi*.

Jews and Greeks

Ten times Paul uses the phrase "Jews and Greeks," always in the same order. Five of these occurrences are in Romans, four in 1 Corinthians, and one in Galatians. Twice the phrase is repeated in close proximity, Rom 2:9–10 and 1 Cor 1:22–24.

Romans 1:16 can serve as the archetype of this phrase.

> I'm not embarrassed by this news, because it has the power to transform those who are persuaded by it, first Jews and then Greeks. God's character is shown by this news to be trustworthy and that leads to having confidence in God, just as scripture says: "The one who decides to live on the basis of confidence in God is the one who gets it right." (Rom 1:16–7)

From the point of view of the Christian doctrine of supersessionism, the "first Jews and then Greeks" implies a narrative in which the good news is first preached to the Jews and then after their rejecting it, God turns to the Greeks or Gentiles (with a capital G; see Barrett, 29). But as we have seen in chapter 5 "To the Nations," these assumptions are not Paul's.

The grouping Jew and Greek indicates that Paul sees them tied together but not merged. The point of view is Jewish, as one would expect with Paul as the author. "First" probably applies to God's judgment. In Rom 1:18 which begins a new section, God's just indignation or wrath (*orgē*) "is being shown against all disre-

gard of God and God's justice." Paul then elaborates the disobedience of the nations and finally in chapter 2 moves to judgment.

> But actually because of your stony and stubborn hearts you're
> compounding the consequences for yourselves that come due on
> the day of God's just indignation, when divine judgment will be
> made clear and when God will pay back each person according
> to what each person has done. (Rom 2:5-6)

The "you" are the nations whose vices worthy of judgment are
fulsomely described in Rom 1:18-32.

> Even though they knew about God, they failed to honor or give
> God what God is due. Instead, their thinking became warped
> and their muddled minds grew clouded. Although they por-
> trayed themselves as enlightened, they became fools. They traded
> the majesty of the immortal God for imitations—a likeness of a
> mortal man, as well as of birds, cattle, and reptiles.
> (Rom 1:21-23; see chapter 13, "Apart from the Law").

Paul makes it clear that the priority of Jew and Greek refers to
judgment in what follows:

> There will be distress and anguish for every single human being
> who does evil, first the Jew and then the Greek; but praise, honor,
> and peace for everyone who does what is good, first the Jew and
> then the Greek, because God has no favorite people.
> (Rom 2:9-11)

The reference to Jews and Greeks in Romans 3 likewise shows
that the context is judgment. When the imaginary Jewish teacher
asks:

> *Interlocutor:* [Well, Paul,] are we Jews then better off than other
> people?
> *Paul:* Not at all! We have already charged that Jews and Greeks
> alike are all prone to wrongdoing.
> (Rom 3:9)

For Paul, if God is impartial in condemnation, so also in generosity.

> For it is in the heart that one comes to have the confidence in
> God that leads to integrity, and it is with the mouth that one
> acknowledges what leads to salvation. Remember that scripture

says, "None of those who put their confidence in God will have cause for embarrassment." There is no distinction between Jew and Greek, because the same one is lord of all and is generous to all who appeal to him. (Rom 10:10–12)

Throughout Romans, the use of Jew and Greek has in mind God's dealing with all at judgment. So then, why not say, "all men"? Why divide humankind into two groups? Paul is clearly trying to point to all humankind, yet he wants to make a distinction, a distinction that he surely thinks is important.

This same usage of oneness with distinction, but without the element of judgment, is present in 1 Corinthians 1. "Since in the larger scheme of God's wisdom the world (*kosmos*) did not come to acknowledge God through its own wisdom" (1 Cor 1:21a). This has been a fundamental plank in his program—humans, the world, cannot attain their own salvation by their own efforts. He has argued that is true of both Jews and Greeks. "God decided to save those who embrace God's world-transforming news through the 'nonsense' that we preach" (1 Cor 1:21b).

Paul then offers an account as to why his nonsensical good news has been rejected:

At a time when Jews expect a miracle and Greeks seek enlightenment, we speak about God's Anointed crucified! This is an offense to Jews, nonsense to the nations; but to those who have heard God's call, both Jews and Greeks, the Anointed represents God's power and God's wisdom; because the folly of God is wiser than humans are and the weakness of God is stronger than humans are. (1 Cor 1:22–25)

Jew and Greek represent two different ways in which the world rejects God's wisdom, the folly of the cross.

Jews seek a miracle (*lit:* signs).
Greeks seek enlightenment (*lit:* wisdom).

Yet in response to the nonsense of the cross, Paul refers to Jews and the nations, in which case nations clearly stands in for Greeks. On the positive side, Jews and Greeks represent all who have heard the good news.

Finally in the baptismal formula in 1 Cor 12:13 and Gal 3:28, the distinction between Jew and Greek is the first one listed as overcome in the Anointed.

Just as the body has many parts and all of the parts, even though there are many of them, are still parts of one body, so is the body of the Anointed. For we were all baptized by the same power of God into one body, whether we were Jews or Greeks, slaves or free, and we were all invited to imbibe the same divine power.
(1 Cor 12:12–13)

The parallel passage in Galatians employs the formula as Paul plays out how difference becomes the same.

So, every one of you who has been baptized into solidarity with God's Anointed has become invested with the status of God's Anointed. You are no longer Jew or Greek, no longer slave or freeborn, no longer "male and female." Instead, you all have the same status in the service of God's Anointed, Jesus. Moreover, if you now belong to God's Anointed, that also makes you Abraham's offspring and—as promised—his heirs. (Gal 3:27–29)

These distinctions no longer count in the solidarity of the Anointed's body, but the distinctions are still real. Paul confidently quotes the baptismal formula because he knows his community accepts it—something on which they will not disagree with him.

Yet we are still back to the same question. Why represent all of humanity, the world (*kosmos*), with the division Jew and Greek? Why is it set in parallel with the slave and free, male and female? These latter divisions represent fundamental divides in the Greco-Roman world. So Paul must also understand Jew and Greek (nations) as a fundamental divide. Why? Is this just an example of ethnic snobbery? I think not. In Galatians he concludes: "if you [Jew and Greek] now belong to God's Anointed, that also makes you Abraham's offspring and—as promised—his heirs." This is our clue: Abraham's covenant.

Two Covenants

Paul apparently sees two covenants descending from Abraham: one covenant for the circumcised and one for the uncircumcised. Part of the problem is that Paul speaks very little about the covenant with the circumcised because he is concerned with the uncircumcised, the nations. Unlike the traditional Augustinian/ Lutheran interpretation, Paul does not see the covenant with the uncircumcised replacing that with the circumcised. Rather in

First Letter to the Thessalonians

This is surely the earliest extant letter of Paul's to survive and the earliest writing in the New Testament. The Thessalonians have only recently "turned away from lifeless images in order to serve the living and real God" (1 Thess 1:9). The letter was written from Corinth around 50–51 CE. Paul responds to some questions they have about those who have died and the return of the lord.

Paul's model the covenant with the uncircumcised fulfills or completes the promise made to Abraham that he would be the father of all nations. Previously that promise had only been partially fulfilled in the covenant with the circumcised. Paul envisions two covenants, the first one with the Jews and the second one with the nations. Both are required to complete God's promise made to Abraham. The first covenant with Israel has been in operation since Abraham and continues in operation. The second with the nations has only now come about with the faithfulness of the Anointed, which parallels and completes the faithfulness of Abraham.

In Rom 1:18–31 Paul does not hesitate to enumerate the vices of the nations brought on by their idolatry and disobedience. Apart from the Anointed, the nations cannot avoid the wrath of God and God's coming punishment. But Romans is not the only letter in which Paul enumerates the state of the nations before they have partaken in the faithfulness of the Anointed. In addressing the Thessalonians, who had only recently abandoned idols to turn to the true God (1 Thess 1:9), Paul contrasts how a man who is in the Anointed approaches his wife compared with a man who is not.

> God wants you to keep your distance from sexual immorality. Each one of you should know how to treat his own wife with respect and honor and not as a sexual object as do nations who do not know God. Nor should you offend or deceive your brother in sexual matters, because the lord is one who will see that justice is done in all such matters, as we clearly warned you before. For our God has not called us to loose living but to a life of virtue.

Therefore, anyone who rejects this is not rejecting human advice but the God who breathes the spirit of goodness into you.
(1 Thess 4:3–8)

A man should not approach his wife as a sexual object, literally, with a passion of desire or lust. The member of the nations before being in the Anointed is controlled by desire, that is, lacks self-mastery. But mastery of desire comes with faithfulness like the Anointed's, as a gift and a call. God has called them to a life of virtue and has breathed the spirit of goodness, literally, has given his holy breath (spirit).

In 1 Cor 6:9–11, Paul provides a remarkable list of vices that characterized the Corinthians before they were cleansed in baptism.

Don't you know that wrongdoers are not going to inherit the Empire of God? Don't let anyone mislead you; neither those who consort with prostitutes nor those who follow phony gods, neither adulterers nor promiscuous people, nor pederasts, neither the thieving nor the greedy, neither drunkards nor those who engage in verbal abuse nor swindlers are going to inherit the Empire of God. And these are what some of you were. But you have been cleansed, you have a new relation with God through the name of the lord, Jesus the Anointed, and through the presence and power (*lit:* breath or spirit) of our God. (1 Cor 6:9–11)

Notice the prominent place of idolatry and sexual immorality. Idolatry leads to uncontrolled desires: "So God handed them over in their cravings" (Rom 1:24). This is Paul's Jewish assumption of how the nations behave without the benefits of the covenant and the law. Or as Paul tells Cephas in Antioch, "We are Jews by nature and not sinners from among the nations" (Gal 2:15 NRSV).

Significantly there is no parallel listing of Jewish vices in Paul's letters. The vice lists apply only to the nations, not the Jews. Jews do not suffer from the consequences of idolatry. "Even though they [the nations] knew about God, they failed to honor, or give God what God is due. Instead, their thinking became warped and their muddled minds grew clouded" (Rom 1:21). Jews, on the other hand, "knew about God," and did not fail "to honor or give God what God is due." As a result, their thinking was not warped nor their minds muddled. So God did not hand them over to their cravings. Thus their covenant with God is working.

Likewise, Paul does not mount an argument about the insufficiency of the Jewish covenant or the Temple, although many New Testament scholars think he does (for example, Jewett, 290). But there is simply no evidence for this. Such a belief derives from a later period after the Temple in Jerusalem had been destroyed. Such an anachronistic view has led Christian scholars to interpret Paul as replacing the Temple with Jesus the Anointed lord.

But when Jews sin, they have a way in the covenant, the law, and the Temple to gain God's forgiveness. In Rom 9:4–5 Paul lists the advantages of the Jews:

> They are Israelites. They were given the sonship, the splendor of God's presence (*lit:* glory), the covenants, the legal tradition, the sacred rituals, the promises. They were also given the patriarchs, and the Anointed is physically descended from them.

This listing of Jewish advantages begins a discussion of the significance of Israel's failure to respond to the good news. But that lack of response does not lead Paul to say that Israel is now in the same state as the nations. They still have their advantages. First of which is that they are Israelites, God's chosen people. They still have the sonship and therefore the inheritance. They reflect God's glory, while the nations "traded the majesty (*lit:* glory) of the immortal God for imitations—a likeness of a mortal man, as well as of birds, cattle, and reptiles" (Rom 1:23). The Jews still have "the covenants, the legal tradition, the sacred rituals, the promises." The covenant is still in place; so is the law and Temple. Paul envisions none of this at risk; it is all still operational. So the implication is not that Israel has failed or that its advantages have been taken away, but that its future is yet to be fulfilled.

There is no hint that even with their rejection of the Anointed they have fallen into idolatry. Their state is very different from that of the nations.

Furthermore, Paul envisions two different covenants, both derived from the promise made to Abraham. The first with Israel encompasses the law as the requirement of covenantal obedience, what Sanders describes as covenantal nomism. The second with the nations is inaugurated by the faithfulness of the Anointed, as whose envoy Paul announces the good news of this new relationship with God and the nations.

FATE OF ISRAEL

More than a half-century ago, Johannes Munck in *Paul and the Salvation of Mankind* (1959) pointed towards the centrality of Romans 9–11, where Paul deals with the fate of Israel, over and against the standard Lutheran exegesis, which saw the climax of Romans at 3:26, traditionally understood as concerning justification by faith. His book signaled the beginning of an important reorientation in the understanding of Romans. Nils Dahl, another Scandinavian who long taught at Yale, made a careful argument that Romans 9–11 "addresses the epistolary situation more directly than in most parts of Romans 1–8" (141). A number of scholars have argued, recently, that the specific situation that Paul's letter to the Romans has in mind is the return of the Jewish exiles after their expulsion from Rome by Claudius in 49 CE and Nero's rescinding of that edict early in his reign, probably in 54 CE.

Paul is addressing, as the title of Neil Elliott's book (20, 96–100) indicates, the *Arrogance of the Nations* at the state and status of the returning Jews. As in Paul's other letters where he addresses a specific situation, in his letter to the Romans he confronts a particular situation in the Roman community. The exiled Jews are returning to Rome, disadvantaged under Claudius and Nero. The community members from among the nations have absorbed the point of view of the empire, and view themselves as at an advantage compared to the recently exiled Jews. As Elliott has observed:

> It is the non-Judean church—not Paul—that announced the "falling" of Israel and conflated that "theological fact" with their own ascendancy as believers in Christ, speaking of themselves being "grafted in" to replace the branches that were "broken off." That ecclesial arrogance is not grounded in any theological perception of Israel that Paul shares with his audience. (110)

Paul inaugurates this discussion by enumerating the advantages of Israel, with which we have just dealt. Those advantages are considerable, as we have seen, and not in jeopardy, even though Christian exegesis often assumes they have been taken away and given to the "Gentiles."

Prior to the announcement in Rom 9:4–5 of Israel's advantages, Paul summarizes the situation of those among the nations who are in the Anointed. Rhetorically it depends upon the pattern of "if now this, how much more to come."

> I regard the sufferings of the present pregnant moment as nothing compared with the future splendor to be revealed to us. For the whole creation eagerly anticipates the disclosure of who God's children really are. (Rom 8:18–19)

But not only creation awaits the transformation, but also those who are in the Anointed.

> We know that the whole creation has been moaning with birth pangs till now; and not only the creation, but we who have savored the first taste of God's power also sigh within ourselves while we await our adoption, the release and transformation of our bodies from their earthly limitations and fate. (Rom 8:22–3)

The "if now, how much more then" pattern governs this whole section. Not only will creation be transformed, but so will the bodies of the faithful. From this Paul draws the conclusion:

> If God is for us, what does it matter who is against us? How can we think that the One who did not spare God's own son (from suffering and death), but allowed this to happen to him for our sake, will not also graciously give us, along with him, the whole world (*lit:* all things)? (Rom 8:31–32)

Paul's principle is straightforward. "If God is for us, who can be against us?" (Rom 8:31 NRSV). The proof follows from the giving of his son in crucifixion. This invokes Paul's apocalyptic scenario in which at the end all things will be subjected to God, which implies that now they are not. The crucifixion demonstrates how out of control the powers of this world are, but they have stirred up God's wrath, and God will act.

> God has put everything under the Anointed's authority. Now when it says that everything is made subject to his authority, obviously the one by whom everything is subjected is excepted. But once all things are subjected to him, then the "son of God" himself will become subject to the one who put everything under

his authority, so that God may be the one who rules everything everywhere. (1 Cor 15:27–28)

This is the ultimate apocalyptic vision of the whole world, all of creation, subject to God's power under his Anointed, his son Jesus. This is indeed looking forward to the final climax of the apocalyptic drama.

What can possibly separate us from the love of God's Anointed? Could it be distress, or anguish, or persecution, or famine, or destitution, or danger, or the sword? As scripture says,
"On your account we are being put to death the whole day long,
we are treated as if we were sheep fit to be slaughtered."
(Rom 8:35–36)

Having spoken of the body transformed, Paul makes a list of physical "sufferings of the present" which are "as nothing compared with the future splendor to be revealed to us" (Rom 8:18). He does not list spiritual realities, but physical realities. Moreover these are realities—"distress, or anguish, or persecution, or famine, or destitution, or danger, or the sword"—could well have been inflicted upon the Jews exiled by Claudius.

Paul now draws his triumphal conclusion:

To the contrary, we completely overcome all of these adversities through the one who loved us. I am convinced that there is nothing in death or life, nothing in the present or in the future, nothing from fallen angels nor from political authorities, nor from any other powerful force, nothing above the earth nor below the earth, nor any other created thing that can separate us from the love of God that has been made known to us through the Anointed Jesus, our lord. (Rom 8:37–39)

In this lyrical fantasy of the powers of the world being overcome, the "us" refers to the nations who share in the Anointed's faithfulness. Immediately afterwards Paul turns to Israel. But we should pause for a second and consider the argument—set aside our Christian prejudice against the Jews. If this is true of the nations who are by nature sinners, how much more is it true of Israel who are the chosen people of God? If they are suffering and have been buffeted by the powers of the emperor, how much more wonderful will be their future transformation? How much more difficult will it be for them to be separated from the love of God? When phrased this way, it becomes evident how much later Christian prejudice against the Jews, the conviction that they have been replaced, has governed the traditional exegesis of Paul's letters. The traditional interpretation takes up not Paul's position, but that of the nations in Rome who have been seduced by Roman imperial propaganda.

True Descendants

After listing the prerogatives of Israel, Paul states:

> It's not as if God's promise has fallen short of fulfillment, because not all those who are physically descended from Israel are Israel, nor are all the physical children of Abraham his true descendants; but as scripture says, "Those who will be acknowledged as your descendants will be through Isaac." That is, the children of God are not the children of physical descent, but the children of the promise are the ones who are considered to be Abraham's descendants. (Rom 9:6–8)

Christians assume that they are the descendants of Isaac, but that is absurd. Paul is restating an argument he has made before. The true descendants of Abraham are marked by promise; like Isaac they are the result of God's promise. Paul makes this clear in referring to Rebekah's two children, Esau and Jacob, by quoting Mal 1:2.

> She was told—before they were born and had not done anything either worthy or worthless in order that the purpose God had chosen might continue to unfold, based not on human accomplishment but on God's choice—"The older will serve the younger," just as scripture says, "I preferred Jacob and rejected Esau." (Rom 9:11–13)

This reiterates the argument made in Romans 4 on behalf of the nations but here is applied to Israel. They, too, are children of promise and election. They were chosen before they were born. This sets the terms of Paul's argument. It is always a matter of God's promise, and God chooses whom God chooses. "So then, God has mercy on whomever God wills, and hardens whomever

God wills" (Rom 9:18). This is not a statement of God's arbitrariness but of his faithfulness to his promise. The promise will out.

Paul asks, what does this show?

> That the nations who did not pursue getting it right [in the sight of God] have [nevertheless] attained it—that is, the getting it right that is based on confidence and unconditional trust in God; but that, although Israel did pursue the law of righteousness, they did not succeed in fulfilling the aim of the law. (Rom 9:30–31)

Paul argues that Israel failed because they did not put "their complete confidence and trust in God" (Rom 9:32). The test for them is still the same test as it was for Abraham, complete confidence or faithfulness (*pistis*) to God's promise. And if God can work the impossible with Abraham, then surely Israel is not lost.

Paul bears witness that Israel has zeal for God, but they lack discernment (Rom 10:2). He describes their situation as like that of the nations: "they miss the point about God's integrity (*lit:* righteousness) and seek to establish their own" (Rom 10:3). They lack discernment about "God's Anointed" who "represents the kind of integrity (*lit:* righteousness) that is the goal (end, KJ) of the law for all who put their confidence and trust in God" (Rom 10:3 SV). The Greek *telos* means completion, end, goal, or even perfection (BDAG). It marks the end point of a progression. Goal, then, is a good translation, and so is end as long as end is understood as end point, not the abolishment of the law.

To show that he is drawing a parallel between Israel and the nations, he quotes Isa 28:16 (LXX) and concludes with Joel 3:5 (LXX).

> Remember that scripture says, "None of those who put their confidence in God will have cause for embarrassment." There is no distinction between Jew and Greek, because the same one is lord of all and is generous to all who appeal to him. As scripture says, "Everyone who appeals to the name of the lord will be delivered."
> (Rom 10:11–13)

Since an appeal to the emperor was the ultimate conclusion of a judgment, the concluding quote probably has overtones of an appeal to the emperor, thus contrasting imperial system with its high stratification and God's system which has "no distinction."

Has Israel Fallen?

So if Israel has stumbled, "Has God given up on the people of Israel?" (Rom 11:1) Paul vehemently rejects this position while pointing to himself:

> I am an Israelite myself, a descendent (*lit:* from the seed) of Abraham, a member of the tribe of Benjamin. God has not given up on the people of Israel whom God already embraced in faithful love (*lit:* knew in advance). (Rom 11:1-2)

Paul is still invoking the argument that implies "if this now, how much more then." How far then has Israel fallen? "Did they get tripped up in order to fall into utter ruin?" (Rom 11:11) Paul once again vehemently rejects this position and argues instead "their misstep is salvation (*sōtēria*) for the nations to make them [Israel] jealous" (Rom 11:11 BBS). In a modern religious context salvation (*sōtēria*) is exclusively associated with the benefits of religion, but the Roman Empire also claims salvation as a benefit of its imperial rule and the emperor (see chapter 5, "Priene Inscription"). Paul maintains that this ultimate benefit, salvation, which has now come to the nations, will make Israel jealous. And so once again the argument: if now they experience a misstep, then "how much more [wealth] will Israel's being brought to fulfillment (*lit:* fullness or completeness) mean?" (Rom 11:12) All of this builds towards the implied argument that Israel is not rejected, but rather Israel's inclusion is the ultimate objective.

Paul reinforces that he is speaking to the nations and that his goal as envoy to the nations is the salvation of Israel:

> I am talking to you from the nations now. In view of my being an envoy to the nations, I make large claims about my ministry in the hope that I may somehow provoke my kinsmen to zealous competition and [in this way] lead some of them to God's fulfillment. If their rejection [of the world-changing message] means global transformation (*lit:* reconciliation of the world), what would their acceptance [of the world-changing message] mean but a return to life from among the dead! (Rom 11:13-15)

Paul's apocalyptic scenario comes into play yet again. The ultimate acceptance of the good news by the Jews will mean nothing less than the resurrection of the dead, the ultimate vision of Daniel and Maccabees of God's dealing with the imperial usurpation of God's rights. For that is what salvation means in this context. This is precisely why in Rom 11:12 Paul shifts from world to nations: "Now if [Israel's] misstep means wealth for the world and if [Israel's] loss means wealth for nations, how much more [wealth] will Israel's being brought to fulfillment mean?" Israel's inclusion will bring on the final reconciliation of the world (KJ) or global fulfillment (SV), symbolized by the resurrection of the dead. Then the world will be right as God created it. "The last enemy to be put down is death" (1 Cor 15:26).

The olive tree analogy apparently originated with the Roman community. They were bragging about being grafted on where Jews had been cut off. Paul turns their analogy against them:

> But if some of the branches of the olive tree were broken off and although you, my friend—a wild olive shoot—were grafted in among the rest of the branches and benefited with them from abundant oil of the olive tree's root, don't brag about the engrafted branches. But if you do brag, don't forget that you don't sustain the root, but the root sustains you. (Rom 11:17–18)

Nothing in Paul's use of the olive analogy indicates that Israel can or will be replaced. Paul pushes the analogy further and concludes once again with an argument based on the pattern, "if now this, then how much more."

> And if they do not persist in their refusal to put their whole trust in God, those branches that have fallen will be grafted in, because God has the power to graft them in again. For if you have been cut from a naturally wild olive tree and grafted into a cultivated olive tree, how much more easily will these natural branches be grafted back into the olive tree from which they came?
> (Rom 11:23–24)

One might rephrase Paul's "natural" language by saying that in his argument Israel is the real thing; the nations, artificial.

Finally Paul reveals the mystery of his apocalyptic scenario. The hardening of Israel, their closed-mindedness, is so that the nations can partake of the benefits of the promise to Abraham.

> So that you will not overestimate your own wisdom, friends, I want you to know about God's previously undisclosed plan: that

a certain closed-mindedness (*lit:* hardening) has come over part of Israel until the full complement of the nations gets in, and in this way all Israel will be brought to God's fulfillment (*lit:* will be saved), just as it is written,

> "The liberator will come from [Mt.] Zion,
> he will eliminate godless behavior from Jacob.
> And this will be my covenant with them
> when I do away with their waywardness."
> (Rom 11:25–27)

Paul eliminates all doubt; in God's plan "all Israel shall be saved" (Rom 11:26 KJ). This is the final act in the apocalyptic scenario. Israel's distress is for the benefit of the nations. Israel may now be an enemy of the gospel, but God loves them because of their ancestors (Rom 11:28). "God has no regrets about the gifts and the invitation offered to them" (Rom 11:29); or, said another way, "the gifts and the calling of God are irrevocable" (NRSV).

Just as Romans 8, where Paul introduced the "if now, then how much more" pattern of argument, ended with a lyrical fantasy of the powers of this world being overcome, so now he concludes this revealing of the end time apocalyptic scenario with a hymn to God's mysteries.

> How inexhaustible are the riches
> and wisdom and knowledge of God!
> How inscrutable are God's judgments
> and untraceable God's ways!
> "Who knew the mind of God,
> or became God's adviser?"
> "Or who gave to God first
> so as to oblige God to return the favor?"
> For everything comes from God, exists through God, and
> ultimately serves God's purposes.
> The glory belongs to God for all time. Amen.
> (Rom 11:33–36)

Israel's Response to the Anointed

If Israel's original covenant with God is still in place and not to be replaced by God's new covenant with the nations, what then should be Israel's response to the Anointed?

In the traditional interpretation, Paul proclaimed a universal gospel of salvation from sin. Since Paul was speaking to the universal human condition, the Jewish response was identical to that of the gentiles: humans are sinful and the solution is belief in Christ. Israel's failure to believe in Christ results in the covenant with Israel being transferred to the gentiles.

This entire scenario is based upon Paul preaching a universal gospel to a universal human. That gospel is a universal solution to the problem of human sin.

This book and much of recent Pauline scholarship has challenged this assumption. Paul proclaims that he is *the* envoy/apostle to the nations and his letters explicitly address the particular situation of the nations in his particular communities, or in the case of Romans, in the Roman community. Even those who think Paul is dealing with the general human situation admit that he is not writing a general theological treatise. Ernst Käsemann in his *Commentary on Romans* acknowledges that Paul's letters are "all occasional letters" (3), but then treats Romans as a dense theological tract.

So what does Paul think the Jewish response to Jesus Anointed should be? Stanley Stowers has asked this same question:

> But what of the Jewish relation to Christ's faithfulness? Here
> Paul's letters provide only hints. One can understand this lack of
> clarity because he writes his letters to gentiles, about the gentile
> situation. Discussions of Israel appear only incidentally. (205)

I agree with Stowers. The problem in answering this question is that Paul does not address it directly, so we are left with hazarding a guess, a situation not uncommon in interpreting the Pauline letters.

Could we not point to Paul himself? Since he was and remained a Jew, should he not provide an example of the expected Jewish response? But Paul is a special case, not typical. In 1 Corinthians 9 Paul protests his freedom as an envoy, asking if he were not entitled to a wage like the other envoys of the Anointed. But he takes none. He is free, yet he behaves as a slave.

> To the Jews I behaved like a Jew so that I might win over Jews.
> To those who are subject to the Mosaic law I behaved as if I were

under that law, not because I really was subject to that law, but to win over those who are. To those not subject to the Mosaic law I behaved as one not subject to it, not because I am not subject to the law of God, but because I am subject to the law of the Anointed, so that I might win over those who are not subject to the law. To the weak I behaved as if I were weak, so that I could win over the weak. I have accommodated myself in all sorts of ways to all sorts of people so that by all these means I might save some. I do all of this for the sake of God's world-transforming news, so that I might have a share in its benefits. (1 Cor 9:20–23)

Paul almost seems to feel himself called to be a chameleon for the sake of the good news. "I have become all things to all people" (1 Cor 9:22 NRSV). Yet he concludes this section by invoking the athlete's model, drawn directly from the language of self-mastery. "Athletes exercise self-control in all things" (1 Cor 9:25 NRSV). So instead of being a chameleon, shifting whichever way to fit the wind, he sees himself as a trained athlete.

I don't run as if I had no goal in mind nor do I box just to punch the air. But I punish my body and make it submit to my aim, so that after I have preached to others I myself do not fail to qualify. (1 Cor 9:26–27)

So Paul is not the model; he is a special case because of his commission to be the envoy to the nations, his call to fulfill God's mission announced by the prophets of old.

Fulfilling that mission is perhaps the key. Central in Paul's understanding of God's plan is the promise made to Abraham. Paul sees two covenants flowing from God's promise to Abraham—one with the circumcised and one with the nations only now fulfilled in the faithfulness of Jesus the Anointed. In his apocalyptic scenario, he envisions a two-step plan, first the Jews, then the nations. The first step has long been in place; now the second step has been put in place.

Paul argues that Israel failed because they did not put "their complete confidence and trust in God" (Rom 9:32). The test for them is still the same test as it was for Abraham; complete confidence or faithfulness to God's promise. Following this logic, for Paul the Jewish relation to the Anointed's faithfulness is for Israel to accept God's plan for the nations. Like the Anointed they should be faithful to God's plan for the nations and accept that God has given to the nations the blessings promised to Abraham apart from the Law. This is why he explodes in the face of James and Cephas' pragmatic solution in Antioch to the threat posed by Jews and members of the nations eating together. He sees the withdrawal of Cephas from table fellowship as a denial of God's plan. Cephas was not behaving as a Jew but as a member of the nations, caving into the demands of Caesar, turning to idolatry.

God has acted; Caesar has been bested; Paul only awaits the lord's descent "from heaven with a loud summons, with an arch-angel's shout and with the trumpet of God" (1 Thess 4:16), and the marching of the nations up to Jerusalem. "But once all things are subjected to him, then the 'son of God' himself will become subject to the one who put everything under his authority, so that God may be the one who rules everything everywhere" (1 Cor 15:28).

In light of the traditional interpretation of Paul that de-manded the conversion of the Jews to Christianity, his apocalyptic scenario does not seem to demand much. But I would submit that it does explain the data we have been examining in this book. God shows no partiality. Both the Jews first and then the nations are made righteous by faithfulness—God's faithfulness to the promise made to Abraham, Abraham's faithfulness, Jesus the Anointed's faithfulness. Both Abraham and Jesus faced death but remained faithful. God remained faithful by giving life to Isaac and raising Jesus from the dead. The nations can participate in a faithfulness like Jesus and thereby gain release from slavery, the yoke of em-pire, and gain life in the body of the Anointed. And all Israel will be saved by remaining faithful to God's promises as expressed in God's covenant with Israel, and now in the new covenant made with the nations.

Paul never fully exposed what it meant for a Jew to participate in the faithfulness of Jesus Anointed because Paul's *apocalypsis/* insight was that he was called to be God's envoy to the nations.

Readings

Barrett, C. K. *A Commentary on the Epistle to the Romans.* Harper's New Testament Commentaries. Peabody, MA: Hendrickson Publishers, 1987.

Beard, Mary, John North, and Simon Price. *Religions of Rome: Volume 1: A History*. Cambridge/New York: Cambridge University Press, 1998.

Branick, Vincent. *The House Church in the Writings of Paul*. Wilmington, DE: Michael Glazier, 1989.

Cohen, Shaye J.D. *The Beginnings of Jewishness, Boundaries, Varieties, Uncertainties*. Berkeley: University of California Press, 1999.

Dahl, Nils. "The Future of Israel." Pp. 137–58 in *Studies in Paul: Theology for the Early Christian Mission*. Minneapolis: Fortress Press, 1977.

Elliott, Neil. *The Arrogance of Nations: Reading Romans in the Shadow of Empire*. Paul in Critical Contexts. Minneapolis: Fortress Press, 2008.

Jewett, Robert. *Romans: A Commentary*. Hermeneia. Ed. Roy David Kotansky and Eldon Jay Epp. Minneapolis: Fortress Press, 2007.

Käsemann, Ernst. *Commentary on Romans*. Trans. Geoffrey William Bromiley. Grand Rapids: Wm. B. Eerdmans, 1980.

Levine, Amy-Jill. *The Misunderstood Jew: The Church and the Scandal of the Jewish Jesus*. 1st ed. San Francisco: HarperSanFrancisco, 2006.

Malina, Bruce J. *Social-Science Commentary on the Letters of Paul*. Minneapolis: Fortress Press, 2006.

Miller, Robert J. *The Complete Gospels*. 4th ed. Salem, OR: Polebridge Press, 2010.

Munck, Johannes. *Paul and the Salvation of Mankind*. Richmond: John Knox Press, 1959.

Stowers, Stanley K. *A Rereading of Romans: Justice, Jews, and Gentiles*. New Haven/London: Yale University Press, 1994.

Chapter 15

Paul's Christian Future

We have finished Paul's story, or at least we have come as far as our best evidence, which is minimal in many ways, will take us. Yet we are not at the end of Paul's story, if for no other reason than we have not reached his death. Even the Acts of the Apostles, which carried Paul's story to Rome, did not report his martyrdom. Paul disappeared into the violence of the Roman Empire and the history of early Christianity.

Who Was Paul?

In the end Paul the person remains a mystery. Putting all the pieces together evades me and I cannot figure out how to get it all in focus. There are too many gaps, too many things we do not know. What Karl Galinsky in *Augustan Culture* notes about writing the history of the ancient world is also true of studying Paul: "the excessive extent to which we have to rely on the few written sources from antiquity too often blinds us to the obvious fact that so much of what went on was a matter of oral discussion" (74). Too much of what we know is episodic, while we pretend it is comprehensive. Paul always will escape our grasp. We end with large parts of the puzzle assembled, but without the last couple of pieces.

Yet I am convinced by our overall analysis. As the title of Pamela Eisenbaum's book has it, *Paul Was Not a Christian*. I think she has it exactly right. But if he remained a Jew, what kind of Jew was he? If he thought of himself as a Jew—and the evidence is overwhelming that he did—did other Jews recognize him as a

Jew? It is not clear that Cephas and James recognized him, and other Jewish envoys opposed him. Paul himself reports, "Five times I received forty lashes minus one from my fellow Jews" (2 Cor 11:24). We do not know whether the "three times I was beaten with rods, once I was stoned" (2 Cor 11:25) was at the hand of Jews. But the five lashings alone indicate considerable conflict with synagogues. Crossan and Reid may be right that he was poaching God-fearers from the synagogue (39–40).

Modern Jewish scholars have also had trouble with Paul. Johannes Schoeps in *Paul: The Theology of the Apostle in the Light of Jewish Religious History* accused Paul of siding with Hellenistic Judaism, rather than the pure form of Palestinian Judaism, as did Samuel Sandmel in his *The Genius of Paul*. More recently Daniel Boyarin in *A Radical Jew* likewise saw Paul as in the tradition of Philo, that is, a Platonist and dualist. Hyam Maccoby, as the title of his book *The Mythmaker: Paul and the Invention of Christianity* indicates, held Paul responsible for the invention of Christianity and anti-Semitism. Maccoby was caught in the traditional Lutheran interpretation. Alan Segal in *Paul the Convert* saw Paul as a Pharisee who converted to another Jewish group that he had been persecuting and came to see it as the true form of Judaism. Where to place Paul within Judaism remains a problem.

Part of the problem is that Second Temple Judaism was not a simple entity. It was not a Judaism but Judaisms. Before the 1950s, scholarship, both Jewish and Christian, understood the religion of the rabbis to be what George Foot Moore is his classic exposition *Judaism in the First Centuries of the Christian Era* called normative Judaism. The discovery of the Dead Sea scrolls shattered this view and at the same time forced scholars to reassess the categories of Hellenistic and Palestinian Judaism, apocalyptic and wisdom. All of a sudden Judaism appeared to be much more pluriform and varied than the model of normative Judaism had allowed. Jacob Neusner in his essay "Defining Judaism" has argued that scholarship needs to "learn how to respect the plurality of Judaic religious systems and speak of Judaisms, not Judaism, or 'a Judaism' when we mean a specific religious system" (6–7). Second Temple Judaism had no central governing authority but a great deal of variation in its differing configurations. Even the Temple in Jerusalem does not provide a central authority, as witnessed by the

Sadducees, Pharisees, and Essenes contesting over its significance and meaning.

Where to fit Paul in all this variation is difficult to know. Before his revelation event he was a Pharisee. Afterwards he continued to view himself as a Jew; some Jews did not; but others did. Even by his own testimony, his place in Second Temple Judaism, after his *apocalypsis*/revelation event was controversial.

Also Paul belongs to a Jesus movement that is on its way to Christianity, but is not yet there and does not know it is headed in that direction. We often speak of early or primitive Christianity, but this is a problematic term. Just as referring to Judaism instead of Judaisms is anachronistic, so we should use the plural for Jesus movements. Before the destruction of the Temple in 70 CE there was no such thing as Christianity; that is, the movement had not yet separated from Judaism. That separation only begins after 70 CE. The name Christian does not begin to be used until the second century and may well be a name others used for them. Paul did not convert to Christianity, but to what did his converts, those members of the nations who belong to the Anointed, convert? Paul argues that they belong to the covenant made with Abraham, but if we are right that he differentiates between two covenants in Abraham—one for Israel, the other for the nations—what is the status of these members of the nations who belong to the Anointed? If they are not Jews, what are they? Eventually this will get sorted out, but not in Paul's day. His apocalyptic scenario masks this problem. Since he does not imagine that it is much longer until the Anointed returns and the nations march up to Jerusalem, he does not have to face the question of group identity. But who did *they* think they were? The debate in Galatia indicates ambiguity. Some clearly thought they should become Jews by submitting to circumcision.

Failure or Success?

If I were to look back on Paul's life, I would be hard pressed to know how to evaluate it. Was it a success or failure?

Opponents

Judging from his letters, it would appear that Paul faced a great deal of opposition. After the conflict with Cephas in Antioch, he never returned to his home base there. His relations with many of his communities were fraught with strife, especially in the case of the communities in Galatia and Corinth.

From the fragments that make up 2 Corinthians emerge a set of opponents whom Paul mockingly refers to as "super-envoys" or "super-apostles" (2 Cor 11:5).

> They, like Paul, use the title envoy/apostle.
> They are Hebrews like Paul.
> They are polished speakers; Paul is not.
> Their preaching is worth paying for; Paul's by implication is not.
> They have letters of recommendation; Paul does not.

One wonders who wrote the letters of introduction. James or one of the pillars? We do not know. Paul engages in an elaborate fool's speech (2 Cor 11:5–12:10) in an effort to refute these super-envoys and bring the Corinthians over to his side. In his fool's speech he returns time after time, often with bitter sarcasm, to his infirmities, not his strengths. He concludes the fool's speech:

> Now more than ever I shall brag most gladly of my limitations, so that the power of God's Anointed might reside in me. So, for the sake of God's Anointed, I accept limitations, insults, calamities, persecutions, difficulties. For when I accept my limitations, then I am empowered. (2 Cor 12:9–10)

This fool's speech reminds us that Paul not only faced real difficulties and conflicts with his communities, but he also faced opposition from other Jewish envoy/apostles as we are reminded by Deiter Georgi in his *The Opponents of Paul in Second Corinthians* (317–19). This forces us to expand our understanding of what was happening in the early Jesus movement. The limiting of apostles to the twelve, as does Acts and the later tradition, misses the complexities of the early movement. It was not all harmony and hymn singing. There was real and deep conflict. Whether we can draw a direct line from the conflict in Antioch or from the men from James to the super-envoys is impossible to know. But both cases indicate continuing opposition to Paul from Jewish envoys.

He evidently never made it to Spain and we have no idea how the letter to the Romans was received, except that it was preserved. That tells us something important—somebody valued it.

The Collection

An important symbol of Paul's response to the opposition in Jerusalem was his collection for the poor in Jerusalem. At the conclusion of the meeting in Jerusalem, Paul had stressed that "their only condition was that we remember the poor—something I was eager to do" (Gal 2:10). Gathering this collection consumed a great deal of energy and years of work on Paul's part, and he had to beg and plead to get the contributions. At the end of 1 Corinthians he gives instructions for the gathering of the collection:

> Now about the money we are collecting for God's people in Jerusalem, you should follow the directions I gave to the communities of the Anointed in Galatia. On the first day of every week each of you should put aside and save up whatever your prosperity may permit, so that contributions need not be solicited when I come. And when I arrive, I will send those whom you have approved, with letters of introduction, to convey your gift to Jerusalem. If it seems worthwhile for me to go also, they will go with me. (1 Cor 16:1–4)

Pulling together the threads from the brief mentions of the collection in his letters makes it difficult to get a coherent picture of what was going on. In the fragment of a letter contained in 2 Corinthians 9, Paul evidences no concern for the success of the collection. "Through the evidence of this generous act of service the Anointed's people in Jerusalem will glorify God for your active acknowledgement of the world-transforming news of God's Anointed and for your contribution to them and to all <of the Anointed's people>" (2 Cor 9:13). Yet by the time he writes the letter to the Romans Paul is concerned. He notes that before he comes to visit those in Rome on his way to Spain, he is going to Jerusalem. "I am going there because [the Anointed's people in] Macedonia and Achaia want to express their sense of community by aiding the needy among Jesus followers in Jerusalem" (Rom 15:26). But a threat or concern lurks in waiting. He requests the prayers of the Roman community, "that I may be delivered from those in Judea who refuse to accept [God's world-transforming message], that the good will and support that I am conveying for the Jerusalem community will be well received by the Anointed's people there" (Rom 15:31). This implies two issues: those opposed to Paul and how the collection would be received.

Who are those threatening Paul's mission? The NRSV translates verse 31: "that I may be rescued from the unbelievers in Judea." Dieter Georgi remarks in his book on the collection, *Remembering the Poor*:

> Paul knew perfectly well what was at stake. He knew what he was doing when, prior to referring to the collection, he mentioned (v. 30) that he might be in danger from the Jews in Jerusalem. (1992: 120)

Besides the fear of those opposed to Paul, the collection itself was a double-edged sword. On the one hand it showed to the pillars in Jerusalem that Paul had lived up to his end of the bargain and physically demonstrated the success of the mission to the nations. The success was marked not only by the amount of money the collection had raised, but also by the presence with the collection of the delegation accompanying it. But on the other hand this very delegation was provocative to Jews in Jerusalem. Again Georgi summarizes the point: "The promised pilgrimage of the peoples had begun to materialize, but without—indeed, in spite of—the majority of the Jews" (1992: 119). Jerusalem had always been the center of the apocalyptic scenario, where the nations would come up to worship at Mount Zion. The collection and its delegation would demonstrate that the end-time event was now in play.

Paul had reason to be concerned. The collection apparently did not have the desired result. He most probably met with at least partial rejection in Jerusalem. Stephan Joubert in his recent study of the collection *Paul as Benefactor* thinks that James and Paul worked out a compromise, basing his argument on Acts (213–15). Not all the communities participated. Did the communities in Galatia make a contribution? The answer is not clear. Did they refuse to contribute or did their circumcision render them no longer from among the nations? Is this another argument that Paul lost?

If the collection was not well received in Jerusalem, does that mean that Paul finished his life as a free agent, unconnected to those pillars in Jerusalem whose status he had disdained? The only mention of the collection in Acts 24:17 is a veiled reference, providing no real help. In the report of Paul's trial before the Roman governor Felix at Caesarea, Paul says in his defense,

> Now after some years I came to bring to my nation alms and offerings. As I was doing this, they found me purified in the temple, without any crowd or tumult. (Acts 24:17–18)

There is no mention of the accompanying members of the nations nor is it at all evident what the purpose of the "alms and offerings" might be. But it is during this visit that Paul's fatal arrest occurs.

He died, of course, without the lord Jesus the Anointed's return. So, yet another disappointment.

Did these events disappoint him, or did he view them as part of a long series of struggles and sufferings in remaining faithful to the Anointed and the Anointed's cross? He stood in the line of Abraham and the prophets, in the line of Jesus. God would be faithful to his promises.

One thing happened to Paul's heritage that he did not live to see. The Pauline communities became gentile and broke the connection to Judaism. As Nils Dahl has noted in his essay "The Future of Israel,"

> What has happened was precisely what Paul warned against. Christian Gentiles made themselves great at the expense of Israel. . . . Gentile Christians soon came to believe that God had rejected Israel, that, much to the advantage of the Gentiles, he had gathered for himself a new people from among them. (157–58)

Perhaps it was better that Paul died before this came to be.

Apocalypsis/Revelation/Insight

We have been pursuing the implications of Paul's *apocalypsis/* revelation. Our analysis of that event/experience as explained in Paul's own words has dictated our path. That path has led us to bypass some normal topics in studies of Paul, for example, Christology or ecclesiology. Those topics derive more from the outline of Christian theology. Paul shows no concern for the Jesus of history (2 Cor 5:16), nor for that matter the Christ of faith. He is interested in what is happening in Jesus as revealed in his *apocalypsis*/insight. His primary titles for Jesus—the Anointed, son of God, and lord—are functional in his usage, not ontological. He does not develop what these titles say about the being of Jesus. For him they tell what God has done or accomplished in Jesus, not who Jesus is ontologically. Paul is more interested in God than in Jesus. God has called Paul. In that emphasis he remains faithful to his Jewish roots.

CHRISTOLOGY

Paul explores the functional or metaphorical implications of his three primary Christological titles: Anointed, Son, and Lord. Paul's audience, undoubtedly, would have understood *Christos/* Anointed as part of Jesus' name, but Paul plays on the traditional Jewish sense of the title. While Anointed implies king, Paul partners Anointed with its opposite implication, Anointed crucified (e.g., 1 Cor 1:23, 2:2; Gal 2:19, 3:1). This partnering of Anointed and crucified exposes the oxymoronic heart of Paul's *apocalypsis/* insight, his good news which is the "nonsense" that Paul preaches (1 Cor 1:20–21).

Son, the title used in Paul's *apocalypsis/*revelation, implies father, as well as heir, implications that, as we have seen, he develops extensively. The notion of son, then heir, is explored in the Abraham cycle, in both Galatians and Romans. The announcement in Gal 3:28–29 that since "You are no longer Jew or Greek, no longer slave or freeborn, no longer 'male and female,'" making you "Abraham's offspring and—as promised—his heirs" can serve as a summary of this Christological exploration. What Paul develops is how the implications of son play out for those who are faithful like the son was faithful.

In Paul's letters there is no evidence of Jesus' pre-existence. In Rom 1:3–4 Jesus is declared to be a son of David according to the flesh and "appointed and empowered as 'son of God,' in accordance with the spirit of holiness, from the time of his resurrection from the dead" (Rom 1:4). This might be a fragment of an early piece of Jesus movement tradition, as Jewett (97–98) among others argues, but it does indicate a two-stage movement in which Jesus only becomes son of God in his resurrection. Again, what Paul develops in the title is its functional implications, not its ontological ones.

The poem-like piece in Phil 2:6–11 is often taken as proof of Paul's high Christology. A movement from heaven to earth and back to heaven has been assumed in these verses, based on the analogy of the prologue of the Fourth Gospel. Ralph Martin's

Carmen Christi is the classic statement of this position. But this is not supportable if for no other reason than nowhere else in Paul is such a pattern evident. Moreover, as Jerome Murphy-O'Connor and James Dunn have argued, the more likely pattern is that of Adam, not the descent/ascent pattern of the Fourth Gospel. Adam grasped at being equal to God. More recently, as Hellerman has argued in his study *Reconstructing Honor in Roman Philippi*, the piece also exhibits an anti-imperial pattern. The emperor furnishes the antitype. The piece is not dealing with a cosmological pattern but represents a movement in status. God, as the Greek literally says, super-exalts the crucified slave, giving him God's own name, lord. But this very title is also an imperial title, and the exaltation mocks the Roman imperial triumphs, as I have argued in *The Trouble with Resurrection* (74–81).

Kyrios in Greek means both master and lord, and Paul plays upon both of these meanings. Significantly, *kyrios* in the LXX and Hellenistic Judaism is used to translate the Hebrew *Adonai,* as well as the Tetragrammaton, God's unspoken name. Furthermore *kyrios* is a title in the imperial cult. We just encountered this double implication in the Philippians poem. Moreover as part of a metaphorical system, master connotes slave, as master and slave are tied together. Mention "master" and "slave" is also implied. Paul refers to himself as a slave of the Anointed. We saw how this worked out in the greeting of the letter to the Romans. Lord has the implication of subject or subjection. This is evident in the conclusion of the Philippians poem, as well as in Paul's apocalyptic scenario as expressed in 1 Cor 15:24–28. But once again, Paul uses the title functionally; he indicates what is happening; he does not speculate on what it says about Jesus.

If we follow Paul's clues, Christology is a subsidiary topic within the main topic of how God is acting, how God remains faithful. Theodicy is the real issue.

In regard to the church (ecclesiology), Paul's primary image is "in the Anointed" and the related "body of the Anointed." He seems uninterested in organizational or institutional needs. Being in the Anointed boils down to a mysticism, to a disappearance of the ego—"It is no longer I who live, but Christ who lives in me" (Gal 2:20 NRSV). It describes the Anointed's crucified body in the world.

Crucified Son

The central insight of Paul's *apocalypsis*/revelation is that the crucified Jesus is God's Anointed son. From that flows everything. For Paul that is a shattering insight that corrodes all it touches. Over and over again, we find it underlying Paul's various positions. It surely made him difficult to argue with. How do you argue with a man with a revelation? To Cephas and James, he probably appeared arrogant. He would not give in. That the crucified one is God's Anointed corrodes the implication of any compromise with the empire. It was the idolatry of the empire, its very arrogance, that led the empire to crucify Jesus, God's Anointed son. To withdraw from fellowship or submit to circumcision or, God forbid, offer a libation to the emperor to placate the empire—that abrogates the good news.

Paul recognized that his insight was nonsense (1 Cor 1:18) by the accepted standards of the empire or the expectations of Israel. But in his view God had consistently sided with losers. Abraham was as good as dead when God chose to fulfill the promise. And Abraham remained faithful, hoping against hope. Likewise in the faithfulness of Jesus, God had acted to fulfill the last part of the promise to Abraham, that he would be the father of nations. Now God had made that possible, apart from the law, for the nations. God had chosen him, one untimely born, a persecutor of the community of God, to be God's envoy to the nations, to bring this good news that was transforming the world. Faithfulness is nonsense because God has identified with the godless.

The Pauls after Paul

While we might not be able to say much more about what happened to Paul, there is much to be said about his heritage. Which raises a strange irony: Paul would have been surprised to know that he had a heritage. His apocalyptic scenario predicted Jesus the Anointed's imminent return to subjugate all things to God, so a heritage was not part of his agenda.

The Letters

Unexpectedly, Paul's occasional and probably in his mind ephemeral letters guaranteed that succeeding generations remembered him. The survival of anything from the ancient world is always an accident and in this case the odds were surely high that they would be lost and forgotten. The Jesus movement at the time of Paul was numerically tiny, probably not on the radar of the Roman bureaucracy. The first Roman official of whom we are aware to take notice of Christians was Pliny the younger in his letter to Trajan in 112 CE.

All of this merely points out the extraordinary fluke of the survival of Paul's letters. We have no idea how many letters Paul actually wrote. The fact that the surviving letters have a connection with Corinth and/or Ephesus suggests that those two cities may have had something to do with their survival and collection. Surely there were other letters about which we know nothing.

There have been numerous proposals for the collection of Paul's letters, although none of them has found general acceptance.

Edgar Goodspeed first proposed in *The Meaning of Ephesians* (1933) that Onesimus, the freed slave of Philemon, was the author of Ephesians and the collector of Paul's letters. Onesimus wrote Ephesians as a cover letter and summary of Paul's theology.

> I don't know how this mere conjecture may strike the reader, but it fills my eyes with tears. The emancipated slave lives to build for his protector a monument more enduring than bronze! (1956: 126)

David Trobisch more recently in *Paul's Letter Collection* has argued that the original collection of Romans, the Corinthian correspondence and Galatians, was made by Paul himself. Trobisch has examined a large number of ancient letter collections that help bolster his argument. Nevertheless, it remains improbable. Such a scheme would make Paul the editor of 1 and 2 Corinthians, hardly likely, and it runs against Paul's apocalyptic proclivities. Given those expectations, what would be the purpose of such a collection of his letters? Yet Trobisch's material on ancient letter collections may contain a key to this problem.

Whoever collected, selected and edited Paul's letters guaranteed his success. The title of Richard Pervo's chapter on Paul's letter collection, "Paul Becomes a Book" (23) intriguingly suggests what happened. The collection of his letters made Paul stand out from all the other early followers of Jesus. Even if he did not know Jesus of Nazareth, he was the only early follower from whom we have any writings. And not just a single letter, but a collection of letters survived. This bestows on Paul an outsized influence on the reconstruction of the early Jesus movement. For many, Paul is Christianity prior to the destruction of the Temple in 70 CE. Only recently has research on the Sayings Gospel Q begun to challenge that reconstruction, as seen in John Kloppenborg Verbin's *Excavating Q* (chapters 7–8). The Q-Gospel offers yet another view of pre-70 CE Jesus movements.

The first collection of Paul's letters started a process that completely altered Paul. It generalized and universalized Paul's letters. It gradually transformed him from a Jewish preacher into a letter writer and a Christian theologian. A new and different Paul replaced the old Paul. This happened because the individual letters were removed from their particular context of addressing a particular community's concerns. The particularity disappears along with the original audience, and the context and the new audience now becomes the whole world. The generalization and universalization of Paul's letters in the context of the collection was inevitable. Only in this way could the letters have survived.

However the collection and editing of Paul's letters came about, and that picture is surely complicated, its effect is clear—Paul became a Christian theologian, and his message became a universal gospel of salvation from sin through faith in Christ, not works of the law. His Jewish heritage was at risk.

Pseudepigrapha

Whether the collecting and editing of Paul's letters preceded the writing of letters in Paul's name or one of these letters was the occasion of the collecting and editing, we do not know. The truth is, we do not know what happened. As is so often the case, we are left guessing, speculating, or finally, silent. The collecting of Paul's letters surely gave prominence to other letters in Paul's name. The collection stimulated efforts to claim Paul. 2 Thessalonians warns of other letters written in Paul's name. The writer warns the reader, "not to be quickly shaken in mind or alarmed, either by spirit or by word or by letter, as though from us, to the effect that the day of the Lord is already here" (2 Thess 2:2 NRSV). This indicates a contest among those writing in his name to claim his heritage, to say what he stood for. All this shows that Paul had become an authority.

Colossians is probably the first pseudepigraphic letter in Paul's name. There are a number of indicators of its pseudepigraphic character.

- Numerous vocabulary and stylistic differences
- Not a single quote from the Jewish scriptures
- No future visits: "I am absent in body, yet I am with you in spirit" (Col 2:5)
- Paul has become the only apostle
- His mission is universal, not local and particular
  (For further details see Collins, 171–80, and Pervo, 64–71.)

Perhaps most significant for the narrative we have been following, Christ is now the head of the church, which embraces the whole world.

> He is the head of the body, the church; he is the beginning, the firstborn from the dead, so that he might come to have first place in everything. For in him all the fullness of God was pleased to dwell, and through him God was pleased to reconcile to himself all things, whether on earth or in heaven, by making peace through the blood of his cross. (Col 1:18–20)

Pervo puts it well: "In a metaphor that would become enduring, Christ as king rules over a hierarchical pyramid, like the Roman emperor" (67). This imperial claim for Christ and his church is likewise expanded to Paul. The readers of the letter are to hold fast to "the gospel that you heard, which has been proclaimed to every creature under heaven. I, Paul, became a servant of this gospel" (Col 1:23). Paul is the minister (*diakonos*) of the gospel, not slave (*doulos*). The shift in vocabulary is noteworthy.

Colossians changed Paul to save Paul. To borrow a phrase from the literary critic Harold Bloom, Colossians is a "strong misreading" of Paul. A strong misreading is both an act of love but at the same time a creation of new space for meaning. Without this new Paul created by the author of Colossians' misreading of Paul, the old Paul would have disappeared. Paul's apocalyptic scenario was no longer working, so the author of Colossians shifted into a different key. The apocalyptic scenario disappeared, and in its place came a more speculative, universal agenda. The vitality of that misreading is demonstrated by its fecundity. It kept alive the original Paul and produced a wealth of disagreement about who Paul was. The Acts of the Apostles, Paul and Thecla, and the Pastorals among others are all contesting for the reading of Paul. Augustine and Luther produced magnificent misreadings of Paul, and we are still engaged in misreading Paul to this day.

Acts of the Apostles

The Acts of the Apostles has contributed enormously to the popular view of Paul.

- The dramatic image of Paul holding the cloaks of those who stoned Stephen
- A Roman citizen from Tarsus
- The vivid story of Paul's conversion, which pictures a blinding light and voice calling out, "Saul, Saul, why do you persecute me?"
- Taught by Ananias
- Works miracles and wonders
- Goes first to the synagogue
- His trials before the Roman governors
- The appeal to Rome

Acts alone tells us this, not Paul in his letters. But a great deal also is missing from Acts.

- No letter writing
- No mention of justification by faith or other important theological terms
- Not an apostle
- No conflict over Torah

The differences between Acts and the letters of Paul are so great that Phillip Vielhauser in a famous essay "On the 'Paulinism' of Acts." suggested that Acts was written by one of Paul's opponents.

One thing Acts denies Paul is his apostleship. While the tradition has taken so many of its clues about Paul from Acts, on this front it has not. Colossians and Ephesians won that debate. The later tradition views Peter and Paul as *the* two apostles, even though Paul is not one of the twelve.

Acts provides the charter myth of Christian origins, as Joseph Tyson explains in an essay "Acts, Myth, and History" in *Acts and Christian Beginnings: The Acts Seminar Report* (15–18), and in that story allows Paul not only a prominent place, but a starring role. As a result, we have a very hard time imagining the early Jesus movement prior to 70 CE apart from Paul.

CANON

Marcion (about 95–165 CE) had a dramatic influence on the literary and theological shape of early Christianity. The Gospel of Luke and the Acts of the Apostles may well be a response to Marcion. Even more surely, the Christian canon consisting of an Old Testament and a New Testament was a direct rejoinder to Marcion's canon, as Jason BeDuhn in *The First New Testament* has recently convincingly argued. Marcion's canon consisted of an *Euggelion* and *Apostolikon*, a gospel and a collection of ten letters of Paul. The orthodox canon's construction of a New Testament divided into gospels and letters surely originated in Marcion's canon.

Canonization continued the process of universalizing Paul by making him into a creedal figure. It also contributed to the singling out of Paul. He dominates the New Testament canon. The following figures point out the significance of Paul in the canon. The numbers in the right-hand column are the number of pages allotted in Nestle-Aland, the critical edition of the Greek New Testament:

Letters ascribed to Paul	154 pages
Acts of the Apostles	88 pages
Total	243 pages

Of the 680 pages of Nestle-Aland, 243 have Paul as their main topic. This works out to 36 percent of the New Testament. This is a significant amount for a person who did not know Jesus of Nazareth.

At What Price?

It is hard to imagine Christianity without Paul. Yet we have seen that this process, which began with the collecting of Paul's letters, changed the perception of both Paul and his letters. In Pervo's phrase, Paul became a book. Without this process from collection to canon, Paul and his letters would have been lost. The question must be asked, at what price? The price paid was considerable.

- Paul's apocalyptic scenario was abandoned.
- The anti-imperial thrust was muted then lost.
- Israel was replaced by the Gentiles.

This is indeed a heavy price. One has to ask if it does not indeed betray the real Paul.

The abandonment of Paul's apocalyptic scenario was inevitable as soon as it failed. The author of 2 Thessalonians, writing in the last half the first century, paints a more vivid apocalyptic picture than Paul himself does, while at the same time other members of the Pauline school have left behind the apocalyptic scenario. Elements of Christianity have flirted with apocalyptic, off and on, to the present day, and it is enshrined in Revelation, the final book of the New Testament canon.

The question has to be faced: what is left of Paul without the apocalyptic underpinning? Does Paul still make sense without it? Rudolf Bultmann's program of demythologization tried to answer this question. He translated the categories of apocalyptic into the categories of existentialism. Bultmann's was a powerful interpretation and some program of demythologization is necessary for those who want to continue to make sense of Paul in the contemporary situations.

In my mind the other two losses are more tragic. The traditional interpretation of Paul saw the opposite of Christianity as Judaism, whereas we have argued that for Paul the fundamental opposition is between the gospel of God and the gospel of Rome. Thus the second and third items on our list are bound up together—Israel and Rome. When Paul's anti-imperial thrust is lost, it eventually is replaced in the Pauline and Christian tradition by an anti-Israel or anti-Jewish thrust. Or it can be reversed. When the church became gentile, it became anti-Jewish and pro-empire. This transformation led to the success of the church, eventually to its recognition and establishment by Constantine. But again, we must ask, at what price?

The history of anti-Semitism is a terrible stain on Christianity and there is no easy way to escape it. Reclaiming the real Paul offers a profound opportunity for Christians to rethink their commitment to anti-Judaism and pro-imperialism. Paul still offers a way forward, but Paul's way demands more than tinkering; it requires a fundamental reconstruction of Christianity.

READINGS

BeDuhn, Jason D. *The First New Testament: Marcion's Scriptural Canon.* Salem, OR: Polebridge Press, 2013.

Bloom, Harold. *The Anxiety of Influence.* New York: Oxford University Press, 1973.

Boyarin, Daniel. *A Radical Jew: Paul and the Politics of Identity.* Contraversions: Critical Studies in Jewish Literature, Culture, and Society. Berkeley: University of California Press, 1994.

Collins, Raymond F. *Letters that Paul Did Not Write: The Epistle to the Hebrews and the Pauline Pseudepigrapha.* Good News Studies, vol. 28. Wilmington, DE: Michael Glazier, 1988.

Crossan, John Dominic, and Jonathan L. Reed. *In Search of Paul: How Jesus' Apostle Opposed Rome's Empire with God's Kingdom.* San Francisco: HarperSanFrancisco, 2004.

Dahl, Nils. "The Future of Israel." Pp. 137–58 in *Studies in Paul: Theology for the Early Christian Mission.* Minneapolis: Fortress Press, 1977.

Dunn, James D. G. "Christ, Adam, and Preexistence." Pp. 74–83 in *Where Christology Began: Essays on Philippians 2.* Ed. Ralph P. Martin and Brian J. Dodd. 1st ed. Louisville, KY: John Knox Press, 1998.

Eisenbaum, Pamela. *Paul Was Not a Christian: The Original Message of a Misunderstood Apostle.* New York: HarperOne, 2009.

Galinsky, Karl. *Augustan Culture*. Princeton: Princeton University Press, 1966.

Georgi, Dieter. *Remembering the Poor: The History of Paul's Collection for Jerusalem*. Nashville: Abingdon Press, 1992.

_____. *The Opponents of Paul in Second Corinthians*. Philadelphia: Fortress Press, 1986.

Goodspeed, Edgar Johnson. *The Key to Ephesians*. Chicago: University of Chicago Press, 1956.

_____. *The Meaning of Ephesians*. Chicago: The University of Chicago Press, 1933.

Hellerman, Joseph H. *Reconstructing Honor in Roman Philippi: Carmen Christi as Cursus Pudorum*. Cambridge: Cambridge University Press, 2005.

Jewett, Robert. *Romans: A Commentary*. Hermeneia. Ed. Roy David Kotansky and Eldon Jay Epp. Minneapolis: Fortress Press, 2007.

Joubert, Stephan. *Paul as Benefactor: Reciprocity, Strategy and Theological Reflection in Paul's Collection*. Wissenschaftliche Untersuchungen Zum Neuen Testament, no. 2. Reihe. Tübingen: Mohr Siebeck, 2000.

Kloppenborg Verbin, John S. *Excavating Q: The History and Setting of the Sayings Gospel*. Minneapolis: Fortress Press, 2000.

Maccoby, Hyam. *The Mythmaker: Paul and the Invention of Christianity*. New York: Harper & Row, 1986.

Malherbe, Abraham J. *The Letters to the Thessalonians*. New York: Doubleday, 2000.

Martin, Ralph P. *A Hymn of Christ: Philippians 2:5–11 in Recent Interpretation & in the Setting of Early Christian Worship*. 1st ed. Downers Grove, IL: IVP Academic, 1997.

_____. *Carmen Christi: Philippians Ii 5–11 in Recent Interpretation and in the Setting of Early Christian Worship*. 1st American ed. Grand Rapids, MI: Wm. B. Eerdmans, 1983.

Moore, George Foot. *Judaism in the First Centuries of the Christian Era*. 2 vols. Cambridge: Harvard University Press, 1954.

Neusner, Jacob. "Defining Judaism." Pp. 3–19 in *The Blackwell Companion to Judaism*. Blackwell Companions to Religion, vol. 1. Ed. Jacob Neusner and Alan J. Avery-Peck. Malden, MA: Blackwell Publishers, 2003.

Pervo, Richard I. *The Making of Paul: Constructions of the Apostle in Early Christianity*. Minneapolis: Fortress Press, 2010.

Sandmel, Samuel. *The Genius of Paul: A Study in History*. Philadelphia: Fortress Press, 1979.

Schoeps, H. J. *Paul: The Theology of the Apostle in the Light of Jewish Religious History*. Philadelphia: Westminster Press, 1959.

Scott, Bernard Brandon. *The Trouble with Resurrection*. Salem, OR: Polebridge Press, 2011.

Segal, Alan F. *Paul the Convert: The Apostolate and Apostasy of Saul the Pharisee*. New Haven: Yale University Press, 1990.

Trobisch, David. *Paul's Letter Collection: Tracing the Origins*. Minneapolis: Fortress Press, 1994.

Tyson, Joseph B. "Acts, Myth, and History." Pp. 15–18 in *Acts and Christian Beginnings: The Acts Seminar Report*. Ed. Dennis Edwin Smith, Joseph B. Tyson and the Acts Seminar. Salem, OR: Polebidge Press, 2013.

Vielhauser, Phillip. "On the 'Paulinism' of Acts." Pp. 33-50 in *Studies in Luke Acts*. Ed. Leander Keck and J. Louis Martyn. Philadelphia: Fortress Press, 1980.

Annotated Bibliography on Paul

By design this book has no footnotes. For the reader, the argument flows in a straightforward manner, which is an advantage. There is no interruption for footnotes or side alleys. The loss for the author is that it is difficult to acknowledge my indebtedness to other scholars and/or to argue with them. This annotated bibliography is an effort to make up for that loss. It represents my take on Pauline scholarship and provides for the reader a guide to further study in the new understanding of Paul. For a more detailed analysis of the history of scholarship in this vein, please take a look at a book I have recommended before: Magnus Zetterholm, *Approaches to Paul.*

Zetterholm, Magnus. *Approaches to Paul: A Student's Guide to Recent Scholarship.* Minneapolis: Fortress Press, 2009.

Traditional Interpretation

The traditional Augustinian/Lutheran interpretation of Paul is well represented in the modern period by a great many commentators, but the classic presentation in the twentieth century is Karl Barth and Rudolf Bultmann. Barth's *Epistle to the Romans* was published in 1919 and a revised edition published in 1922 (English translation 1933). Barth rejected the liberal German Protestant theology he had been raised in, because he saw it supporting German nationalism which led to World War I. He used his commentary on Romans to rethink his theological heritage, arguing that the God revealed in the cross of Jesus said "No" to every human achievement. This gave rise to dialectical theology and later neo-orthodoxy. Barth's influence on theology in the twentieth century is hard to overstate. Whether that influence is positive or negative, I leave to the reader's consideration.

Rudolf Bultmann was undoubtedly the most important and influential New Testament scholar of the twentieth century. While initially allied with Barth and dialectical theology, they parted ways over neo-orthodoxy. Bultmann's program of demythologization involved translating the worldview of the New Testament into the categories of existentialism. This can be seen in his magisterial treatment of Paul in the first volume of his *Theology of the New Testament*. For him theology is anthropology, so he divides his treatment of Paul into two sections, "Man Prior to the Revelation of Faith" and "Man under Faith."

Bultmann's students carried on his program. Günther Bornkamm's *Paul* attempts a biography of Paul, while aware of the problems in such an effort. Ernst Käsemann's *Commentary on Romans* is a dense and important theological commentary in the Bultmannian tradition.

Barth, Karl. *The Epistle to the Romans.* Trans. Edwyn Clement Hoskyns. London: Oxford University Press, 1933.

Bornkamm, Günther. *Paul, Paulus.* Trans. D. M. G. Stalker. New York: Harper & Row, 1971.

Bultmann, Rudolf Karl. *The New Testament and Mythology and Other Basic Writings.* Ed. Schubert Miles Ogden. Philadelphia: Fortress Press, 1984.
> A collection of essays on Bultmann's program of demythologization.

_____. *Theology of the New Testament.* 2 vols., combined. Trans. Kendrick Grobel. New York: Charles Scribner's Sons, 1951.

Hammann, Konrad. *Rudolf Bultmann: A Biography.* Trans. Philip E. Devenish. 1st English ed. Salem, OR: Polebridge Press, 2013.
> An important biography and study of Bultmann. A must-read for those interested in this important New Testament scholar and theologian in a progressive mode.

Käsemann, Ernst. *Commentary on Romans.* Trans. Geoffrey William Bromiley. Grand Rapids: Wm. B. Eerdmans, 1980.

_____. *Perspectives on Paul.* Trans. Margaret Kohl. Philadelphia: Fortress Press, 1971.
> A number of specialized essays on Pauline topics.

Call

In the aftermath of World War II and the Nazi holocaust, many Christian scholars began to explore the implications of that event for Christian theology. They felt that Christian theology must come to terms with anti-Semitism and anti-Judaism in the Christian message. For many Paul was the proper place to begin. The clarion call that sounded the shift in the interpretation of Paul was Krister Stendahl, "The Apostle Paul and the Introspective Conscience of the West" (first published in Swedish in 1960, English 1963). A long time professor and dean of Harvard Divinity School, he argued that Paul was not tormented by his inability to follow the law, and instead, relying on Phil 3:6, saw himself as blameless before the law. This undercut a major plank in the Lutheran interpretation of Paul. He clearly showed that Paul did not have to be interpreted as against and rejecting Judaism. His later essay on "Call or Conversion" is a classic (in *Paul Among Jews and Gentiles*). Stendahl remained interested in Jewish/Christian relations to the end of his life.

Stendahl made two major gains. Paul was not obsessed as a Jew with his inability to fulfill the law; as Paul himself says, he was blameless in regard to the law. And Paul was called to be an envoy of the Anointed, not converted to Christianity.

Stendahl, Krister. "The Apostle Paul and the Introspective Conscience of the West." *Harvard Theological Review* 56 (1963) 123–44.

_____. *Paul Among Jews and Gentiles*. Philadelphia: Fortress Press, 1976.

> A collection of his essays on Paul, including "The Apostle Paul and the Introspective Conscience of the West" and "Call or Conversion." It is still well worth reading and a good place to start in understanding the new scholarship on Paul.

Judaism, Paul, and the Law

If Stendahl's essay began to define a new way of viewing Paul, E. P. Sanders, a professor at Duke University, in *Paul and Palestinian Judaism* demonstrated that Judaism was not a legalistic, works bound religion as demanded by the traditional Augustinian/Lutheran interpretation. He defined Judaism as "covenantal nomism." This understanding of Judaism represents a definite gain. Between Stendahl and Sanders, it was difficult to see how the traditional interpretation could stand. While Sanders did not present a convincing analysis of how Paul should be interpreted, we know how Judaism cannot be understood.

In 1982 the British scholar James D. G. Dunn gave a lecture entitled "The New Perspective on Paul." He accepted Sanders' description of covenantal nomism, while noting that Sanders had really failed to grasp a new Paul. He correctly critiqued Sanders for maintaining the traditional opposition between Paul and Judaism, thus undercutting his own analysis of covenantal nomism. Dunn set out to take Sanders seriously and to understand the implications for interpreting Paul. While making a real effort to understand Paul as not in opposition to Judaism, Dunn still is trapped by what appears to be a theological need to oppose Judaism and Christianity. He argued that in the opposition between faith in Christ and justification by the works of the law, Paul objected to Jewish particularism.

N. T. Wright, a prolific author, has followed along in his fellow Englishman's footsteps. While Dunn coined the term "the new perspective," Wright publicized it. Like Dunn, he accepted Sanders' analysis of Judaism and also tried to interpret Paul in light of this new understanding of Judaism. He argued that Paul did not convict Judaism of being either legalistic or bound to works-righteousness. For Wright, somewhat like Dunn, Israel was guilty of relying upon its literal descent according to the flesh as its guarantee of being in the covenant.

Both Dunn and Wright were correct to accept Sander's description of Judaism and they both made important contributions in showing how covenantal nomism helped in understanding Paul, but in the end they remained too committed to the Christian paradigm; they needed for Paul to be at some important point in opposition to Judaism to preserve the universal nature of salvation in Christ. To really deal with Sanders' conclusions about Judaism, a more radical program was needed.

Lloyd Gaston was prepared to take that radical step with what he called a hermeneutic of experimentation. In his book, *Paul and the Torah*, he proposed that Paul as apostle to the gentiles was addressing non-Jews and was not concerned with Jews. This is the fundamental methodological step that breaks the impasse. For him, the problem with Israel is that they have not accepted God's plan for the gentiles. There are then two separate covenants—one for Israel and one for the nations.

Stanley Stowers moved in this same direction with an in-depth study of Romans, *A Rereading of Romans: Justice, Jews, and Gentiles*. His study is more ambitious than Gaston's, but he makes the same methodological moves. He argues against the consensus that the Letter to the Romans was addressed to a mixed community. Paul is only addressing the gentiles. Having written his dissertation on Paul's use of the diatribe form, he explores the use of speech-in-character and the importance of self-mastery for understanding Romans. Time and again, Stowers shows how the traditional reading of Romans has failed to understand Paul.

Dunn, James D. G. *The New Perspective on Paul.* 2d ed. Grand Rapids: Wm. B. Eerdmans, 2007.
> A collection of Dunn's essays including the essay that initiated the "new perspective" on Paul.

_____. *The Theology of Paul the Apostle.* Grand Rapids: Wm. B. Eerdmans, 1998.
> An accessible account of Dunn's interpretation of Paul.

Gager, John G. *Reinventing Paul.* New York: Oxford University Press, 2000.
> He pushed hard on the issue that Paul was not rejecting Judaism and insisted upon understanding Paul within the contours of Judaism.

Gaston, Lloyd. *Paul and the Torah.* Vancouver: University of British Columbia Press, 1987.

Sanders, E. P. *Paul and Palestinian Judaism: A Comparison of Patterns of Religion.* Philadelphia: Fortress Press, 1977.

Stowers, Stanley K. *A Rereading of Romans: Justice, Jews, and Gentiles.* New Haven/London: Yale University Press, 1994.

_____. *The Diatribe and Paul's Letter to the Romans.* Society of Biblical Literature Dissertation Series, vol. 57. Chico, CA: Scholars Press, 1981.

Wright, N. T. *Justification: God's Plan & Paul's Vision.* Downers Grove, IL: IVP Academic, 2009.

_____. *Paul: In Fresh Perspective.* 1st Fortress Press ed. Minneapolis: Fortress Press, 2005.

_____. *The Climax of the Covenant: Christ and the Law in Pauline Theology.* Minneapolis: Fortress Press, 1992.

Faith of Christ

This debate around a seemingly small point of grammar has critical implications for understanding Paul. Sam K. Williams and Richard B. Hays started and maintained this line of research. The debate between Hays and Dunn at the Society of Biblical Literature meeting in 1991 marked the high point in the debate in which the best case for both sides was made. These two essays are still a good place to start in understanding what is at stake.

Dunn, James D. G. "Once More, PISTIS CHRISTOU." Pp. 730–44 in *Society of Biblical Literature 1991 Seminar Papers.* Society of Biblical Literature Seminar Paper Series 30. Atlanta: Scholars Press, 1991.

> Dunn, who had been influential in initiating the new Paul studies, here backs the traditional understanding of "faith in Christ."

Hays, Richard B. "Justification." Vol. 3, pp. 1129–33 in *The Anchor Bible Dictionary.* Ed. David Noel. Editor-in-Chief David Noel Freedman. New York: Doubleday, 1992.

> This dictionary article is a good summary of Hays's position.

_____. "PISTIS and Pauline Christology: What Is at Stake?" Pp. 714–29 in *Society of Biblical Literature 1991 Seminar Papers.* Atlanta: Scholars Press, 1991.

> Part of the debate with Dunn, Hays defends the translation of "faith of Christ."

_____. *The Faith of Jesus Christ: An Investigation of the Narrative Substructure of Galatians 3:1–4:11.* Chico, CA: Scholars Press, 1983.

> An important dissertation devoted to the issue of meaning of "faith of Christ."

Williams, Sam K. *Jesus' Death as Saving Event.* Harvard Dissertations in Religion. Missoula: Scholars Press, 1975.

> The dissertation that can be said to have started the debate, but is much more wide ranging, as its title indicates, in its implications than just the "faith of Christ."

_____. "Again Pistis Christou." *Catholic Biblical Quarterly* 49 (1987) 431–47.

Paul in the Empire

If Paul is only speaking to the nations and if his opposition is not Israel or its Torah, then what is he opposing? A group of scholars have recently suggested that Paul's real opposition is the Roman Empire. Neil Elliot has been exploring this in a number of books, but especially in *The Arrogance of Nations*. The subtitle tells all: *Reading Romans in the Shadow of Empire*. John Dominic Crossan and Jonathan Reed also explored this same issue in an interdisciplinary fashion, bringing archaeology and the material culture to bear on the interpretation of Paul. The subtitle of their *In Search of Paul* summarizes their thesis: *How Jesus' Apostle Opposed Rome's Empire with God's Kingdom*.

The Fortress Press series, Paul in Critical Contexts, has published a number of important works (Neil Elliot, an editor at Fortress, edits this series). Brigitte Kahl has been especially good at showing how the conflict between the gospel of God and the Gospel of Rome functions in a semiotic model. Since this line of research has not yet matured, the reader must be willing to labor through a good deal of technical jargon, but the effort is worth it.

Crossan, John Dominic, and Jonathan L. Reed. *In Search of Paul: How Jesus' Apostle Opposed Rome's Empire with God's Kingdom*. San Francisco: HarperSanFrancisco, 2004.

Elliott, Neil. *Liberating Paul*. Minneapolis: Fortress Press, 2006.

_____. *The Arrogance of Nations, Reading Romans in the Shadow of Empire*. Paul in Critical Contexts. Minneapolis: Fortress Press, 2008.

_____. *The Rhetoric of Romans*. Minneapolis: Fortress Press, 2000.

Kahl, Brigitte. *Galatians Re-Imagined: Reading With the Eyes of the Vanquished*. Paul in Critical Contexts. Minneapolis: Fortress Press, 2010.

Oakes, Peter. *Reading Romans in Pompeii, Paul's Letter at Ground Level*. Paul in Critical Contexts. Minneapolis: Fortress Press, 2009.

Jewish Scholarship on Paul

Jewish scholars have long been interested in the Apostle Paul. Given the influence that interpretations of Paul have had on Christian understandings of Jews, these studies of Paul are frequently efforts to understand Christian anti-Semitism or anti-Judaism. They have generally followed two strategies. In 1914 Claude Montefiore, protesting against the understanding of Judaism implied in the Augustinian/Lutheran understanding of Paul, argued that the religion of the rabbis was not a religion of legalism and works, thus anticipating the work of Sanders. Many Jewish authors have continued this protest. The second strategy was to figure out how Paul fit into Judaism. What kind of Jew was he? In general they opt for understanding Paul within the context of Hellenistic Judaism, frequently as similar to Philo of Alexandria.

> Boyarin, Daniel. *A Radical Jew: Paul and the Politics of Identity*. Contraversions: Critical Studies in Jewish Literature, Culture, and Society. Berkeley: University of California Press, 1994.
> > This is a brilliant study of Paul that understands him as a radical dualist in the mode of Philo.

> Eisenbaum, Pamela. *Paul Was Not a Christian, The Original Message of a Misunderstood Apostle*. New York: HarperOne, 2009.
> > An intriguing and important study that benefits from the studies of new Paul.

> Maccoby, Hyam. *The Mythmaker: Paul and the Invention of Christianity*. New York: Harper & Row, 1986.
> > Sees Paul, as the title indicates, as the inventor of Christianity and anti-Semitism.

> Montefiore, C. G. *Judaism and St. Paul: Two Essays*. London: Max Goschen, ltd., 1914.
> > An early effort to protest against the understanding of Judaism implied in the traditional interpretation of Paul.

> Nanos, Mark D. *The Irony of Galatians: Paul's Letter in First-Century Context*. Minneapolis: Fortress Press, 2002.
> > Nanos' two books, like that of Eisenbaum, could easily be in the group dealing with the new perspective on Paul. He sees Paul as a Torah observant Jew whose churches/communities where in some way Jewish. Both of his books and many essays are provocative and challenge taken-for-granted positions.

_____. *The Mystery of Romans: The Jewish Context of Paul's Letter*. Minneapolis: Fortress Press, 1996.

Rubenstein, Richard L. *My Brother Paul*. New York: Harper & Row, 1972.
> Deeply influenced by Krister Stendahl's understanding of Paul, Rubenstein makes many sympathetic interpretations of Paul.

Sandmel, Samuel. *The Genius of Paul: A Study in History*. Philadelphia: Fortress Press, 1979.
> An important Philo scholar, Sandmel sees Paul within the tradition of Philo of Alexandria.

Schoeps, H. J. *Paul: The Theology of the Apostle in the Light of Jewish Religious History*. Philadelphia: Westminster Press, 1959.
> Argues that Paul is best understood within the context of Hellenistic, not Palestinian, Judaism.

Segal, Alan F. *Paul the Convert: The Apostolate and Apostasy of Saul the Pharisee*. New Haven: Yale University Press, 1990.
> A fascinating and important study of Paul with many insights.

COMMENTARIES

The last half of the twentieth century saw the inception of some important commentary series in English, ranging from very scholarly to more popular. What follows is by no means exhaustive, but commentaries that I have found useful.

Betz, Hans Dieter. *Galatians: A Commentary on Paul's Letter to the Churches in Galatia*. Hermeneia. Philadelphia: Fortress Press, 1979.
> Almost encyclopedic in scope, but traditional in interpretation.

Williams, Sam K. *Galatians*. Abingdon New Testament Commentaries. Nashville: Abingdon Press, 1997.
> An insightful commentary.

Keck, Leander E. *Romans*. Abingdon New Testament Commentaries. Nashville: Abingdon Press, 2005.
> While a commentary written for preachers, Keck attains a very high level of innovative scholarship. Well worth a read. A summation of a lifetime of scholarship on Paul and on important issues he has changed his mind.

Reumann, John Henry Paul, ed. *Philippians: A New Translation*. The Anchor Yale Bible, vol. 33B. New Haven/London: Yale University Press, 2008.

Argues for the edited character of Philippians and is very good on Phil 2:6–11. An important commentary.

Jewett, Robert. *Romans: A Commentary*. Hermeneia. Ed. Roy David Kotansky and Eldon Jay Epp. Minneapolis: Fortress Press, 2007.
A massive commentary, especially good on the rhetorical structure, but in the end a traditional view of Paul.

Dunn, James D. G. *Romans 1–8*. Word Biblical Commentary, vol. 38a. Dallas: Word Books, 1988.

_____. *Romans 9–16*. Word Biblical Commentary, vol. 38b. Dallas: Word Books, 1988.
Interesting to watch Dunn struggle with the new and the old Paul.

Index of Scripture

About the Author

Bernard Brandon Scott (Ph.D., Vanderbilt University) is the Darbeth Distinguished Professor Emeritus of New Testament at the Phillips Theological Seminary, Tulsa, Oklahoma. A charter member of the Jesus Seminar, chair of Westar Institute's Christianity Seminar, and former co-chair of the Bible in Ancient and Modern Media Group at the Society of Biblical Literature, he is the author of several books, including *The Trouble with Resurrection* (2010), *Sound Mapping the New Testament* (with Margaret Ellen Lee, 2009) and *Re-imagine the World* (2001), and editor of *Funk on Parables* (2006).